Praise for the First Edition Of *To Timbuktu for a Haircut*

"In the magical-travel-names department, Timbuktu undoubtedly holds the trump card — Marrakesh, Kathmandu, or Zanzibar are mere runners-up — but Rick Antonson's trek to the fabled desert city proves that dreamtime destinations are found in our minds just as much as on our maps."

— Tony Wheeler, co-founder of Lonely Planet and author of *Bad Lands: A Tourist on the Axis of Evil*

"*To Timbuktu for a Haircut* is a great read — a little bit of Bill Bryson, a little bit of Michael Palin, and quite a lot of Bob Hope on the road to Timbuktu."

— Professor Geoffrey Lipman, former assistant secretary-general of the United Nations World Tourism Organization

"There are three kinds of people. The people who make things happen, the people who watch what happens, and then there are the people who wonder what happened. With this book, Rick Antonson has made things happen in West Africa on a remarkable journey to and through a part of the world most of us may never experience.

Great characters, great stories, and truly great adventures. Not to mention ... a great read."

— Peter Greenberg, former travel editor, NBC's Today,
current travel editor, CBS News

"The remarkable combination of Rick Antonson exploring the ancient mysteries of Timbuktu matched with the rich culture of Mali that he captures so well ... makes a page-turner from start to finish. Rick's underlying story confirms my own experience in that amazing land."

— Jerry W. Bird, editor, Africa Travel Magazine

"I thoroughly enjoyed reading To Timbuktu for a Haircut from cover to cover and had difficulty putting it down. It is truly an engaging book. Rick Antonson indeed captures the essence and intricacies of Malian culture, as well as the flavour of what it is like to travel through West Africa 'roughing it.'"

— Professor Musa Balde, CEO, Timbuktu
Educational Foundation

"Anyone planning a trip to Africa should put Antonson's book on their packing list right after malaria tablets."

—National Post

To Timbuktu for a Haircut

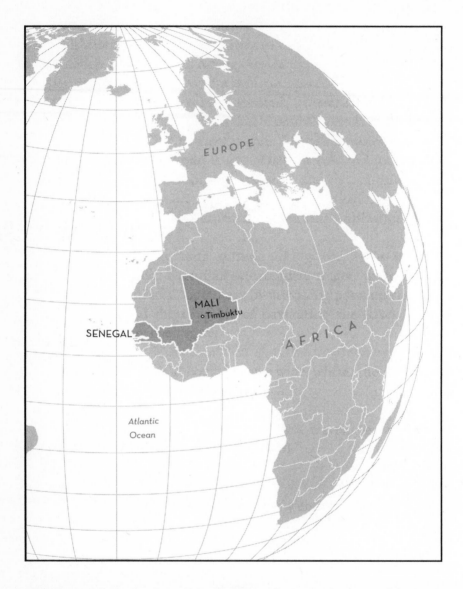

Timbuktu is thought of as the most remote place in the world. This historically rich city, today in the country of Mali, houses 700,000 ancient manuscripts from the 14th and 15th centuries. The author traveled in Senegal and Mali.

To Timbuktu for a Haircut

A JOURNEY THROUGH WEST AFRICA

RICK ANTONSON

Foreword by Professor Geoffrey Lipman

Skyhorse Publishing

Skyhorse Publishing books may be purchased in bulk at special discounts for sales promotion, corporate gifts, fund-raising, or educational purposes. Special editions can also be created to specifications. For details, contact the Special Sales Department, Skyhorse Publishing, 307 West 36th Street, 11th Floor, New York, NY 10018 or info@skyhorsepublishing.com.

Skyhorse® and Skyhorse Publishing® are registered trademarks of Skyhorse Publishing, Inc. ®, a Delaware corporation.

www.skyhorsepublishing.com

Front cover photo: iStockphoto/Thinkstock

10 9 8 7 6 5 4 3 2 1

Library of Congress Cataloging-in-Publication Data is available on file.

ISBN: 978-1-62087-567-4

Printed in the United States of America.

Contents

To Brent and Sean — two sons, two travellers, two friends — who believe in my every journey, even those in the wrong direction. And to Zak, my Dogon guide and Mali friend. May the three of you meet one day over the long pours of a Tuareg tea.

Part of the author's royalties from To Timbuktu For A Haircut: A Journey Through West Africa *will go toward preservation of the endangered Timbuktu manuscripts.*

About this 1830 engraving, taken from René Caillié's Travels Through Central Africa to Timbuctoo, *the French explorer wrote: "Two enormous heaps on the outside of the town appeared to me to be also collections of dirt or rubbish. Many a time I ascended to the tops of these hills to obtain a complete view of the town and to make my sketch."*

Certainly, travel is more than the seeing of sights; it is a change that goes on, deep and permanent, in the ideas of living.

— Miriam Beard

Foreword

TO TIMBUKTU FOR A HAIRCUT IS A GREAT READ — a little bit of Bill Bryson, a little bit of Michael Palin, and quite a lot of Bob Hope on the road to Timbuktu. It has adventure — in the form of a journey into the unknown. It has knowledge — a wealth of information about the geography, history, and sociology of a fascinating land, its people, and their culture. It has discovery — of a hidden treasure trove of ancient manuscripts that tell of a civilization long forgotten that, in its day, rivalled modern-day mega-states. And it has romance — the love of a man for his quest, his encounters, his profession, his family, and for the essence of life itself. Once started, you simply don't want to come to the end.

The story is compelling. And it's told with passion, with self-deprecating humour, and with a strong sense of respect for the seemingly barren land where daily life is a constant reminder, to the rest of us, of the importance of the United Nations Millennium Development Goals and of our global commitment to halve extreme poverty by 2015. Rick Antonson's personal odyssey is peppered with commentary on issues that are geopolitically relevant, and his insights as an industry professional into those issues' links with travel are right on the mark.

The reader truly feels a part of this journey, beginning with Rick's agonized midlife decision to spend a month without work, without BlackBerry, without family and business obligations.

Next comes the germination of the big idea of chasing a childhood fantasy in "Darkest Africa" and then the bizarre travel planning with its self-imposed requirement to do it the hard way, accompanied by a pivotal local agent who makes Fagin in *Oliver Twist* seem like St. Jude, the patron saint of travellers. Finally, there is the truly fascinating adventure itself — travelling overland to a city that at its peak rivalled London or Venice as a trading centre.

The story flows easily and lucidly, blending local community minutiae with serious global issues such as the disparity between haves and have-nots, shown in the dull monotony of a handful of rice as breakfast, lunch, and dinner. The author shows us the contrast between today's survival-of-the-fittest, market-based society and a railway carriage or hostel in Mali where you can leave your belongings with strangers. He reveals the awesome Sahara Desert's creep into Timbuktu, demonstrating one of the most serious sides of climate change. And he evokes the radiant, innocent beauty of the smile on the face of a child who receives one of Rick's seemingly endless supply of memorabilia, reminding us that children everywhere are so different in the conditions into which they are born, but are so alike in their characters, and that we owe the children of Africa a seriously better future.

We follow the adventure by train, Land Cruiser, riverboat, camel, and quite often on foot. We feel the weight of the overpacked knapsack, share the camaraderie of fellow travellers stuffed into a dank railway carriage, and experience vicariously the misery of basic sleeping, eating, and sanitary facilities. We begin, too, to understand why the word *travel* is believed to be a derivative of *travail*, the French word for *work*. And as we read of the early explorers, we marvel that so many kept searching for the legendary city even as they were mowed down by climate, terrain, and hostile inhabitants.

Yet we also discover how tourism really works at its basic level, where a journey can help provide jobs and export income in another country that has few other service exports — whether it's the author travelling for leisure or the film crew who share part of his journey travelling for business. And we understand graphically what every extra dollar of tourism revenue can mean to a family that lives on less than a dollar a day in a country that is saddled with debt and disease and has few chances to compete in world markets. We see the endless pain of abject poverty that is everywhere, the horrors of AIDS as it decimates families, and the barbarity of female circumcision, which is still widely practised across the continent. And we learn about the pain of river blindness and read the fantastic story of a drug company that puts pure humanity ahead of pure profit.

We meet a cast of characters that Shakespeare would have been proud to bring to his pages: Mohammed, the travel agent from hell, who puts the trip together in a way that maximizes his profits and minimizes his client's comfort and quality; the priceless Zak, the tour guide from heaven, who becomes a companion and a confidant and who takes the author on his own tour so that he can experience the traditional hospitality of his enchanting family; the coquettish Nema, whose hidden sensuality is a nice addition to her skill as a chef, creating palatable dishes from a handful of basic ingredients and finding ingenious ways to incorporate onions into everything despite her employer's aversion to them; and an array of bit players who add colour to the journey at every stop.

If there is a hero in this tale, it isn't the author or any of the characters he meets along the way. No, what is heroic here is Mali itself and the indomitable spirit of its people. A land that has seen kingdoms come and go, Mali has a history as proud and rich as any country on the planet, but it is a nation that has also been dealt an incredibly tough hand by nature. Mali is a land with some of the most evocative place names on earth — the unyielding Sahara Desert, the seemingly endless River Niger, and the mysterious Timbuktu, an ancient capital of a long-lost empire — and it is a nation that has remarkably proud people, including the famed and feared Tuareg warriors, along with their equally celebrated Berber ancestors. Chronicled in these pages are the people of Mali, whose men love football and life, whose women are tireless and possessed of enduring perseverance, and whose cheerful, loving children, above all, anxiously reach out to touch the hands and hearts of strangers.

Timbuktu turns out to be a bit of a disappointment, though, given its status as a World Heritage Site. It is a surprise to learn that for hundreds of years it was a primary marketplace on great trade routes driven by gold and, above all, salt, which, in economic terms, was the oil of its day. It is equally amazing to read about Timbuktu's rulers, who could destabilize global commerce by dumping gold in what was then a world commercial hub in Egypt. And it is also interesting to discover that Timbuktu was once home to scholars who were the leading lights in the fabled Muslim academic community that brought us so much of our science, mathematics, and literary heritage. Most traces of this culture have disappeared, however, as time, sand, wind, shifting markets, and escalating poverty have taken their toll and will continue to do so.

But the author finds two great compensations. One is his side trip to the remote Dogon region, the most memorable part of his journey, where the rugged beauty of the countryside and the charm of its long-suffering people capture his heart and mind. In a world where nature-based and community-based ecotourism is the Holy Grail, there is surely untapped potential. The other compensation is his rediscovery of the ancient manuscripts, which tell of the great days of Timbuktu and its role as a centre of learning, trade and, of course, tourism of its day. It is a "rediscovery" because a central purpose of the journey (other than the literal and figurative haircut) was to visit the libraries and peruse documents that have been described in archaeological terms as similar in importance to the Dead Sea Scrolls. What the author finds is that the papers and records are suffering from serious neglect, are far more numerous than imagined, are far more meaningful as a record of civilizations past, and are sadly in need of urgent action to save them from destruction by the desert. True to himself, he has committed to support the international campaign to save the manuscripts, including the donation of some of his royalties from this book.

So there you have it. *To Timbuktu for a Haircut* is a great read, a mine of information, and a fascinating insight into travel at its most fundamental level. In this book we see how tourism can be a learning experience and how it can act as a way to break down barriers between people and between nations and allow them to understand one another better. The author puts it this way: "At its core, travel holds immense hope for a better world. Two hundred and eighteen countries call this tiny planet home: each of us is but a step or two away from a person in every one of those nations, perhaps family, a friend, or a fellow traveller. Tourism, more than any other industry, can bring people together to celebrate differences."

But the reader is left with one nagging question: despite the glories of its past, is Mali and its hardy population, now existing in a different world characterized by extreme poverty, destined to remain that way, or is there a chance the world community can help the children have a better life? The answer that flows through every chapter of this book is that that we simply have to help.

World leaders have made great promises of change in the recent past, particularly in the case of the Rio and Johannesburg Earth Summits, the Monterrey Debt Summit, the Millennium Development Goals, the emerging Doha Development Round, and the Bali Climate Change Framework. In all this grand global design there is a massive promise to transfer funds, build infrastructure, and supply technical know-how to developing countries generally and to African nations specifically. The United Nations family, the Bretton Woods institutions, the World Bank and IMF systems, as well as the G8 and industrialized states, are committed to implement this development agenda by 2015.

If tourism were to be given a prime place in this support network, Mali and countries in the same poverty trap would have an area of proven wealth and job creation as a stepladder to sustainable development. The policymakers and bureaucrats who will be responsible for such a paradigm shift should start their research on the following pages.

Professor Geoffrey Lipman
Former Assistant Secretary-General
United Nations World Tourism Organization
Madrid, Spain

Timbuktu's most famous landmarks are three mosques. This minaret has been often remudded since its creation hundreds of years ago. The mosques have been cited as "unique earthen architecture."

Preface

IF I'D THOUGHT TO TRAVEL TO TIMBUKTU ANY later than I did, this book probably wouldn't exist. The fabled city is once again as dangerous for foreign travelers as it was centuries ago.

In early 2012, as the Arab Spring's revolutions crested in North Africa, their unintended consequences tore into the landlocked nation of Mali, including the city of Timbuktu. Within the year the northeastern two-thirds of Mali, an area approximately the size of Texas, was threatened or controlled by an alliance of the nomadic Tuaregs and the upstart Ansar Dine (Defenders of Faith), a franchise of sorts under Al-Qaeda in the Islamic Maghreb (AQIM). That perilous situation would hold into 2013.

Far away, secure in my home country, I emailed my Malian friend Zak, who years earlier had been my guide to Timbuktu: "Are you safe?"

"Am safe," he replied. "Village has fear."

This fear had spread to Timbuktu as well. The ancient city, a UNESCO World Heritage Site, despite remaining famously remote, became a daily news item on the Internet. Concerns for its future led to its being identified as "a looming disaster." Another resident of Mali, unable to flee the recent assaults by extremists, exclaimed: "Truly we are living in misery."

A new afterword for this Second Edition of *To Timbuktu for a Haircut* explains the unfolding and ongoing struggles taking place in Mali today. Though you and I can no longer travel there freely as I did not so long ago, there are ways in which we can help, and they begin with an understanding of the people and culture of Mali and why Timbuktu matters. My hope is that the story of my own travels in West Africa might bring a more human perspective to the reports of violence and political unrest coming out of that region and that one day, a journey to Timbuktu may once more be a worthy—and safe—quest.

Rick Antonson
New York, June 2013

INTRODUCTION

Touch a Map of the World

WHEN I WAS A BOY, EVERY OCCASION MY FATHER left the house was important. I and my older brother would pester him: "Where are you going, Daddy? Where? To work? To church? To the store?" And in the vernacular of the day, or perhaps with a flippancy meant to silence us, he would say what I believed to be the truth: "I'm going to Timbuktu to get my hair cut."

So began my own feeble notions of travel. With the irrefutable logic of a child, I understood that one day I, too, must go to Timbuktu and get my hair cut. After all, how far could it be?

Fifty years later, a world away, I walked a path among mud homes as old as time, baked by a dry heat that choked my breathing. It was impossible to tell the sand from the dust unless you stood on it. A young boy was setting up a chair with a missing leg in front of his parents' house. Sand piled by the doorway, nudged there by desert winds that pushed relentlessly through these village streets. His left foot suddenly slipped over the edge of the path's centre ditch. The slip almost caused him to fall into the shallow sewer. He noticed me as he regained his balance, and I stopped and looked into his eyes. We were only a metre apart. The youngster, maybe five years old, stared down my greeting. His eyes widened in a glare of determination. He crossed his dusty arms and clasped each defiant shoulder with a scraped hand. Sand and drool encrusted his lips in loose granules. The rose colour of his tongue showed and he did not smile. I felt like the first white man he'd ever seen, and not a welcome visitor. His face proclaimed his proud independence. He knew that whatever had lured me to travel there was hollow. But he did not know that I was looking for a shop where I could get my hair cut.

It was my wife's idea. I had time available for being away the coming January, all of it, and Janice didn't. For half a year we'd talked about my taking a solo journey. But her interest began to fade when the topic of "What *I'll* do" reared its head. We were in Prague to hear the International Olympic Committee's decision naming the host destination for the 2010 Olympic Winter Games. My colleagues and I had launched Canada's Vancouver-Whistler bid six years earlier and were now part of the Canadian delegation. Janice and I arrived in the Czech Republic two days in advance, near midnight. In search of a late dinner, we walked on the cobblestones of the Charles Bridge, looking into the dark waters that flowed beneath. The roadway led us to an open but near-empty restaurant, where our lives were unexpectedly changed within minutes. While waiting for our grilled chicken over pasta we talked about *the bid* and then anything but *the bid.*

My wont at such times was to compile a mental list of projects I could accomplish within a month. Friends had suggested everything from a long walk to a short sailing voyage; my family advised a month's vow of silence in a Tibetan monastery. It must change you, people said; you'll come back better for the time away. Whatever you do, don't stay home and do chores.

Our wine arrived before the meal, and without any preamble, I said to Janice, somewhat desperately, "It's only six months away. I've got to pick something to do and start getting ready!"

Her eyes clouded. A pause stilled the air. Exasperated, she finally said across the table: "Why don't you just go to Timbuktu."

Stunned by the perfection of her suggestion, my head jerked. I could feel my lungs fill with oxygen. "Brilliant," I said. My heart took stag leaps. "Absolutely brilliant." We looked at one another. Janice sipped her red wine, unsure of what she had wrought.

"I'm going to Timbuktu," I committed, so profound was the image. "Just as soon as I find out where it is."

Touch a map of the world. Move your hand to Africa. Press a finger to unfamiliar West African names like Benin, Togo, Burkina Faso. Look north, above Ouagadougou, to the nation of Mali, and there, near the River Niger, find the most ethereal of names, Timbuktu.

It is easier to point out countries of terror and despair, of dictators and abusers. The facts of sub-Saharan Africa are awful, the past mired in exaggerations, the future one of faint hope. Perhaps we understand Africa only marginally better than those who, in the not too distant past, hid their geographic ignorance by filling in the uncharted voids on their maps with sketches of fantastic monsters.

To exploration-mad societies like France and England in the eighteenth and nineteenth centuries, Timbuktu lay at the unknown edges of cartography. Its sheer unassailability challenged even their most intrepid travellers. It acquired such an aura that even today many people believe Timbuktu is fictitious. It is assuredly not.

Our globe's most exotically named travel destination is rooted in the language of Berber, though it has been distorted to the point that only myth explains its genesis. I've found it commonly written as *Timbuctoo, Tombooctoo* or *Tombuctou, Tombouktou*, and less often *Tumbyktu, Tembuch, Tombuto, Timkitoo* or *Tambuta*, as well as the word used here: *Timbuktu*. The most frequently used label is the French, *Tombouctou*, which one finds on Mali maps and postcards.

In Tuareg folklore, the place began with an old woman who looked after the nomads' well when the men went trading or hunting. Tuareg Imashagan, desert people, first set camp in Timbuktu around A.D. 1000. Their well, *tin* in Berber lingo, provided water that was free of the illnesses they contracted nearer the River Niger, where they grazed camels and cattle on the burgo grass, and it became their preferred spot. As summer annually gave way to autumn's temperate rains, these nomads moved on and left their goods in care of the old woman, commonly referred to as *Bouctou*, which translates as "woman with the large navel." It was her well, and thus her name, that became renowned. The linking of proprietress and place formed "TinBouctou." *Timbuktu*, one of the world's finest names, is "the well of the lady with the big belly button."

Africa in 1829, prepared by the cartographer Sidney Hall, working from geographical information available to Europeans at that time, which demonstrates how limited knowledge was regarding the continent.

ONE

Scarcely Visited Places

DEREK, A FELLOW I'D ONCE WORKED WITH, serendipitously showed up at the office two months before my intended departure. Our talk turned quickly to his travels in West Africa three years earlier.

"Were you in Mali?" I asked.

"Yes, Burkina Faso, Mali, Senegal."

"Did you go to Timbuktu?" I probed immediately, already sensing that my travels to Africa, even maybe Timbuktu, might lose the novelty I coveted.

"No. It's inconvenient, and in West Africa that means expensive travel."

Derek, with the shaggy locks of a part-time drummer hanging to his collar, and his fellow traveller, Chris, short, entrepreneurial, invigorating, agreed to meet me later at the pub and share their photos and travel savvy.

"Chris was mugged," Derek said before the beer arrived.

"Lost my money," Chris added, shifting off a suit jacket. "It's a good idea to carry an old wallet filled with cards you don't need and a little currency. Give it up right away. The robber will leave."

"And what if you're mugged a second time?" I asked.

"That'd be a problem."

"Moneybelt's best," said Derek. "And slip your leg through the pack strap when you sleep. Take postal tape so you can wrap your parcel if you leave anything in a safety deposit box — it's the hotel staff that steal. Take your own lock for the room doors."

Derek took a long pull on the beer as soon as it was set before us and honed his stare directly into mine. "West Africa is a place to keep one eye open when you sleep."

I gave him a long wink to demonstrate my understanding.

"But Burkina Faso was wonderful. Felt welcome," said Derek.

Chris countered. "I'd say the Dogon was the most special. Never felt in danger." I'd read of this area only recently, its astonishing history and two-hundred-kilometre stone escarpment, and worked it into my rough itinerary.

Noticing my enthusiasm, Derek cautioned: "Travels in Mali, however romanticized, are rugged."

When they urged me to spend a day at the Slave Trade Fort in Dakar, I finally made a formal declaration that my trip was about Mali.

"Mali is one of the world's throwaway countries," Derek declared. "Ignored. It's like Mali gets second seating at UN banquets."

"But," said Chris, harking back to Dakar, "you will be in Senegal, right?" I nodded. He continued: "Once, there was a train running from Dakar to Bamako. Doesn't run anymore."

My heart sank. My silence remaining unexplained, they jumped to provide another advisory.

"They *may* have a smattering of English," Chris observed. "I hope your French is good. Be prepared, theirs is different. Doesn't sound like ours."

Mali is a francophone country. The guidebooks were emphatic that knowledge of French is essential, especially in the remote regions. Derek said, "Often in Mali, the people don't speak either French or English. The country has more than thirty indigenous languages. All you need to do is learn Bambara, or Bamana, the most common one." He grinned wickedly.

For anyone who travels, not to have a second language is a social hangnail. Now it would prove even more problematic. Pursing my lips for vowels and gurgling consonants unsettled me, but I did not want to be a unilingual wanderer among "uneducated" people who were nevertheless conversant in four languages. I must brush up on my high school French.

"Pack small," advised the already compact Chris. It was a comment that led Derek to say, "Take breathable pants. And polypro sox. Shirts, too. You're going to be a sweaty bastard, and you'll want that damp off."

"And Malian officials check your passport and your yellow fever certificate with equal interest," warned Chris. "Lacking either means denied entry."

I jotted everything down. "What did you wish you'd taken?"

"Well, we were better prepared than that Scot," began Chris.

"Park ... something Park," said Derek, finding it funny. "About two hundred years ago."

"Mungo Park," I said. The irascible Scot was much on my mind: explorer extraordinaire, he twice failed to reach Timbuktu.

"That's him. Provisioned with beads to barter, a thermometer and an umbrella," claimed Derek.

"And the other Scot, the British major," prodded Chris. "A bit odd, too."

"Laing?" I asked, knowing it must be. Many British explorers attempted to find Timbuktu in the early nineteenth century, but he stood out. "Alexander Gordon Laing?"

"That's him," Chris replied. "Prepped for a year and left England without his medicine chest or writing quills." They both looked at me. "You know these guys?"

The months since I'd returned from Prague had been consumed with research. Park, Laing, and a host of others had become intimates, but I'll get to that. "Now, you two — what did you forget to take?"

"Safety pins. Ziploc bag to keep my passport dry. A Petzl," Derek said, mimicking the forehead lamp that coal miners wear for the convenience of keeping their hands free while having a flashlight that moves wherever their head looks.

"Food is iffy," said Chris. "Take pâté in a can, maybe Tabasco to liven up the rice. And powdered spices. They're easy to pack."

"Ah, and a large towel. I'd have loved that," Derek added.

They launched me on repeated trips to Mountain Equipment Co-op, Three Vets outlets, and The Travel Bug Store. Their most instructive talk was about attitude: "You get by, you just do. It all works out."

We each have horizons. I had to ask, "Weren't you tempted to try to reach Timbuktu?"

"It seemed impossible," Chris said, as though offering a business evaluation.

"Just too far from everything else," Derek explained.

I heaved a sigh of relief. My dream was safe.

It was true, I had little idea where Timbuktu was. Janice and I left Prague two days after her late-night admonition. Flying home to Vancouver, still leery of thwarting the travel gods by discussing my newfound destiny, I searched the in-flight magazine's map of the world. No Timbuktu there. Transiting Heathrow homebound, I ducked into a W.H. Smith bookstore. No *Guide to Timbuktu* there. Perhaps an atlas would help. The index got me to a page showing West Africa. I found Timbuktu, Mali. Mali? Africa, in that part of the continent, was often still referred to as French West Africa. Post-colonial name changes had translated French Sudan to Mali. This had occurred ten years after I was born; I just wasn't paying attention.

Entering "Timbuktu" into the bookstore's computer identified fewer than a dozen books, most of them out of print. Some had the word in the title but no relevance to the place; an eye-catching marketing game, a dog's name, a fictional concept, and other misuses hampered my search. I purchased the *Lonely Planet Guide to West Africa* and fondled the pages referring to the elusive country of Mali. There I found a useful reference to a once-central place reduced to a geographic curiosity.

Back home, I scoured my bookshelves, pulling out every book on Africa and thumbing its index. They showed my now-favourite place in an unfavourable light, unworthy of the hard travel it would take to get there. But it was *there*, it had once been grander than words could tell, and it seemed to say, "Find me if you can."

Timbuktu would be dismissed today if it weren't for the symbolism of its name. In the fourteenth century, the fabled city was a commercial hub that encouraged scientific and religious scholarship above all else. The cribbed history: salt from the north was traded for gold from the south; tobacco came too, then slaves. Timbuktu was the "Rome of the Sudan" and the "Athens of Africa," more prosperous in its heyday than Paris or London. Then began the myths of "streets paved with gold," the cornerstone of a legend that European explorers would one day lay bare. No sense of that legendary past remains in time-worn Timbuktu.

Travelling to Timbuktu had become my obsession. When one's work commands sixty hours every week, there is an imbalance apparent to all but the culprit. Henry David Thoreau, pondering this issue in *Life Without Principle*, piqued my guilt: "There is no more fatal blunderer than he who consumes the greater part of his life getting his living." It had become "the job that ate my life." That was not how I wished to see myself, not how I yearned to grow old. Every day seemed to be about other people, and I wanted to leave that behind, even if only temporarily.

Flying a hundred thousand kilometres each year for two decades, travel for me meant air, not ground. A term as chair of an international travel association doubled those travels from Bali to Liverpool, from Quebec City to Sydney. I often gave speeches about the world of travel, and moved in a style distanced from the rigours of a traveller's self-reliance. My visits were hurried and tinged with regret. My memories were trifling. In Cuba to deliver a lecture on travel, I was greeted by a crawling Mercedes and an English professor as guide each time I stepped outside Havana's National Hotel. That could only distort my expectations. Checking into the Los Angeles Biltmore Hotel to chair a travel conference, I was shown to the five-hundred-square-metre President's Suite. Travelling in this way skews priorities and shaves principles. I watched harried colleagues become "oft travelled" rather than "well travelled." For all my moving around, I was a travel amateur.

Trips had begun to blur, which saddened me. When trips move quickly — a hazard when many are adjuncts to business obligations — one anticipated the fun of reflecting almost as much as the being there (something sad in that line, but let it be). Postponed reflection left many a trip taken without closure. What had happened to the tingly feelings that had once been brought on by strange places? And the insecurities? And anxieties? What would I amount to — a transient with an asterisk?

I dreaded the thought of an unfinished life. What was more, it had been too long since I'd trudged up mountains in Nepal, snorkeled with fairy penguins in the Galapagos, driven a dogsled in the Yukon, or ridden horseback with a herdsman to his village in Mongolia. My train travels, which had happily included the hardships of the Trans-Siberian railway, were now as easy as a recent, smooth Amtrak ride from New York to San Francisco. Yet I was convinced that in one's rocking-chair years, travels will count as much as friends, only a little less than family and much more than money.

Being past mid-ocean in my life's crossing, I felt there was only a limited time left to do what I wanted. Ernest Hemingway wrote, "There are some things which cannot be learned quickly, and time, which is all we have, must be paid heavily for their acquiring. They are the very simplest things, and because it takes a man's life to know them, the little new that each man gets from life is very costly and the only heritage he has to leave." You die with regrets, not from them. Others might brood in your nursing-home years, but I would not. Timbuktu and the re-education of a traveller had begun.

On the History Channel's web page I came upon a link to the feature "Threats to the Survival of Timbuktu." The most precious legacy of Timbuktu, it said, was the city's centuries-old manuscripts, which were under threat. "In closets and chests throughout the southern Sahara, thousands of books from Timbuktu's ancient libraries are hidden, their disintegration delayed by the dry desert air yet threatened by insects and the annual humidity of rainy seasons."

Their words became dust, their pages crumbled, and their bindings turned to powder. Finding out about these manuscripts set my pace and became a motivation for my journey. My itinerary now included researching the perilous state of these books and manuscripts, and the efforts underway to protect them. My journey now had the aura of a treasure hunt.

I decided to go in search of the Timbuktu manuscripts.

The wanderer in me was ready, brimming with anticipation. Paul Theroux's *Sunrise with Seamonsters* said it well: "It is a ridiculous conceit to think that this enormous world has been exhausted of interest. There are still scarcely visited places and there are exhilarating ways of reaching them ... It is every traveller's wish to see his route as pure, unique and impossible for anyone else to recover ... The going is still good." That was me and Timbuktu.

In Cape Town, South Africa, a few months earlier, I'd found a book tucked away in a travel supply store. Ross Velton's *Mali: The Bradt Travel Guide* fuelled my desire. Jealousy sprang to the fore when I encountered Michael Palin's newly released *Sahara* in the Johannesburg airport. I flipped nervously through its pages. Palin had been there, with the BBC in tow, as part of a year's venturing back and forth throughout the Sahara.

As I'd hoped, my reading broadened my knowledge. In medieval times, Timbuktu had been central to African trade. The benevolent leaders of the Malian Empire endowed the city's universities. Under the Songhais, books were plentiful and knowledge was a source of wealth and pride. Timbuktu was Africa's capital in all things spiritual, commercial, and intellectual. It was this image of an imagined utopia that glued itself on European minds through rogue, hearsay reports and rumours that reached willing believers. The Timbuktu of the fourteenth century lived on in the dreams of Europeans for centuries. It was a fascination distorted by distance.

It was September, four months before my departure, when late-night fears first crept beneath my sheets to plague me. "Hyenas and wild cats are widespread," I'd read that day. The thought of lingering on a dark, lonely road, struck with the bad luck of missed transport, progressed to a vision of a black-backed jackal, fangs bared, staring me down.

Tales of atrocities emanating from sub-Saharan Africa did nothing to quell my fears. ("They let the man free in the jungle, as he asked; but not before hacking off his arms and legs.") I rationalized that I would be in Saharan Africa, but then a guidebook warned about the danger of being left alone in the desert unless you were willing to pay surcharges demanded by the (about to disappear) guide. Now, like

Dashiell Hammett's Sam Spade, "I don't mind a reasonable amount of trouble," but "reasonable" was beginning to seem like a concept I couldn't take for granted.

Health issues and travel are inextricable. The travel industry facilitates the worldwide spread of communicable diseases. Twisted together, perpetrated by tourism, are SARS, AIDS, West Nile virus, Norwalk, and a host of other unwanted experiences.

Medical clinics specializing in travel health and safety have the deserved "first-stop" reputation when strange lands beckon. Safety and precaution are the only methods to defeat worry.

"You're going to the armpit of Africa," the prim doctor said, as I rolled up my sleeve for the first injection. "We can only do so much for you." She was as thorough as she was adamant. Whether one is concerned about sleeping sickness (trypanosomiasis by a less say-able term) or other insect-carried diseases, avoiding insect bites is key. "Take a mesh to drop over your hat when walking, and wear light *porg* shirts and pants sprayed with DEET." Her non-medical prescriptions included advice on taking a mosquito net for my tent, spraying it with permethrin before I left the country, and carrying ample repellant and bite salve. They added weight to the packing list.

Her succinct warnings abounded: "Swim only in the ocean or your bathtub." Best simply not to submerge in stagnant water; stick with hot showers.

I looked into the eyes that cautioned with more sincerity than her words did.

"But stay out of fresh water," she stated. "You court a parasitic infection that will ruin your trip and live in your body for months afterwards."

She worked through a series of health issues, and for each item she passed me a pamphlet or prescribed medicine: malaria is preventable (though it can be fatal) — begin doxycycline two days before departure and take it daily on your journey, plus every day for a week post-trip; stay away from fruit. Bacteria and viruses often lead to what she called "traveller's tummy," a euphemism that makes it none the more pleasant a volcanic experience — begin taking Dukoral two weeks prior to departure, and repeat one week before.

"And in case that gets worse, I've something that will bung you up," she offered. And so it was that I packed blockage pills (ciprofloxacin), mindful of her advice: "If you have to use them, you should probably seek medical attention."

The ability of Hepatitis A and B to damage your liver lengthened my list of concerns. The specialist reviewed the "meningitis map" on the wall of her windowless office, showing clearly that West African travels take you there.

She continued with clinical efficiency. Typhoid. Boosters for measles and tetanus-diphtheria. And she took the time to ensure that I'd had a one-time polio vaccine, as most westerners have had as a child.

Motor vehicle accidents kill or injure many in West Africa, and the doctor's related concern was that local medical treatment, if required, may not resolve all problems or may create new ones. She provided me with syringes in a packet and signed a note of permission for me to carry them. Despite this provision, she advised: "Don't have an injection if you can avoid it. Take packaged oral medication if at all possible."

I was leaving her office with a satchel of material (everything from tensor bandages for strains, to salves for cuts and burns) and a healthy dose of advice when she added, "Of course, the food. Avoid street vendors. Drink only bottled water with sealed caps. No ice. Never. And stay away from unpasteurized dairy products."

All in all, fairly comprehensive travellers' paranoia.

The desire to travel is often motivated by a curiosity about someone else's home; the novelty of learning about those whose daily life is markedly different from our own, even though we share a planet. Every day I tapped into the Mali news website, tracking headlines about the cholera epidemic, updates on the tuberculosis outbreak, and news about the locust gathering.

"FLOODS DAMAGE ANCIENT TIMBUKTU" shouted the morning's BBC World Edition when my sons both flipped it over on e-mail. Alarmed by the heading, I opened the folio to follow a story weeks in the making and just as long in reaching our part of the world. (Neither CNN nor the CBC nor Fox News carried the story; hands up, those surprised.)

Heavy rains had pounded the seamless earth beneath Timbuktu, and the water had nowhere to drain. Instead, it puddled around the base of earth-built walls, wound through the maze of narrow streets, and flushed into the open sewers. In one home, it seeped through the mud foundation, surprising and drowning two children.

One hundred and eighty mud buildings (*banco* is the local term for this construction) were destroyed. The edifices slowly folded back to earth. They would be rebuilt around their wooden doors and splintered shutters. More expensive homes, built with limestone foundations and walls, were spared. But the nightmare was not over. It was predicted that the River Niger would overflow its banks, displacing a million Malians in fishing villages along the water's edge.

One afternoon a Malian entry visa was happily secured to the last blank page in my passport. So I made my currency arrangements. Travellers cheques are cumbersome to use in that part of the world. VISA withdrawals would take two days to authorize. I tucked U.S. dollars, British pounds, and Euros into my money pouch, since West Africa's currency was not available at Heathrow, let alone in the street exchanges of London or Cape Town. The currency is known as *Communauté Financière Africaine* (equally explained as *Colonies Françaises d'Afrique*), the franc CFA or, in local parlance, *seffe*. It is available only in the member nations of the West Africa Monetary Union, which regularly expanded its participating countries, contributing to the economic good, the travellers' convenience, and the disappearance of indigenous currency art. The exchange rate was 500 *seffe* to one U.S. dollar; 650 to one Euro, and 400 to one Canadian dollar.

At work, I never prepared for business travel. My arrangements were made for me; I checked my tickets on the way to the airport to find out which airline I was on, looked at my hotel information in the taxi at the other end to get an address. This trip would be different. I would make my own arrangements.

There is no book called *What to Pack for Your Trip to Timbuktu* so I rummaged through websites, mined bookshelves, and eventually compiled a suitable list and began to assemble my travellers' paraphernalia. My first concern was food. I envisioned myself emaciated on the road to Timbuktu, unable to carry on. I purchased cartloads of granola, energy bars, peanut butter. Thinking of a dry throat in the desert, I stocked Gatorade, chewing gum, and lozenges.

Choosing a backpack created another conflict: capacity versus functionality. I chose a High Sierra of singular orange, ensuring that it would not be mistaken for any other backpack. Not much chance of that; resting on the floor, it towered past my waist. A case encompassed its full width and length, and two end packets completed its ability to hold thirty kilos. The straps were wide, sturdy, and tucked behind a flap when not needed. A handle slipped out at the top for pulling the backpack, suitcase-like, on thick wheels. But now it seemed too large for the journey; I was disenchanted with how many comforts it could carry. I spent two months trying unsuccessfully to get rid of it, to replace it with something smaller and more manageable.

Once a week I worked a trapline of outdoor and mountaineering stores, vetting necessities: along with clothing suited for the desert night's temperature of five degrees Celsius or the midday's thirty-five, I gathered travel trinkets like crampons and lanyards, whether I needed them or not. (I did not.) At home, the floor of my room became littered with waterproof matches and candles, water purification tablets, and gauze strips.

In addition, I would carry a day pack. In a sop to good practice and paranoia, I duplicated many items in case one pack got lost. These essentials I chose carefully: maps, medical supplies, copies of important travel documents.

But still, fearful thoughts awakened me at night. A racing heart, images of tigers (there are none in Africa), and threatening faces resulted in the resolution to pack a sheath knife, sturdy and familiar from camping trips; a danger if stolen. Swiss Army knives won out — one for each pack.

The Bradt Guide mentioned a European-based company that relied on someone in Mali to make local arrangements for their once-a-year, eight-person tour through Burkina Faso, Mali, and Senegal. Through this company I got the name of Mohammed, who owned a travel service in Mali. It took a number of unanswered e-mails and a further direct prod from the European company before we were connected.

Mohammed was, however, a fountain of information. Timbuktu would be reachable with effort, time, and money. On the cheap, delay and frustration often ruled. You could travel on the River Niger for three days from Mopti to the small port of Korioumé in a long, thatch-roofed boat (*pinasse*), loaded with trade goods and people, smelly and uncomfortable. Then hitch a ride by road for seventeen kilometres to the arched entrance of Timbuktu. It seemed the right way to earn that achievement. Alternatively, there was a decent (in African terms) road from Mopti to Douentza — a distance of about 185 kilometres — followed by a day's drive via four-by-four north from Douentza to Timbuktu. My preferred plan was the river route heading to Timbuktu. (If you want to make the travel gods laugh, show them your plans.)

My first e-mail to Mohammed outlined my ideas. "I leave in a little over a month. While I'm quite keen to be on my own as much as possible, I'm mindful of the need for arrangements for river travel. And for a guide and driver between Timbuktu and Bamako, though I don't wish to involve guide costs when they're not necessary." I sketched a possible travel sequence, a noncommittal itinerary.

Mohammed's reply positioned it all nicely and proposed an overland route to Timbuktu as the best strategy. "This is the busiest time. Options are scarce. After Timbuktu we will get you on *pinasse* and send you back to Mopti. You will definitely need a guide for Dogon Country and Djenné, but after that it is your discretion." He ended with an apology for "the delay in our response." I trusted him.

There was a ghost train in West Africa. The Lonely Planet guide told of tracks between Dakar, Senegal, on the Atlantic coast, and Bamako, the capital of Mali. It hinted at twice-weekly passenger service. Sorting out this train trip became, for me, symbolic of the unreliable information about this part of the world. Once I found it, the train did everything it could to vanish from my plans.

Although Timbuktu exists, there is a common sense that it is, in fact, nowhere. The train took on the same characteristic. Every reference was different. One book stated that the rail line existed but that the once-upon-a-time passenger service no longer did. An independent website said the train ran only on Wednesdays. Another source was emphatic that since departure was chronically unreliable, travellers should make other plans. A government website implied that the train existed. A recent travel article said, "It is no longer there to be ridden."

One story stipulated that if you did have the choice between taking the rumoured Wednesday train or the purported Saturday train, take the former: first, it derailed less often; second, it had fewer thieves.

I e-mailed Mohammed to ask if the train ran and, if so, when it departed. His wife replied that when it did, it was dangerous. "You are definitely very ambitious in your endeavors to travel to Mali!" she began. "With your desire to delve into the Malian culture and language you will win many hearts," she said. "I do not advise travelling by train between Senegal and Mali. It is extremely uncomfortable, chaotic, and no matter how careful you are, you are bound to have something stolen. There are many ways to be adventurous, but travelling this train is not a fun one."

"As to the train," I replied, "I need to do this." My youngest son, Sean, who has travelled by rail in many parts of Eastern Europe, said to me, "Don't pack anything you're not prepared to have stolen." I mentally prepared to re-provision in Bamako if the worst happened. My air bookings were made into Dakar rather than Bamako, solely to take advantage of the possible train trip. Mohammed's wife captured the image well: "It sounds certain to be sadder than any train I've been on."

A U.K. conference on business tourism presented me with another opportunity to speak about tourism's international obligations as well as its potential to bring prosperity to tourism destinations. In London on a Monday, with another presentation scheduled that Friday for Tourism Edinburgh's annual meeting, I seized two research days mid-week at the British Library.

In the rare book room, I felt I would at last find the obscure facts I needed. I sniffed the ambience and grazed among the shelves. The room smelled of thinking. I searched titles on the computer, working through the list I had compiled from countless bibliographies and references. With a click of the computer mouse, the books I requested were pulled from mysterious, hidden shelves. Then, surrounded by walls of leather-bound volumes and silent fellow readers, I sat on the research bench, anticipating the impending facts and stories. The reader's light came on at my designated seat, beckoning me to the library counter, where the first six books were ready for my perusal.

The pages consumed unnoticed hours. I gulped words as a parched throat would water. I flipped between books without discipline, a hungry man at a smorgasbord. When I settled down, it was with books I'd sought in stores to no avail, and older tomes not available at other libraries.

The next day in the rare book room, I fondled an 1813 edition of Mungo Park's *Travels in the Interior of Africa*. Gently placing it in a felt easel to protect its fragile binding, I opened the gatefold map of Park's West African travels, its edges brown with frail markings. There was no mustiness, only the harmony of age and paper.

If I were to live a borrowed life, I would have chosen Mungo Park's. He, more than anyone, symbolizes to me the adventure traveller. History credits him with sighting the River Niger and determining that it flowed, contrary to educated thinking in Europe, eastward. Inland. I read through his book anxiously, only to find that, despite all his preparations and tenacity, Timbuktu had eluded him in both 1795 and 1805.

After two long days of reading, I left the British Library unshaven and bleary-eyed, my mind filled with archaic phrases, dismal stories, and haunting images.

It was raining, and I walked two kilometres in the freshness. In the night's damp I reached Stanford Books and Maps off Leicester Square, hidden behind a reconstruction of its facade. On the second floor, I found myself in Africa. Shelves and tabletops offered dozens of books on the continent.

Park's *Travels* waited on a wood shelf in a recent edition with an afterword by Anthony Sattin. Again I was struck by the coincidences that informed my preparations, as Sattin's book *The Gates of Africa: Death, Discovery, and the Search for Timbuktu*, was my history bible.

Stacking my coat, Park's *Travels*, and an English map of Mali for purchase, I browsed the African titles. In a shipping box not yet off the trolley lay an untouched *Rough Guide to West Africa*. I debated the guide's £18 cost against the fact of already having two other editions of the book. What hints or directions could be new? I picked it up and thumbed through it, looking for information on train service between Dakar and Bamako. This was my most reliable test for unreliable details and conflicting information.

Muttering hope, I skimmed and found *The Express International*. That was the train Malians were responsible for, the Saturday train, my hoped-for-against-hope Dakar departure. I read that this train "has not been in operation for several years." My disappointment was confirmed; my route would not work as planned.

Then, the *Océan-Niger*. An enchanting name for a Senegalese operation of mixed reputation. The guidebook called this trip a "gruelling journey — one of the last great train rides in Africa." It ran! On Wednesdays. It was the *only* train from Dakar to Bamako. One of my problems was solved as another was created: four extra days in Dakar, as my arrival date there was fixed with an air ticket. Now, it seemed, so was my departure from Dakar. At least it would be by train.

Then I came across a confusing statement about the train: "At the time of writing ... the service appears to have ceased operating entirely." Time of writing? I paged the book for its publication date. It was that very month. This must be true. *The Lonely Planet Guide to West Africa*, published a year earlier, suddenly seemed as dated as my dream.

I was a month away from my trip and oblivious to an event that would reshape my travels. Standing in Stanford's, I flipped further in the guidebook and learned about the "Festival au Desert," a Tuareg celebration of Malian music, which would take place from January 9 to 11. Tagged as the "most remote festival in the world," it promised Ali Farka Toure and boasted that Robert Plant had performed there the year before. Well, if Robert Plant could make it, so could I.

Sitting on the warm bookshop floor on a cold London night, I saw for the first time the name Essakane, the village where the Tuareg would stage their festival. This oasis, with two hundred inhabitants, was in the Sahara Desert, sixty-five kilometres northwest of Timbuktu. Should I rearrange my dream trip of trekking in the Dogon Country, then routing back to Mopti and making slow travel by the River Niger to Timbuktu? If I travelled to Timbuktu by road, I could arrive earlier and go to the festival. But no, the approach to Timbuktu should be arduous, earned.

I bought *The Rough Guide to West Africa* and began making plans for passing those unwanted days in Dakar before the Wednesday train departed, *if* it departed.

By the third week of December, my efforts were being stymied by not wanting too much structure. My Mali connection, Mohammed, promoted the Festival au Desert in a reply e-mail and proposed an itinerary that would get me to Timbuktu a week earlier, and by land rather than by river. The delayed train departure from Dakar cramped my schedule further. I would not get to Bamako on time, and I was faced with abandoning my original route. My explanation of that conundrum frustrated Mohammed. His latest began huffily, "We are not sure exactly what you want from this trip."

I could see his point.

But Mohammed's efforts, which I had solicited, veered toward more control than I liked. He intended to be in Bamako the week I arrived. If neither of the two (perhaps mythical) trains ran there from Dakar, I'd take a bus across Senegal or fly from Dakar to somewhere in Mali. My decision to leave such arrangements until I was in Africa increased Mohammed's frustration. Finally, his impatience showed: "We suggest we meet you in Bamako the day after you arrive and plan out your journey to Timbuktu." He offered to inform the Wawa Hotel, a place I could not find referenced in any guidebook, that I would show up at the hotel that week on an unknown day.

I accepted his offer. At this stage, my confidence in Mohammed was high (which gave it room to slip, and room it would need).

The most consistent advice I had received was to have a guide and prearranged driver for overland travel in either direction between

Bamako and Timbuktu. Guidebooks and history persuaded me to include the River Niger and *Le Pays Dogon* in my trip. Mohammed repeatedly urged venturing to the once-famous trading centre of Gao, a settlement in the remarkable beauty of river and desert, as well as other places he said were of interest to tourists. I declined them all. He relented.

Within each of us are character traits that grow with risk. I sensed my risk was shifting from that of a quest to that of trusting this man. I considered scuttling his role, which in fact I'd sought. But having someone local was my linchpin of safety. I committed to wiring him money.

Unwrapped Christmas presents were strewn about our mountain cabin the days before I left North America. Most were intended to be useful to me in my quest: our nation's flag in pins and iron-ons; *L'Alchemist* for my French reading on the trip, as it tells of the traveller's search and finding; a Leatherman knife-tool that could fix, cut, or prod most anything living or mechanical. And, from son Brent, a rare copy of Brian Gardner's book *The Quest for Timbuktu*, my most informative history lesson. From Janice, *Hemingway in Africa* by Christopher Ondaatje. It occurred to me that perhaps one could read these books and avoid the pending turmoil of the journey, but I brushed away the unworthy thought.

There was, as well, a French-language map of Mali. Although I'd thought an English-language map would be better, or at least comprehensible to me, this gift was inspired. Few Malians would have been able to point me the right way on an English map.

Another gift was a pocket watch that clamped shut to keep out the sand. I have not worn a watch for thirty years, having once been late and missed a departing airplane that crashed. Time seemed to move along fine without having me watch it. Despite that, I packed the timepiece when my family suggested that this was about safety; sometimes catching transportation does rely on punctuality.

A friend, his wisdom anchored in his family's exile from Uganda, offered advice in a noisy pub just before I departed: "For each of us there are two destinies." I swallowed the remnants of my beer while his mug remained full; I listened. "One is the destiny you pursue," said Abdullah, finally taking a drink. "The other is the destiny that pursues you."

At that point in my life, there was no more fitting symbol for travel destiny than Timbuktu. It spoke of "beyond," of "difference," and "silence." Abraham Cresques's 1373 map of West Africa made the first delineation of Timbuktu. Since then, *Timbuktu* has meant "can't get there" to Westerners, and every traveller dreams of having been to such a place.

I was fully aware that my personal quest paled in comparison with those who had gone before and with notable contemporaries who explored uncharted caverns, climbed unnamed mountains, and engaged in peculiar escapades of discovery. I admired those who did that; respected their skills, fortitude, and stick-to-it-iveness. My journey had a clear motive: the betterment of self and the topographical freedom that Timbuktu implied. And I was realistic. As one journalist had recently written, "It takes a lot of effort to get to Timbuktu."

On a snowy New Year's Eve in Vancouver, in a convenience store displaying a half-burned-out Western Union sign, I wired Mohammed the promised payment. I was prepared for Bambara and French, but not for that store owner's Cantonese. He declined my credit card and wanted cash. I fought the crowds escaping the closing of a nearby shopping mall to find a bank machine and obtained the funds. But my pre-trip ordeal was not yet over. In his first efforts as a Western Union franchisee, the clerk managed to send my payment to Bulgaria. After taking half an hour to reverse this transaction, he succeeded in getting it to Mali. The money was sent simply to a name in a land. *Mohammed (last name), Mali.* That was it. A peculiar trust. At eight o'clock I headed home in the freezing dark to a cooling dinner and an even cooler Janice. Understandably, her patience was near an end.

I was ready to go to Timbuktu the next day, a little afraid and tremendously excited. That night I prayed. "God, just don't lose track of me."

Mohammed's wife said of the Dakar-Bamako trains that they are "certain to be sadder than any train I've been on."

TWO

The Origin of Myths

BOARDING THE FIRST-CLASS COACH OF *THE EXPRESS
International* in Dakar in the afternoon heat was complicated by a
boarding platform of rocks, divots, and garbage. The task was made
even more difficult by the fact that the cars were not numbered. The
train was coloured the green of a grocery store awning last washed
in the 1970s. It would carry me east to Bamako, Mali, where I'd
make arrangements for travel to Timbuktu. My coach was close to
the diesel engine, nearer the fumes but with a smoother ride than
the trailing coaches. The cement walkway of potholes and skips
ended well before it reached the highest-priced coaches. From there
it was strewn with rubble for three more lengths, after which I
found a vaguely identifiable attendant dressed in everyday clothes.
He seemed as surprised to be proffered my ticket as I was to learn
that he was in charge.

"*Un billet?*" he demanded, staring at me suspiciously.

"Here, try this," I said, thrusting my ticket papers his way.

"*Oui. Quatre,*" he said. And I climbed aboard in search of my
berth.

I edged down a narrow corridor filled with people. Roomette
(a loose use of the term) "Four" had been replaced with its alphabet
counterpart, "D," lettered in dribbled paint.

Nudged aside by a family hustling off the train before it
departed, I entered my roomette to face a blunt man, black muscles

bursting his black shirt. He seemed twice my size and half my age. He pointed to the lower berths to indicate they were both taken. He was intrusive; he had simply got here first. I resented him immediately. Eyes locked, neither of us moved. I thought, okay, I'm about to be flattened.

"Then help lift my bag," I groaned, stabbing it with a finger and swinging my head to indicate the two top bunks that were now mine.

He hoisted it atop all by himself, smiled, shook hands as a victor would, and introduced himself as Ebou. His Dakar friend, the custodian of the other low berth, poked in and grinned with a handsome mouthful of teeth. "Ussegnou," he said by way of self-introduction. He was bigger and blacker than Ebou, and his face glistened in an easy sweat.

The train jerked, throwing the three of us together. The six hundred pounds of us could barely turn around in our roomette. My journey jostled to a start.

I was 2,123 kilometres from Timbuktu.

It was my good fortune to be on the train at all. Only the Saturday train existed! At least this week.

Arriving in Dakar near 11:30 the previous night, I fumbled my way through customs, past beggars, all the while shying away from loud offers of "taxi" in order to find a rickety bus, more rust than paint, that promised to drop me at the Sofitel Dakar Teranga hotel.

I asked a fellow standing nearby, "Does a train run from Dakar to Bamako?"

He shook his head. Then, in a language I'd never heard, he spoke to a dishevelled man leaning against a lamppost with no lamp. The man's answer sounded pleasant but emphatic. "He says maybe Wednesday. Me, I don't think there's a train anymore."

The bus bumped from airport brightness onto craggy pavement and spotty streets on its run to downtown. It stopped at a poorly lit entrance to let off two passengers, leaving me alone on the vehicle. Fifteen minutes later it wound into the driveway of my hotel.

After checking in, the question still nagged. "Is there a train to Bamako?" I asked the frumpy hotel desk clerk, a young woman who was more smiles than help. We duelled in English and French. Something I said in French was a laugh line, and she swung around in her chair, straightened to an attractive pose, and spoke in a third language to a giant man behind the counter. He shook his head, not seeing the humour.

Then, he reconsidered, scratching his grey temple. "Yes. I think there is a train." He was the hotel's night manager, and maybe he wanted the train to run as much as I did. His left hand slowly dropped from his forehead and scrunched his mouth and chin into an indecisive frown. "But she says no." His head twisted to face the telephone operator, who had overheard my question.

"There used to be a Saturday train," he said. "Go to the station in the morning and find out." With that he turned and walked to the other end of the counter.

A currency machine accepted my VISA card and disgorged sufficient *seffe* that I no longer felt the peculiar vulnerability that comes from carrying only U.S. dollars in a foreign country. I downed a Senegalese beer, stuffed some West African currency in my pocket, and headed to bed.

Even my jet lag–addled sleep could not dull the sense of immediacy I had upon waking the next morning. Leaving behind an unmade bed and a large pack stuffed in my room, I strolled out of the hotel lobby holding a styrofoam cup of coffee with powdered milk and a teetering lid, and carrying my small day pack. My goal: train station at sunrise. My prayer: that there was a Saturday train. My sub-prayer: that it didn't leave at sunrise.

I was learning local names and trying my tongue with them. Tannis was a huffy porter helping as the doorman. He whistled for a taxi. Getting in, I uttered one of the few French phrases I was confident about, clearly directing to *Le Gare de Dakar*. The driver looked puzzled, but nevertheless delivered me to a place he didn't believe I needed to go. The streets were deserted all but for the coffee vendors setting up their stalls and the morning bread merchants on bicycles. Ten minutes from the hotel we swept in front of a shabby building, once proud, and perhaps once a landmark. It looked unused. I could only conclude that this was the train station.

"Train?" I asked, paying the driver.

"Non," he replied, pocketing my money.

Under the trio of high arches, the dank station's iron gates were open. I walked beneath the *Arrivée* sign, where a solitary woman and her mop played at the concrete floor. The building's foyer felt as old as the railway's first arrivals, who had come in 1923 from the then colony of French Sudan and its capital, Bamako. At the far end of the room, a dowdy man sat on a stool, his face against a window, speaking to a man behind it. I walked toward them through stale air and saw a handwritten departure schedule taped to the window frame, through which they kept talking. There was no glass. Both old men wore threadbare clothes. Mr. Gitta. Mr. Sarr.

I sputtered my questions about Dakar to Bamako, first in French then in English as though to reassure myself, since they just kept nodding. In this *franglais*, I was hearing and confirming.

"Train ticket?"

Nod.

"Train today?"

Nod.

"Train ticket? Single? Bamako? Sleeping Car? Today?"

Nods.

"Aujourd'hui?" I tapped at the counter to ensure I was not creating a problem through wishful thinking. Emphatic tap again. *"Aujourd'hui!"*

Mr. Sarr slipped off his chair and leaned a finger to the hand-scrawled schedule. The paper was scruffy and looked tentative. "Yes. Today," he said in English.

It was true. Saturday. 1:50 p.m. Dakar, Senegal to Bamako, Mali. Thirty-five hours. I exclaimed in delight. They snickered at my giddiness.

A few hours later, diesel fumes filled the air as we lurched along the route first begun in 1907, more than 1,200 kilometres away, near Bamako, after years of political deliberation. We were moving in discomfort, but I welcomed this after spending two hours standing in line with hundreds of Senegalese and Malians, all of whom were barred from the shade of the station until shortly before departure. It is a wonder to me that a train of fourteen coaches, carrying that many people, could be kept a secret. The factor at work here was irregularity, the on-again, off-again unreliability. Would it run next Saturday? Who knew?

"Ebou," stressed the keeper of the lower bunk after I mispronounced his name. His mellow voice reverberated in our small chamber, and I got his name right the second time. Ebou was a walrus of a man. His head barely fit the Boston Red Sox cap he wore. His smile was so broad it seemed like an extra row of teeth. As the train bunted underway, he grinned at my large pack, which I'd crammed onto one of the top bunks. I'd sleep on the other one.

Ussegnou was a quiet man with a slow smirk that morphed into a grin; he had a cautious enjoyment of all things. His eventual laugh showed a pink tongue. It was difficult to gauge where his forehead gave way to the baubles of hair; his scalp was a melding of darks. His baggy shirt hid the amount of room he required.

The three of us, each at least six feet tall, sized each other up. If our luggage could breathe, there'd be no air left. We realized that we were stuck with each other. Into this crowd came first the hand and then the head of the conductor, jabbing the still air of the upper mattress that held my pack. Beneath his armpit a seventeen-year-old snuck into the roomette.

"*Bonjour,*" the young man laughed. "Pierre," he introduced himself, aware that he'd been thrust into our room against our wishes. Pierre was full of energy and at home in our midst immediately, despite the presence of my bag on *his* bunk. Ebou and Ussegnou each grabbed an end of my pack, shifted it across the room, and crammed it into the corner of my bed, leaving barely enough room for my bootless feet against the metal ceiling. Pierre sprang from the floor to his berth in an effortless arch, landing seated, his feet dangling to a stop in unison. He was a professional dancer with an African troupe. Between gigs right now, Pierre was on holiday to stay with family near Bamako. He ran his hand through the field of tufts on his scalp and leaned back to the corner of the wall. He bent to mould himself against it. A gold chain gleamed around his neck, outside his T-shirt. "Where you from?" he asked in practised English. And our answers flowed as we settled in.

Grime covered the window, doubly so because the dirty top pane had been pushed down in its sleeve behind the stationary one. We could see more clearly through a jacket than through the eons of smoke encrusted on this double-glazing. From the top half of the window, where I leaned into the slow breeze of the train, I could see the intermingling of people and garbage near the track. Goats ate rubbish, children tossed plastic bottles as toys, women hunched over fires, men peed as they faced the train, their backs to the sign *Défense d'Uriner*, telling me I was not the first to sense that this could be a health problem. It was their life. This day's only difference was the ghost train moving among them.

We aimed for Thiès and from there toward the border between Senegal and Mali.

Pierre was beside me at the window, upwind, as the train gained speed. Just in time, he turned his head in to ask a question and avoided a faceful of spray. Frequent train travellers call the wispy moisture "The Christening." Pierre knew it was fizz blown from the front coaches' flushed toilet. He tightened his lips and grunted.

In the fourteenth century, before the European Renaissance, Timbuktu was home to Africa's religious, intellectual, and business elite. Timbuktu, the centre of enlightenment, was attuned to the Africa of its day in a way unlike any European city's relationship to its continent. The city's commercial success financed the creation of schools, among them the prestigious Koranic Sankor University, in what is now seen as the culture's golden age. Up to two hundred thousand people lived at one of history's great crossroads on the fringe of the Sahara. But today, with the desert's sands eroding the city, fewer than twenty thousand souls call it home.

In the beginning, there was salt. For millennia, at various times and places, salt has been a treasured source of power and wealth. Thought to influence both female fertility and male potency, it has long been an important element of religious ceremonies, superstitions, and medicine. Before its preservative qualities saved food on distant journeys or in storage, it was used to stabilize mummies. Whether derived from brine or hard salt, its ownership has brought prestige, prompted wars, and provided tax revenues.

Salt coins have even been used as currency. But, while the uses and supply of salt are plentiful, its locations and availability were not always so, thus its disproportionate value until a century ago.

Salt caravans from Tegusa, almost two thousand kilometres away, crossed the Sahara southward, laden with Mediterranean merchandise to swap at Timbuktu, close to the River Niger's water commerce. There, the caravans would meet northbound traders to exchange their goods for gold from southern African mines in Banbuk and Boure.

In a common trading scene, a pile of salt tablets would be offered, and its visual impact weighed against an offered stack of gold. Over days of unhurried negotiations, traders would add gold ingots or take pieces of it from this pile. In response, or when pre-emptive bartering served their purposes, salt merchants would enlarge or diminish their own stack. Guarded night and day, the resulting mounds reflected the patient deliberations. The individual salt tablets, carved from the mines in rectangular blocks, weighted nearly ninety kilograms each. It is said that on occasion, a given weight of gold was traded for an equivalent weight of salt.

Tribal differences often defer to trade needs. Bruce Chatwin, in West Africa, observed that trade functioned as "a language which prevents people from cutting each other's throats." The Songhai met in Timbuktu with the Fulani, who traded with the Wangara, all of them leery of the Tuareg and reliant on the Arabs.

Merchants and nomads also arrived on the River Niger with all manner of goods: weapons, cooking utensils, foods, and medicines. Slave trading — African slaves for African owners — existed prior to the American and European trade in slavery and Timbuktu offered a convenient venue for the exchange. Timbuktu, the marketplace, soon became permanently settled.

While documents exist from the time when the expansive Ghana Empire of the eleventh century controlled Timbuktu, it was when the Malian Empire emerged in the early 1300s that the city became infatuated with the written word. This was the beginning of its intellectual reputation, created by the Mandigo Askia dynasty. Later the Songhai, proud descendants of Askia, ruled with a merchant fleet and military vessels to dominate Timbuktu's culture and trade. With its Muslim scholarship, and unparalleled influence on the central Sudan, as well as rumours of wealth and powerful knowledge, Timbuktu attracted unwanted attention.

The Moroccans sent an army of four thousand into the Songhais' tranquil desert community in the late sixteenth century. The plundering Moors exiled religious leaders and burned libraries; religion is the devil's left hand when it comes to destruction. With the death and the deportation of scholars, thousands of books and manuscripts went to Fez and Marrakech. Basil Davidson's perspective in *Africa: History of a Continent* is this: "If their invasion cost the Moroccans much more than it was worth, it cost the Songhai its place in history. For it demolished the unity and the administrative organization of the state, and while it left Timbuktu and Gao and Djenné as considerable cities, it robbed this civilization of its vitality."

Trade shifted like sand dunes, taking the trans-Saharan caravans farther west. Eventually Portuguese traders undermined Timbuktu's commercial supremacy by providing ports on the west coast of Africa and ships capable of navigating the River Niger. Timbuktu's decline had begun.

"I'll tell you a story," said Ebou, his eyes wide, white, and watching to see if I'd believe him. "It is true."

I smiled. "Okay."

"This very train, a few years ago, was travelling fast, then slowed. Near a village it popped off the rail."

"Popped?"

"Yes. Derailed."

"Was anyone hurt?" I asked, reasonably enough.

"No, nothing like that. That's not the story."

"Okay."

"Only the last car popped off the track. And it was slowing down. It dragged a little and then stopped. It would take a day, longer, for the repair crews to come. Everyone was anxious to go. Word went out to the village and to nearby places. Three hours later, there were many people, mostly men and big children."

"You're not going to tell me ..." I started.

"Yes, it is what you think. They all together lifted the train back onto the track."

My expression must have conveyed my disbelief.

"It is true," he repeated.

Ebou was a shoemaker. His family name, Coldonneur, reflected that. He said he had sore feet, which seemed odd, but I said nothing while offering powder and a salve from my medicine staples. He appreciated that.

The train's occasional village stops let a few locals on board and as many off. Vendors rushed the tracks beside the train. They handed up for sale cloth sashes, cooking oil, oranges for refreshment. Children acted as porters, their heads balancing platters of corn. Or they asked passengers for permission to collect our empty bottles.

From in the crowd and onto the tracks stepped an astonishingly beautiful woman in a yellow dress. Ussegnou saw her first and nudged us in time to catch the elegant toss of her right foot as she stepped on a wooden box to make her way into a coach.

Cash and carry sales continued well past the train's warning whistle, from ground to window through outstretched arms. The train moved off, slowly at first, and the sellers ran alongside, closing deals. Their bartering was clipped short by the steel wheels.

"Rick."

It was Ebou. His dusty fingers were pulling aboard two loaves of the freshest bread. His hands twisted and tore the baguettes in two. Crumbs scattered everywhere.

My French worked when I worked at it. Ebou took the lead, describing himself as *mon professeur* for the coming days. He taught phrases, repeated French words for objects, and had fun with my ineptness. My fellow travellers' English was better than my French, and they were more confident in it. They didn't feel silly trying to help me learn. I began to relax, having fun with the repetition, and that they liked.

Our train stopped again. To the window we went. It had been only fifteen minutes since the last station stop, and the throng of merchants pressed their wares on us. Atop heads were baskets of fruit, baskets of meat, and baskets of smaller baskets. The heads were old, they were young. They were all women's heads.

Again Ebou spotted the stunning woman we'd noticed earlier. She stepped briefly off the train and retrieved something from a man. She had a new red sash wrapped around her hair. It hung over a bare shoulder above her yellow shift. How could the drape of cloth on skin say so much?

Later, lying in my upper bunk with my stocking feet wedged to the metal roof above my pack, I recalled my initial unhappiness about the crowded roomette. I wrapped it in my mind and tossed it aside. I could see clearly through the open window, and if I were on a lower berth I'd have to look through a pane soiled with smoke that had been ironed on by the wind. The roomette's dome light didn't work. The reading lamp sputtered. The fan had been torn from the ceiling. The radio on a lower bunk carried the Senegal soccer game, audible everywhere on the train. The train wobbled. "It's like a ferry boat!" Ebou exclaimed, rocking, his sea legs strong. I was starting to love this place.

Pierre asked about our destinations.

"Burkina Faso," Ebou answered. "Friends are there. We'll visit them, help them farm. Maybe two weeks."

"And where are you travelling?" Pierre asked me.

Ebou leaned into the conversation before I could answer, presuming the train's destination was mine. "Why Bamako?"

"I'm going to Timbuktu," I said.

"*Tombouctou,*" Ebou corrected. And with awe, added, "It is very far."

I listened to them talk among themselves, and noticed my frustration with the West Africans' French accent. I asked about French words that Ebou said were not French. They were speaking Bambara, interspersed with French phrases and uttered with a French lilt. Their conversation and the slapping of wet branches on our window lulled me to sleep.

By the time of our next stop, a bond had been forged. One day into my travels, despite all the warnings I'd received in the previous months, I trusted my bunkmates with my pack and left the train. Every time we stopped for fifteen minutes, each of us wanted time on the ground, mingling and wandering in the market. The only

THE ORIGIN OF MYTHS

workable way to do this was to have one of us stay on the train, watching everyone's bags. We took turns. It was a train with thieves, but I knew that none shared my room.

Ebou elbowed me to look at the woman yet again. Three stops, three sightings. She had entered our realm and did not even know it. Looking past her and thirty metres along, I got a sense of our train's exterior: weathered green trimmed with "stainless" steel that had found a way to stain.

Not having the confidence to buy cooked meat, I moved close to a fire and looked in the market at the meat on the coals. It smelled fine. Smelled, though. Ussegnou was pulling brochettes of goat meat off a stick and into the glove of his bread loaf. English banter filtered his French as he held it up to me. "Try." It looked delicious. I declined.

I held out a handful of *seffe*, and it was picked clean by the wizened fingers of a woman with crinkly skin around her eyes. She gave me four loaves of her freshly baked bread. It was a warm gift for our roomette, ensuring we'd all sleep in crumbs that night. When I handed a loaf to each of my roommates back in our *couchette*, they set theirs down, untouched, and continued breaking from the one I'd started: the bread would stay fresher longer that way. And I realized that everything I ate on this trip would be shared with my roommates. And almost everything I drank.

Our perches, except for sleeping, became interchangeable. You leaned where you wished, lay where you pleased. From a lower bunk I scanned the roomette realizing I'd never, ever, been in such filthy surroundings. It was like a drunk tank without the spittle. But it was home for now, and I was starting to settle in.

The sun was setting in shades of purple. I flopped sideways on the lower bunk to catch its last rays and landed on Ussegnou's radio, bending the antenna. His big hands cradled it as he would a small bird that some klutz had wounded. "No problem," he said, assuaging my guilt. "No problem." Then he smiled, widely, and calmed the room.

Taking in the aisle's fresher air, Ebou and Ussegnou leaned into the window space. Each had one arm over the other's shoulder. They had a brothers' camaraderie. I plunked my chin into the crest where their shoulders met. Out our window was the Sahara, source of three hundred million tonnes of dust every year. Sixty percent of the world's dust blows around West Africa.

Ussegnou pointed through the open window as the tracks curved, and the front of the train came into view. Rooftop passengers were crouched in a silhouette on the first coach. They started to disappear as a cloud hid the moon. I thought about how differently we travel to the same destination. Night covered them.

"What are you thinking?" Ebou asked later, catching my long stare and breaking my reverie. I looked across the train's floor to the lower bunk and at his face. His eyes searched me. He was not merely trying to be polite.

"I was thinking about travelling," I said.

He took that to be a mistake on my part, a daydreaming of trips to come. "No one is promised another journey," he said. "Enjoy the one you're on."

In the hallway of *The Express International* I met a Frenchman. In the manner of the French, his English was very good and he politely relinquished his mother language so that we could converse. Alec was his name. Maybe thirty-five, his age was made more vague by his balding head and narrow cheeks. A crumpled packet of cigarettes was stuffed in his shirt pocket. He had lived for six years in Chad, Nigeria, and Senegal. It was his first time on this train. He sipped a red drink, a local beverage he'd purchased at the last train stop. "*Bissap*," he said. It was semisolid liquid, sealed in a small plastic bag, or so it seemed. "The other is ginger," he pointed to a Senegalese man holding a similar package. It was browny-green, and the man sucked at it from a bitten-off corner. My distaste must have shown. "They are boiled, then frozen," he said, pausing to reassure himself. "At least in theory."

I declined his offer of a sip.

"Doesn't bother me," he boasted, patting his stomach. "I've had whatever I'll get."

He asked how far I was going. "Timbuktu," I said.

"*Tombouctou,*" he corrected.

Train travellers Ebou, Matthew, Pierre, Alec, and Ussegnou.

"Have you been?" I asked.

"Never. I was never near enough." That from a man who had travelled most of West Africa.

Matthew, his friend, came from their roomette into the corridor, unshaven, the arms of his sunglasses stuffed in the bushy sides of his hair. He was thin enough that even with his blue shoulder pack he didn't take up too much corridor space. Alec motioned at me. "He is going to *Tombouctou*."

"I've thought of that," Matthew said. "Too far."

Seven hundred years ago, there was a dramatic shift in the world's awareness of Timbuktu, one that reset the salt-and-scholarship centre's reputation. The Sultan of Mali was Mansa Kankan Musa, whose empire stretched from the Atlantic Ocean eastward to what is today northern Nigeria and from what we know as central Mauritania to the border of modern Ivory Coast. It would take a year to cross Musa's kingdom by camel. Timbuktu was then wealthier than Moscow or Madrid.

The sultan undertook a journey in 1324 that would establish the remarkable association of Timbuktu with unfathomable wealth. A Muslim, he decided to visit Mecca. He crossed the Sahara Desert in the company of sixty thousand people, each responsible for carrying and protecting a three-kilogram rod of gold while travelling to Cairo with "the greatest caravan in history." Mansa Musa's 180 tonnes of travelling gold had a profound impact, as he spent and gifted his way across Africa. According to the *UNESCO General History of Africa*, "When he stopped in Egypt, the Egyptian currency lost its value. Word of incredible richness spread rapidly beyond Africa to Europe."

A few decades later, the Moroccan Ibn Battutah, "the world's greatest traveller," visited Timbuktu. Having spent a lifetime travelling from country to country via every mode of transit then imaginable (and guided by the dictum "Never follow the same road twice"), his writings were sought by royalty and learned men — and they were believed. His reports of his visit to Mali in 1353 were the first outsider's eyewitness account of Timbuktu. The "City of Gold" acquired a reputation that would take five centuries to lose.

Almost two centuries later, in 1526, the Moor Leo Africanus, who reportedly traversed 120,000 kilometres in his almost continuous journeys around the known world, visited Timbuktu as an emissary of the Sherif of Fez. His account, *The History and Description of Africa*, is based on his two trips to Timbuktu and extensive travels in the north and west of Africa. Written in Spanish and eventually published in English, the *Geographical Historie* rightly placed the African metropolis near the River Niger, at the time a river whose source, flow, and mouth were unknown to the Europeans.

Leo Africanus's tale of Timbuktu was in keeping with the popular perception that vast glories awaited visitors to this city. Never skimpy on superlatives, he wrote of Timbuktu, "The inhabitants are exceedingly rich." Refreshing the public's palate, he proclaimed, "The coin of Timbuctoo is gold ..." Europeans needed little else to dream of trade and to imagine a primitive people who might be easily subdued by their power. His more modest description of the homes, "built of chalk, and covered with thatch," rang contrary to the images Europeans wanted, the embellishments missing, and it was ignored. The impression of unimaginable wealth would endure for three more centuries.

But Africanus told the truth as well: "There are many judges, doctors, and clerics here, all receiving good salaries from King Askia Mohammed of the State of Songhai. He pays great respect to men of learning. There is a great demand for books." Curiously, though, given the extent of markets for gold and salt and other valuables, Africanus claimed that "more profit is made from the trade in books than from any other line of business."

Galbraith Welch, writing in *The Unveiling of Timbuktu*, quotes Africanus as referring to "golden scepters and plates used by the King of Timbuctoo, some whereof weighted 1,300 pounds." Welch observed: "It is perhaps not too much to say that in the whole annals of literature there is not another passage which has conduced more materially to the progress of geography."

Out the train's window, Africa was black. In the north, the sky bent the Big Dipper off-side.

"We're not a quarter of the way there yet," Pierre said with a child's impatience. It was ten o'clock and cooling.

"We'll get there Monday, not Sunday," Ussegnou agreed. I munched a granola bar in my upper bunk, not sharing — worse, not thinking to share in my desire for nourishment.

The train stopped at Guinguinee. Two of us jumped off, landing near a cooking fire. My flashlight skimmed the mounds beside the tracks and canvassed the food stalls, following the tiny glows in the row of *brazier* fires. Matthew paused at several stands selling bottled water, gently twisted the caps of their product to test the seal and returned every bottle. All were suspect. His flashlight settled on a table of fruit. "Watermelon appeal," he announced. "Feel this." He tossed a melon to me, letting go at the last minute.

"Heavy," I said, accepting its weight.

"Too heavy. The locals fill them with water to make it seem worth more." And we both realized it was not water from a sealed bottle. "They sell sealed water in the dining car. And beer," he told me.

I was surprised. "There's a dining car?"

"*Oui.* Behind us. We just had dinner there."

"Dinner? Really."

"*Très bien,*" Matthew added as we climbed back into the vestibule.

At the roomette I found Ebou and Ussegnou eating cooled meat bought through the window. They sliced open the afternoon's bread and made a sandwich.

"Like some?" Ebou offered, handing it my way.

"I'm going to the dining car," I announced.

"There's a dining car?" Pierre asked from behind.

Putting my shoulder to the heavy metal door leading to the next wagonlit, I pushed and it opened. At first I thought I was seeing the effects of a brawl. A man lay on the bar top, another was asleep on a stool, and two more sat in silence and looked angry. I woke the slumbering man behind the bar.

"*Bière?*"

"*Non.*"

"*Non?*"

"They're out," said Alec, who happened to be tucked against the wall. "Or it may be that we're *toobabs*," he suggested, using their word for white foreigner.

Through the entrance I found the "dining room" portion of the coach with seven men crowded into a four-person booth, yelling about football. The rest of the room took its tone from that noise. This group had cornered the beer supply. Every seat was taken, save for one in the shadows at the end of the room. I took it. From there I surveyed the space. The windows were dim with night and grime, inside and out. Everyone seemed finished with their dinner. Cards were played. A student reading a book titled *Le Petit Voix* sat across from me.

The waiter in village attire walked over to me and I boldly ordered. "*Le petit déjeuner, s'il vous plaît.*" In for a penny ...

A hesitation. He came back and showed me a can of peas. I nodded. What else would you do? Peas and what? Unsure of what I'd ordered, I watched him go to a hole in the wall at the end of the coach a metre from my back. It was a half metre square and pitch dark behind. He talked to the darkness. A tiny light sparked and wavered, its glow focused down. Propane hissed.

I tried. *"Un bière?"*

A beer was clipped open before me. The waiter gave me a cloth napkin, which I thought was a nice touch. Used, mind you. Next, a plate with chicken, browned from frying, and spaghetti arrived. Clumped nicely at the side, peas. I had an immediate curiosity about hygiene and the likely dishwashing scenarios on board. I pulled from my day pack the knife and spoon I had scrounged from British Airways. Handy. I pushed the peas on the plastic knife and slipped them in my mouth, as Mom forbade. With one finger I held the chicken as I carved sinew. Missing a fork, I wound spaghetti around the knife. It was all quite tasty. I broke my spoon to fashion a spear and poked the chicken.

Finished with my meal, I moved the plate aside, where the waiter retrieved it and I reconsidered the place. It was a converted baggage car. People slept sitting up. Across from me, the silent student wrote. One table's bench seat was broken. It had a sturdy end, adjacent to the wall; the other end slanted to the floor.

The train lurched. I noticed the waiter eating his meal. Or, rather, eating what I'd left on my plate.

The possessions I'd left in *The Express International*'s roomette for the past hour while "dining" did not concern me. If they were to be riffled, they had been. I left the dining car knowing they hadn't.

In the car's aisle, I stepped over a sleeper. The dining car ended with a once-silver door, which I pulled open. It slammed shut behind me. All was shiny-dark in the vestibule where I waited. It was impossible to see, but I stepped in one motion over the floor plates that joined the two coaches, straddling the gap between them precariously. The other door would not budge. Mid-stride, I pushed. Then pulled. The gap widened in the dark. My feet shifted involuntarily on the metal sheets as they waltzed frantically in the train's winding. I leaned against the door, but had poor leverage; my feet were spread too far apart. We were moving at fifty kilometres an hour. There was a small porthole in the door, missing its glass, and I poked my head through, hoping for help. A porter sat in the dark on the other side, barely visible. He motioned me to slide. This opened the door.

My three companions were asleep. The window was shut and the room was filled with the staleness of exhaled air. It smelled of train iron, old mattresses, and odours you could taste. I pulled the window's steel frame down as far as it would open. Cool, fresh air poured in as one of my Senegalese roommates tossed in his bed. I'd wakened him. Hoisting myself up to the top bunk, I heard Ussegnou say, "Rick, Rick, use the ladder." I landed ungracefully, but the bed absorbed me. "I'm in." Ussegnou, the calm, gentle poultry farmer, rolled over.

I fell asleep to the measured *clack-click*, the sound of the train crossing the small welds that held the rails together — a rhythm lost to North America and much of Europe, with their modern, seamless rails.

Suddenly there was shouting and a scuffle in the hallway. We were all awake and out of the room, a crowded foursome with our backs to the doorway. About ten feet down the aisle, two men struggled with each other, fists flying and shoulders slamming. One man, in military fatigues, kicked the other's legs out from under him. A second official arrived as the man buckled, and he put his knee into the fallen man's calf. "He won't show his papers," Pierre whispered.

"Your passport, Rick?" Ebou asked. He looked very worried.

"In the pack," I said, tapping it for emphasis.

"When they ask for it, give it. If he asks for a thousand *seffe*, it is not normal, but give it. That's for his coffee."

Back in our room I noticed that someone had closed the window again. We all climbed into bed, me last. Before I went up top, I lowered the window once more. There was a resigned silence, one I did not understand.

THREE

The Quest for Timbuktu

I WOKE TO THE TRAIN'S FILTH. THE BATHROOM was at the end of the passage where our coach connected to the next. It was functional to the point of austere, and uncared for. I passed it on my way to the dining car for my morning coffee.

Alec and Matthew were sitting on the same side of a table and I took a seat opposite them. The side I sat on was the diagonal bench, its aisle end on the floor, broken. I perched on the incline as Alec mixed and poured me a *café au lait*, all powdered, and offered me his bread and jam. Matthew said, as though I needed to be warned, "Enjoy. Near the Sahara, every meal tastes of sand."

"Explain the coffee," I asked, as Alec reached across the table for a fresh sleeve of instant. "I expected some of the world's finest in Africa. So far it's all powdered. Does that change in Mali?"

"Keep searching," said Alec. "Nescafé is both the bane and the saviour in these parts."

"Bane?"

"There's supposed to be a boycott. It's aimed at Europe more than West Africa. Many years now. It's a boycott against the commercial pushing of powdered milk to replace the breastfeeding of newborns. Anger at the parent, Nestlé. Anger at the offspring, Nescafé."

"But they grow coffee here," I said. "Mali exports it."

"Ivory Coast is right next door," said Alec. "Largest coffee producer in Africa."

"Nescafé is just easier. It's everywhere," Matthew said. "You'll be hard pressed to find Malian coffee."

Bringing up another nagging issue, I pointed to the obviousness of my busted seat. Alec sighed, "It is their way," as though repairs were not a national trend. I was in an awkward posture and turned my back to the window for a brace, stretched my legs floorward to the aisle and shoved a slippery cushion beneath me. On the other side of my angled bench, facing the table behind me, was a Senegalese man in a tar-black robe. He was arguing about yesterday's football match. Every time he gesticulated, he bounced up and down, propelling my side's teeter-totter. I sipped the hot coffee slowly, carefully.

Matthew slunk in his seat, wearing the same clothing as yesterday. "We didn't think this passenger train ran anymore."

"In Dakar, I was told it had started up again only recently," I said.

"Ah," he said, smiling. "You can see the refurbishments."

The teetering seat jolted and my coffee splashed on the table. Matthew used a napkin to mop it up.

"A traveller I met had once taken the train from Dakar to Bamako, but not the passenger trip," Alec began. "He and his wife booked on a commercial run, sleeping with the cargo. They were shown to a container, huge, empty, and cheap. Inside it they set up their tent for the trip. At Thiès they were surprised to find goods being loaded into 'their' container, but adjusted their space by moving the tent." He leaned over the table to pour me more coffee so not to disturb my precarious seating, adding the powdered milk and stirring for me as he talked. "At the Kayes station stop, more storage got loaded into their shrinking compartment. At each stop, their accommodation was reduced by new cargo. By the last one hundred kilometres, they had about two square metres, behind shipped goods and uncomfortably close to the container roof."

We all laughed, knowing it could have been us, eager to travel by train and naive about the arrangements.

"These are true stories," Alec promised us. We knew another tale was coming. "A traveller boarded in Bamako in the popular section of the train, crammed with passengers, over one hundred in the coach. As the train jerked forward he saw he had left his bicycle on the platform. Jumping from the rolling train, he grabbed the bicycle and ran alongside the moving train, gaining slightly on it, hauling his bike with him. A Senegalese man reached out the window and took hold of the handlebars, clasping the bicycle to the side of the coach. Another hand reached out the doorway and hauled the traveller onto the train."

Alec paused for coffee and Matthew observed, "That is how they would do it."

"True," Alec said. "Rope was found and the bike was tied to the outside of the coach and lashed around a widow's frame, where it stayed for the entire trip."

Long before the "Timbuktu Rush," that international competition for the glory of discovery, bloomed late in the 1700s, the destination enthralled Europeans. Their romantic anticipations were not replaced by knowledge until death and dysentery had struck many of those adventurers seeking to be the first to reach the Forbidden City. Government sponsorship of sorties came with the expectation of eventual trade. The salt, the gold, the slaves — all were financial motives. To those were added national prestige, as both France and England sought a countryman to "discover" Timbuktu and return safely to Europe.

In 1788, an independent London group known as the Saturday Club more formally established an entity of exploration and took the name "Association for Promoting the Discovery of Inland Parts of the Continent of Africa," soon known as the African Association. Its specific goals were to explore the River Niger and to reach Timbuktu, the finding of the latter held to be that period's great geographical challenge. It determined resources and retained adventurous travellers to serve its mandate. Its most notable explorer was Park, who failed to reach Timbuktu on either of his journeys.

Within two decades in the eighteenth century, forty-three European expeditions were launched in search of Timbuktu.

Instead of success, they brought death in the Sahara, on the River Niger, or in little-known Malian villages. Their brazen entry sparked retaliation at the hands of suspicious people defending their territory. Frenchmen serving as an armed front for commercial interests drew attacks by itinerant bands that feared losing control of trade and politics. And the British often fell victim to the ignorance of health through their arrogant dismissal of the desert's extreme temperatures or stagnant waters; mosquitoes to them were irritants, not carriers of malaria.

The cost in English lives alone was exceptional: one hundred died in 1816, a year when two government-sponsored expeditions faltered. The British debated whether it was proper form to proceed across the Sahara as an explorer while in disguise. Some argued that it was important to be evidently British, to the point of travelling as British officers properly attired in woollens for duties in London while sweltering in West Africa. Most risky of all was to travel openly as a Christian, a faith distrusted by the Africans. Thus it was not long before the interior of Africa became known as "The White Man's Grave."

Geographical "firsts" abounded two hundred years ago, and the acknowledgement of such achievements was as much about scientific findings as about the individual prowess. Recognition and rewards were often substantial. The character traits of the nineteenth-century explorers ranged from bravery and ambition all the way to lunacy, self-aggrandizement, and a befuddling detachment from reality.

I sought out the stories of the early Timbuktu explorers and used their records as my trip primer, as guides to the rigours of the journey and the attitudes required to accomplish it. Five names stand out in the European search for Timbuktu in the nineteenth century. The Scot Mungo Park, of course. I will cross the River Niger upriver from the place where the Tuareg ambushed his final expeditionary force. The American Benjamin Rose (alias Robert Adams), whose forced trek in the open desert was relentlessly cruel. Alexander Gordon Laing (often referred to as Gordon Laing), the Scot who travelled a circuitous route with a singular goal. Frenchman René Caillié, a man of incredible diligence. And the

German Heinrich Barth, of whom it can be said that he put to rest the era's preoccupation with the myth of Timbuktu.

Additionally, in the European quest for Timbuktu, there is a first arrival: Gordon Laing, a captain (and a major, but only in Africa) in the British army whose motivation was notoriety. The thirty-three-year-old explorer left Tripoli for Timbuktu, arriving there in 1826. Sheikh Al Bekây favoured Laing with hospitality, a dramatic change from Laing's encounters with Tuaregs on his desert travels, where he had been badly misled. He described Timbuktu as the place he "discovered," and therein lies the motivation for travellers there still today: stepping aside from what one's colleagues or family expects in order to do something different, perhaps singular. It is said that the home Laing lived in can still be found in Timbuktu today.

The Scramble for Africa frequently consisted of well-funded, harebrained expeditions for reaching Timbuktu. Success even eluded astute and capable explorers, their fame in death hollow compared with the glory they sought. Unable to attract government funding, commercial support, or military backing, the Frenchman René Caillié was forced to make extraordinary preparations in order to be the first white man to both reach Timbuktu and to return safely to Europe. He did that in 1828, at the age of twenty-nine. Caillié developed an affinity for the natives and a desire to be like them. He lived for an extended period in what today is Guinea in order to learn the Muslim culture, became fluent in Arabic, and was not suspected to be European. Disguised as an Egyptian, he ventured to Djenné on the River Niger and from there to Timbuktu. The place where Caillié stayed while in Timbuktu appeared on the map in only one of my guidebooks. Perhaps because it was a nondescript home and because his time there was a mere two weeks, the structure was not one of the main destinations for travellers, though I felt I must go there.

In 1853, with costs underwritten by the British government, a German, Heinrich Barth, headed south across the Sahara from Tripoli. Experienced and curious, he had all the attributes of a tenacious traveller and has been called "one of Africa's greatest explorers." The arduous crossing, inevitable delays, and repeated

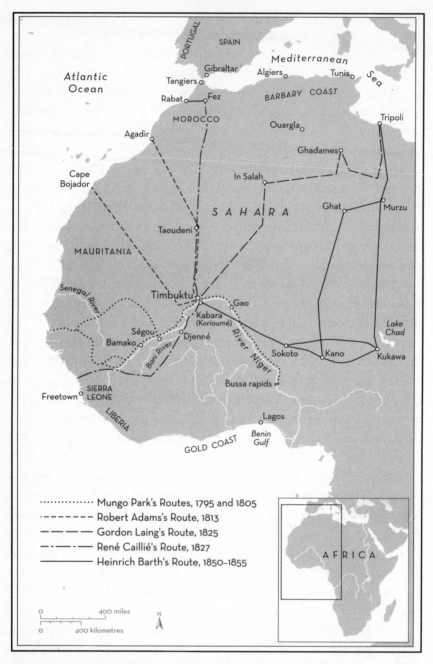

*Europeans knew Africa in the early nineteenth century as "The White Man's Grave,"
where many explorers perished in search of trade, honour, and fame. Those whose
journeys are shown here represent diverse backgrounds: two Scots, an American, a
German, and a Frenchman.*

dangers did not dissuade him. Ineffectively portraying himself as an Arab, his Christianity was tolerated in Timbuktu upon his unlikely arrival, but only through the benevolence of Sheikh Al Bekây. He was permitted to stay for eight months, after which he journeyed in difficult circumstances to Europe. The story of his stay and the resulting sketches were reportedly given a modest display at his one-time residence, which I intended to visit in Timbuktu.

La Frontière — the border — between Senegal and Mali was formally passed by *The Express International* at Diboli in the early morning. We stayed on board while the Senegalese locomotive was changed to a Malian one. Customs officials strolled through the train, knocking on doors to wake the sleeping or reluctant, and took our passports with the promise of return at our first stop. Not having our passports made me and my fellow travellers uneasy; a lost passport was reason enough for deportation by the very officials who might "lose" them.

The train bounced along the warped tracks and finally halted at Kayes a few dry hours later. Kayes has been called Africa's hottest town, with temperature readings up to fifty degrees Celsius. The heat stifled breath and thought. We were roughly halfway to our destination, geographically, if not time-wise. Uncertainty about our train's departure time made us anxious to retrieve the stamped passports.

Paul Theroux has said, "The border is drama, misery, real life, strangeness, and the actual sight of the dotted line one sees on a map. But it is usually the farthest distance from the capital, and so highly revealing of what a place is like." I had to agree. At the back loading dock of a mud-and-wood warehouse, West Africans frantically sought the return of their identity cards. African-nation workers and non-Malian itinerants jumbled with other foreigners wanting their passports. An official in a short-sleeved shirt with mock epaulets held a fistful of passports as he stood on a loading dock. Another in the same abbreviated uniform emerged on the deck above the crowd with two hands full of documents and the self-satisfied smirk of officialdom that is detested the world over. At their most coordinated, these two alternated the call of a country and a name. More often, they shouted over each other's announcements, their words colliding. Mayhem ensued, with people on the ground yelling helpful directions regarding which passports were currently being retrieved. Their words flew noisily, voices crashing against one another. Identity cards passed from hand to hand over the heads of a hundred people toward back-of-throng individuals waving when they thought they heard their name. A third official came through a separate doorway. His effort at efficiency added confusion. Then a fourth showed up.

"De Luzy. France," called a border guard flaunting a passport. It was Matthew's. We pointed at his waving hand. His proof of nationality was secured.

"Antonson. Canada." I heard new acquaintances shout my whereabouts to the petty official, who threw my passport to a black hand in the crowd. It was fumbled, caught and flipped in the air to a lady, from where it moved like a hot potato over half a dozen hands in a black wave and into mine.

A customs guard mispronounced the next surname, tried to say it again louder, and then added, "United States." At the building's corner stood two women, retreated from the fray, seemingly Americans in early adulthood. They were out of earshot and looked nervous. I moved their way, asking the pony-tailed brunette, "You American?"

"Yes," she said as if it were a secret. Her friend looked pale from the food, frail and worried. She shied a step backward. "Why?"

"I think they called your passport," I offered.

When they returned with their booklets, they linked arms as if to make their presence appear larger. They were bound for Bamako, and from there a straight return to Dakar, by air. The midwesterner was a Peace Corps worker in Senegal, the other a shell-shocked friend visiting from stateside.

"I wanted to go to Timbuktu," she said as we chatted about my goal. "But my supervisor refused to sign permission papers. It's very dangerous, you know. She threatened to cancel my entire trip when I suggested it."

"Timbuktu," her friend sighed poetically. "Forever far away."

Matthew and Eric walked by and cocked their heads, "Rick, come. We're going to get our passports stamped." Sure enough, nothing had been added to the documents that the officials had held for hours. Not a whisper of ink to signify our entry. And that oft-advised "It's a turn-back offence" warning? The Yellow Fever certificate was still in my pack on board the train. My French companions had been told by a Japanese university student that the police station would stamp passports. We wanted this odd accreditation for our journey, unsure if it was a souvenir or a validation.

Kids stopped us and offered frozen fruit juice in plastic bags the size of a fist. We wove around three women balancing bananas in pink plastic pails on their heads, shouting "*Nanasa-be* (banana-here), *Nanasa-be*." Matthew found the police corps at ease in front of a black-and-white television, where two French football teams were engaged in a match. Their building was a privileged location and enjoyed the broadest shade trees of the city. While two policemen were delegated to find the stamp and ink pad required to emboss our passports, Alec and Matthew argued for their favourite teams. A static, flipping image on television, maddening to me at home, brought joy to the *gendarme*.

Mindful that we were now out of earshot of the train's thin whistle (assuming there'd be such a courtesy), the three of us ran toward the station's tracks. As we neared, we could see through a fence that locals were boarding. A man palmed his hands in a groundward motion and said, in French, "It's not leaving."

We re-crossed the street, ordered three colas and a firm-topped bottle of water, and watched the football match continue on another static television screen. Drinking the healthy water, I downed my daily anti-malaria quotient.

Football transcends the utter nonsense of political ruin in Africa, providing fans with spirit and belief in their countrymen. The Africa Cup of Nations had been held in Mali the previous year, bringing new stadia, national pride, and a burp of economic renewal. As I travelled a year later, this pan-African series of contests played on transistor radios, on television sets, and in arguments over millet beer.

Making our way back to the train, we ran into the Japanese couple against the backdrop of our grungy transport. We exchanged stories, and the Kyoto student nodded slowly toward my French friends. He leaned his head my way, looking at me uncertainly, and then nodded some more. "Timbuktu ... ahh ... unreachable."

The Big River, as the locals called it, flowed under a train trestle as we ventured through *labrousse*, the French name for the bush country. The train hunched forward and sidled along the Sénégale River to more arid lands. Into the evening we stopped at a village near the river.

"Eight more hours to Bamako," announced Ebou, the optimist.

"Ten," countered Pierre, smiling his awareness of the train's poor reputation.

"Twelve hours," anted Ussegnou in a guess that would come closest to the actual.

Sunglasses deflected the grit thrown by the moving train toward our open window as dusk claimed the scene. The engine's headlamp glowed in the desert dark.

The train stopped abruptly and our coach argued, bunting its displeasure against the car in front. It was Ebou's turn to watch the bags, and Pierre, Ussegnou, and I leapt down to the platform of dirt. The scene engulfed us immediately, and we each went our separate way. It was very dark, and the way was pitted; there was hawking and unintended shoving.

A chain of cooking fires lined the track, commas in a sentence that described a land, a people, a way of life, an economy, families, and hierarchy. Each fire hole was stoked with twigs: every offering was different. My flashlight found a skewer-covered grill and would not let go. The charcoal flared under droplets of grease. My light skimmed across the choices. I took three kebabs and rolled them away from the others, setting them above the highest flame, and instructed the squatting grandmother that I wanted to keep these morsels cooking, to what I believed would be a singed, safe crispness.

A boy, maybe ten, called out from behind me as I tended the mystery meat. He had bread to sell and had been following me. His baguettes were large, and I took one that cost more than it should have but was still less than its value to me. The young seller scampered into the night. I tore the loaf in half to make it sandwich-sized. Then I split the bread the long way with my thumb and forefinger. I sheared each of my personal skewers of its blackened meat into a bread mitt.

"Sauce?" (I'm sure that was the intention of the Bambara word). The cook tipped a bowl toward the meat.

"Non merci," I hastened, loudly and stupidly repeating it in English. One stomach adventure at a time.

"Rick!" It was a yell. I swivelled. Distracted, I hadn't noticed the train's movement. Pierre hollered again from the train as it moved away, gaining speed. *"Rick!"* I ran toward Pierre, one hand outstretched his way, the other protecting my dear dinner and my day pack. He gripped my fingers, then my wrist. Tight. And he hoisted me up the closed stairway, steel wheels clicking at my heels.

Eventually my adrenaline gave way to calm, and I eased into the best meal I'd had since my arrival in Africa. Ebou, Pierre, Ussegnou, and I crouched on the lower bunks, sharing my food. They laughed at the inanity of my near miss and peppered me with echoes of my misspoken French.

There is a woman's walk, a call to attention. The striking woman who had made cameo appearances at the earlier station stops walked past our roomette, and then back to her roomette. It seemed that she was travelling with her father, and we hoped he was her father as she was young, boldly attractive, and a rarity; he was none of these. She was in her late teens, he a father's age. "Beautiful," said Pierre.

"As pretty as God would be willing to make a woman," Ebou added.

Pierre was the first to flirt with her, simply asking if she'd like to visit with him and his friends. *"Non,"* she replied, and then he laughed at her rebuke and she fell in with his infectious giggling. Ussegnou apologized for any misinterpretation, saying, "Join us, it is innocent." And this solidified an evening's visit.

For a couple of hours, the four of them mirthfully told stories in their language. I eavesdropped while reading on my top bunk. I was a shadow on their tableau, and that was fine. Every once in a while, they'd include me in a story, telling me the punch line in English so that I wouldn't be left out of the laughs. Ebou formally introduced Jeniba to me, saying that he was my professor and that she could help him teach me French. She did not even smile at this notion.

I left them in the room and walked in the coach's empty aisle. I felt alone with my thoughts of the coming weeks' unknowns and the happy attainment of a Saturday train departure from Dakar. It had worked out, after all. It now meant four more days in Mali. That opened my travels to new possibilities.

Ussegnou's bent radio aerial gave the announcer a fuzzy voice for the football game, and I noticed this as I retraced my steps to the roomette. I heard Ebou and Jeniba cheer. Ebou shouted the final score to me, twice. Jeniba arched as she rose from her seat on the bed and left for the night. All three of my roommates leaned out the roomette to watch her walk away.

We dimmed the lights and readied the beds. Pierre and Ebou sang a Senegalese ballad with a happy mellowness. Ussegnou joined their quiet singing and hummed the melody. In our two days together, our French conversation had gone from *vous* to *tu*.

The window in our roomette was up full, closed tightly. I struggled with the window frame and finally pulled it down to elbow height, and leaned out into Africa for the night's benediction. Stars and a moon and comrades. I was starkly aware of my good fortune. All went quiet, even the rails seemed sensitive. After a while, I stepped back and started to climb into my bunk.

Ebou closed the window against the rushing air. I reached back and trimmed it down to half.

"Rick," said Pierre. "Are you not cold at night?"

"Hot, not cold," I said.

"I woke," he said, with a mock shiver, "in the middle of last night. You lay snoring. Asleep. No jacket. Me, I'm so cold."

"Cold. Very cold," added Ebou, shaking himself.

"Me? Me, I'm freezing," said Ussegnou.

"Canadian: one; Africans: three," I said, signalling the ratio in our room with my fingers. "For Africa, this much," I moved the window closed in proportion, stopping at three fourths. The top quarter was left open for upper bunk air, "And for Canada, *un peu*."

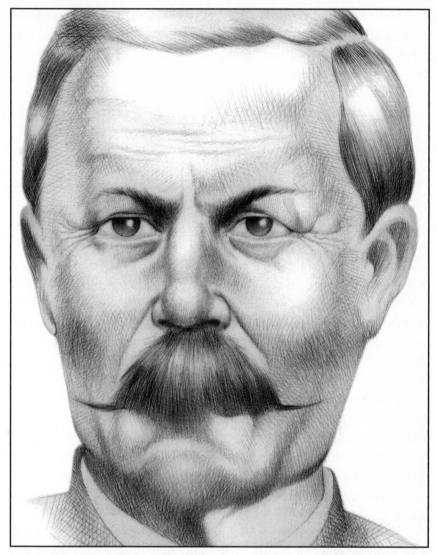

In 1880 Colonel Paul Flatters, "a middle-aged, under-employed officer in the Bureau Arabe," led a disastrous French mission to chart a route for the ill-conceived Transsaharian Railway.

Had the Frenchman Paul Flatters been successful in his 1880 mission, I might have boarded my train in Algeria, on French-laid tracks for the Transsaharian Railway, disembarking at Timbuctoo Station.

The world today has travel corridors, routes carved for convenience or commerce, predetermining where most of us can or will take our journeys, our vacations, our travel experiences. France believed that a railway connecting the Sahara's north and south, a line across the awesome desert, would bring commercial and military benefits similar to those that trains were then bringing for North America — a colonial mindset that would eventually be expressed as "Eurafrica." It led to the greatest disaster to befall an expedition in the Sahara.

Flatters was a respected lieutenant-colonel, experienced in the desert and, approaching forty, considering final efforts to claim a significant career achievement. Although he was long tempted by the lure of Timbuktu, his earlier submissions for support of an expedition under his leadership had been declined by the French government. Now, on a journey of conquest and trade, France provided funds for seventy-seven troops, *tirailleurs*, and assorted engineers, guides, and native Algerian porters. They embarked with three hundred camels southward from Ouargla, an oasis and marshalling centre in Algeria. Defining a railway route across the Sahara Desert for trade and travellers was their only mandate.

Six weeks later, low on water and sensing how desperately poor was the proposal for this railway, Flatters sent his last dispatch, though he did not know it at the time, from remote Inzelman. The style of the wandering Tuareg had been welcoming to the Frenchmen. The Blue Men of Africa shadowed Flatters's group as it moved across their territory, the Tuareg having no idea that Flatters's engineers were surveying for a railway.

In need of water, Flatters accepted the Tuaregs' advice that he and most of the camels go with them to a nearby well while the remaining troops set up camp and unpacked the supplies. The entire Tuareg contingent left with Flatters and his party of thirty-six to find the promised water. The appearance of nearly one hundred men behaving as a military unit had been a sufficient deterrent for the Tuareg up until that point. But once they had separated into two units, the French were vulnerable.

On the slow move toward the oasis, the Tuareg attacked Flatters's men with swords, killing Flatters and most of the Frenchmen with

him. Many of the natives were captured, some murdered. A few
escaped and made their way to where the main force encamped and
told of the massacre. A young Lieutenant Dianous, terrified and
confused, was now in charge. His decision, based on a pitiful lack of
options, was to retrace their two-and-a-half-month journey back
to Ouargla.

The Tuareg weighed on Dianous's mind. Scouts returned,
confirming the patient following by these nomads. Dianous,
his fellow Frenchmen, and the Algerians were well armed and
confident that their ammunition supplies could ward off the
Tuareg. But within two weeks of embarking northward, they
were without food. They were starving and chewing the leather
straps and beltings of their luggage. It was then that the Tuareg,
in a gesture of desert hospitality, gave the remnants of the once-
powerful French force a gift of dates.

Soon the men writhed in agony. Many went mad, and some
ran into the desert. The dates had been poisoned.

Disoriented and distressed, the surviving soldiers broke their
next night's camp before dawn and began to march toward a big
well within the day's reach. An hour after moving into the horizon,
the desert sun rose, the sand's surface glimmered, and a strong line
of Tuareg, mounted on their camels, waited.

The Tuareg hovered in this threatening position for a long
time, until advancing suddenly. Charging into the volley of
French musket balls, they suffered heavy casualties. It was not
their expected victory. But the Tuareg's retaliation to the French
rebuff was immediate and horrific. They slew those prisoners they'd
held alive from the Flatters incident. Shocked and demoralized,
the Frenchmen watched the killings just out of musket range.
Then, from a Tuareg sniper, a bullet pierced the desert air, striking
Dianous. He fell.

An anguished sergeant assumed responsibility and led a
switchback course for the near-dead, who remained under his
command. It is said that he shook the Tuareg at the edge of
their lands. Those soldiers who could walk, stumbled north. In
desperation, they killed and then ate their weaker comrades. When

the brain-addled sergeant himself could barely walk, he, too, was killed and eaten by those he'd led.

Four months after they had left to find a suitable route for the Transsaharian Railway to connect European markets with the gold-rich trade cities of the River Niger, tattered traces of the *tirailleurs* found their way into a north Saharan village. France's dreams of a railway evaporated with the tales of these half-mad survivors.

In the early 1900s, France faced the challenge of mollifying the renegade Tuat tribes under Moroccan claim. If it was to effectively influence the Sahara, its military operations required a means of regular supply. "Paradoxically, the Transsaharian could not be built until the Tuat was firmly under French control, and the Tuat could not be controlled until the Transsaharian was in place," writes Fergus Fleming in *The Sword and the Cross*. Should France build a railway?

It did not, and not until 1965 was a Trans-Saharan Railway again proposed. But the idea was just as quickly dropped. The Trans-Saharan Railway is now unthinkable as much for the inhospitable geography of shifting sands as for the shifting politics, or the lesser cost and convenience of air travel. One of the few safe travel predictions for Africa's future is that it will not include the phrase, "All aboard for Timbuktu."

No travellers fall into easier conversation than do train travellers. Paul Theroux observed that "train travel is the last word in truth serum." Eye-to-eye contact, known departure points, and a sense that when you leave, the train stays behind with your stories and secrets, all add to the candour.

Ussegnou began. "Your travels are long, Rick. Do you not work?"

"I have time off," I said, and rolled over in my upper bunk.

"Do you not work?" he repeated.

"I work in travel," I said.

"You're working now?" He saw the looseness in my life, and I could see that he wondered at the relevance of my job. I felt defensive.

"No. This is my holiday. I will go back to work when my vacation is over."

"And then your work is more travel?" I sensed Ussegnou's bemusement.

"Why in Africa?" he asked into the darkness. "Because we are poor and you are not?"

FOUR

From Here to Timbuktu

A JOLT ON THE TRACKS WOKE US AND ANNOUNCED our arrival in Kita. It was early, dark. We were still 185 kilometres from Bamako. I rolled over and felt a loaf of bread crumble under my weight. Unable to see, I slipped off the top bunk, my hands exploring to find the doorway, and headed into the dimly lit corridor. I hoped for coffee with milk. Hot water was available in the dining car, but the serving staff was preparing for our arrival at the Bamako terminal and therefore not in the mood for serving. Two washed mugs sat on the bar, and I took one. Powdered milk filled a tumbler in the corner and I shook a clump of it loose. A pile of sugar was spilled on the counter. I scooped that into the cup as well. The porter pushed a broom around the chairs and a half-used packet of Nescafé fell from his trouser pocket. I picked it up off the floor and sprinkled the granules into my cup.

West of Bamako, we skirted the Manding Mountains, home of the once-mighty Malinké, custodians of the Mali Empire. The train's chugging made one marvel at those who crossed that barrenness on foot or camel. My disembarkation point neared, first with glimpses of garbage and then with struggling buildings that seemed to not want to be noticed.

The platform in Bamako was a chaos of litter and colour and shouting and bags being shifted by strange hands. Neither our delayed departure from Dakar nor the disruptions en route were unexpected. The scheduled thirty-five-hour trip had taken over ten hours more. Everyone pushed and elbowed to get off the coaches and into the crowd of greeters and hawkers.

"You should travel with us," Ussegnou proposed as we shunted our bags to the platform, and I knew he meant it. "Meet our family. Stay with them. Then come to Burkina." They'd offered this a number of times as our train travel neared its end. Now, with our packs resting by our sides, this was their last offer of camaraderie.

"It would work," said Ebou, as his strong hand gripped mine.

"I already offered Rick to stay at our place," Pierre said to them in French and then in English. His kindness was as simple as theirs — an invitation for me to hitch on and meet their friends, to travel some.

"I'd love that," I told them sincerely. "But, you know, I've got to get to Timbuktu."

Stern hugs, last laughs, and Ebou said, "Safe passage." They melded with the flow of people and were gone.

When Matthew and Alec jostled through the roiling bodies, shook my hand and left, I found myself alone. My journey was suddenly a crowded remoteness. I swam by myself in the current of black people, men moving cargo and women in dresses that screamed colours as loud as the insistent hucksters.

My appetite for disorder peaked and waned with my breathing. My first impulse was to sit down and watch it all, capture the turmoil. Crates of luggage moved on worn wheels over the concrete walkway, suitcases were inadvertently shoved in front of people, tripping them. Families bumped aside anxious passengers, and everyone hugged or yelled directions. My second impulse was to secure transport to my hotel before all the taxis disappeared. I watched from the platform, heavy backpack by my side and rucksack over my right shoulder, looking for a vehicle.

And there, far away in the middle of the car lot, where vehicles came in dust, loaded in dust, and left in dust, was Jeniba. Around her, people dodged cars and taxis aimed at people. I hauled my backpack across the ground and said hi. She was nonplussed. This was her town, and her countrymen — my friends were gone. She did not speak English well. We verbally fenced *en français*.

"Do you know the Wawa Hotel?" I asked.

"There's *non* such *l'hôtel.*" Jeniba turned away slightly, like she wanted to lose me. She was neither keen to help solve the problem of the hotel's location nor interested in my plight. I wondered if my three days without a shower played into the relationship.

I grappled with my Lonely Planet French/English book to get delivery right. "It's near the old bridge," I said. "*Pont des Martyrs.*"

"*Non.*"

I wrote the district's French name on paper and showed it to her, offering my pen for her unwilling reply. But she was waiting for someone to meet her, and that might be what showed when her green eyes squinted in frustration. Or she maybe found dealing with me a chore. She did, however, consent to read my scrawl and rearranged the alphabet. We asked a taxi driver if he'd heard of the Wawa.

"*Non.*" And he loaded a black man's possessions into his trunk.

Again, to another driver.

"*Non.*" Since they didn't know the hotel name, they didn't want me.

Jeniba was now into the game. Her stunning face, taffy-toned skin, and erect pose garnered attention. Everyone looked at her. I'm the only white guy, and with an orange backpack, so you'd think I'd be noticed as needing a taxi, but I'd have been missed like so much dust if I hadn't been standing next to her.

Thrice more Jeniba stared down a running driver, her look as compelling as a shout, and showed him the paper with "Wawa Hotel" written on it.

"*Non.*"

Doubtful.

Tenth time lucky.

"*Oui,*" and I hustled after a man with missing teeth, missing hair, and a quirky assurance that he knew the whereabouts of a hotel no one else did. I turned around to thank Jeniba, but she was walking away, her bag carried by a man her age; I guessed dad-on-the-train got ditched. A dozen men lingered on her sway.

Basking in the front seat of the taxi was a fat lady emblazoned with clothing of reds and greens and blues, wrapped with a yellow cloth over her shoulders. Her smile ran from ear to ear as she dilly-bobbed her head around and talked to me in a language of hiccups and burped syllables. She was ready to go, anxious at the driver's delay, surprised at me climbing in. Bags aplenty crowded my seat in the back of the ancient car, held together by rust. I forced my bag over hers to make room. The lady gasped at the funniness of my orange backpack.

The taxi coughed smoke out of its exhaust pipe, and we had driven only thirty metres on blacktop before the driver swerved. We bounced down a dirt road for five minutes and then abruptly turned onto a goat path. The lady and the driver giggled like former lovers over every small thing, and he eventually dropped her off in a yard filled with dusty people. They seemed to find it hilarious that she was home.

Off we went, the car's shocks a little more absorbent without her weight. Fume-laden streets, honking vehicles, and goats accompanied us through town, over a bridge and closer to where the driver's rapid French made me believe I was going. I realized I should have begun *Alliance Française* lessons a month earlier; practised my diction, done my homework even. *"Parle lentement, s'il vous plaît,"* I said, using my verbal safety kit: "Speak slowly, please."

A hand-painted sign announced the Wawa Hotel. The driver pointed to it with such emphasis that I felt he was as surprised to see it as I was. We bumbled to a stop at a doorway in an alley, and dirt sifted everywhere. A child who had watched us arrive sized up the situation and disappeared into his house.

A high wall flanked the front of the hotel, keeping it back from the road and enclosing it within a courtyard. Two leafy trees broke up the inside space between the wall and a low deck, with several wicker chairs, which led to a lobby area. To the left of this, as I toted my bag toward it, was what looked to be a counter. Behind the counter I found a man sleeping on a desk. I woke him.

He fumbled through scraps of paper and finally showed me a note that had my name on it. I took this to be my reservation, and when I nodded the man seemed disappointed. He said I was to be there not *that* day, but *that* week. He explained in French that there wasn't an empty room, but there might be one later.

"Today?" I asked.

"No," he said in French. "Maybe tomorrow."

"Café?" I asked, seeing chairs set up around cloth-covered tables near a kitchen. I had the traveller's willingness to let things unfold as long as a beverage was available. I rushed for nothing.

The clerk brought hot water and a sleeve of Nescafé. The child who'd watched the taxi arrive appeared with a basket of fresh bread. I hadn't realized how hungry I was and quickly ate all of the bread, only then finding the butter that would have melted swiftly on the hot loaf. The child left to get another.

"Is Mohammed here?" I asked for my Malian contact by his full name, as this was the hotel where we were to meet. Might that be today? The clerk sloughed off to rouse Mohammed. I walked past the counter and leaned against a ledge as emotional tributaries flowed together in the muddy pond of my gut: one stream each for happy, uncertain, curious, and anxious. I wanted a reliable guide and a flexible itinerary, and the coming hours should deliver all of that. Mohammed sleepwalked from the hallway, rubbing his nose and yawning, led by the night clerk.

Face to groggy face, we sized one another up and adjusted the images we held from the tone of exchanges. All of a sudden I was wanting little, expecting less.

Mohammed was young, touching the upside of thirty, handsome enough. He scratched sleep from his eyes; the pupils were like date pits. He misplayed his confidence by not smiling.

"Been up all night. It's very busy. I'm very busy. Many people come this time of year. I went by the train station last night. Thought you might be on it. Didn't you say later in the week? Went to the airport to pick up three for a tour. I'm tired. At the station they said the train would be an hour late. I went back. That was ten hours ago. I've had no sleep. You're four days early. Want coffee?"

Belatedly we shook hands.

He was an Arabophone, a Francophone, an Anglophone and, as an afterthought, a Malian. He spoke to those about him in several languages. I got the English. To me there was a measure of respect in his voice, as I had yet to pay.

Mohammed slouched at the nearest of four empty tables, his feet splayed. His hands were lankier than his body. The slump took a lot of room, and his mood was like a fourth language. We talked over the itinerary. As I slurped coffee he told me what he thought I should do now that I was there. Every suggestion from me was rebuffed as to its inconvenience, "but something can be done." There was the faint echo of a cash register ring in his voice each time he said that. It reinforced my pre-departure concerns about his easy e-mail chitchat regarding costs and his predisposition to charge more for every possibility. I should have been more scrupulous.

"After Timbuktu, we will get you on the *pinasse*, and send you back to Mopti," Mohammed said, implying the efficiency of a FedEx shipment.

"Tell me more about the boat," I asked.

"The *pinasse* on the Niger is for you and two couples, one from the U.S.," he said, as though that was reassuring.

I balked. "I've no desire to spend time in Mali with other people from North America."

He demurred. "Okay. We can change that. They will be at the festival. Just two of them. But okay." The closer I got to Timbuktu, the more accessible it seemed, the less novel my doing.

"Good, change it," I demanded.

"You must pay more."

"For what?"

"For not having others in the *pinasse*."

"Others are fine," I said. "Just not North Americans. I'm here to learn."

"You must go to Gao."

"Not my interest," I said. "Maybe more days in the Dogon."

"Three days is enough in Dogon," he advised, clipping the option. "You need to see Lac Faguibine in the desert."

I was getting to know Mohammed.

A broken muffler burst the morning quiet, and a car clanked to a stop outside the hotel. Minutes passed before the vehicle emptied and three Malians slumbered into the courtyard. A traveller walked in their midst. He tipped a pith helmet my way and smiled wearily at Mohammed.

Mohammed said to me, "That's Dennis. I arranged his trip. Talk to him. He will tell you I'm good."

Dennis's Japanese heritage showed in his eyes, skin colour, and round face. He had just returned to Bamako after a month in Mali. He was content and self-assured, though cautious toward Mohammed. He held a day pack in a lazy grip, his stocky body giving no sign of deprivation. We shook hands, his clasp firm. He was keen on going home but willing to share a few lessons with me before he went.

While one of the helpers hauled his bag to a room, he relaxed in a wicker chair in the lobby. I joined him there, flattened my cushion, and started my questions.

"Yes, I was in Timbuktu," he replied to my first. "You must go."

"I will. I am," I said, disheartened. My quest was intended to be singular, and so far I'd been pleased that the others I'd met had not ventured there. Dennis had just dashed part of my hopes. Yet I was equally encouraged by this fresh source of knowledge and asked more.

"The Dogon, yes," he replied. "The Niger? Of course."

This man has taken my trip.

Mohammed ducked around the corner, looking for me. His chin pushed his lower lip to a concerned pucker, as though he figured my talking with Dennis might not be a good idea after all. We had negotiations to finalize, and Mohammed was anxious. Dennis rose to find his room. I walked to the hotel's reception area and rested against the counter, my back to the wall, and faced an overconfident Mohammed, his mouth that of a jackal; a twitch, a pounce.

"Fuel is extra," said Mohammed.

"Extra?" I looked at Dennis, who was only a few metres away, within hearing. He shrugged, as I learned all do upon leaving Mali.

"I wanted to meet you to explain these things," said Mohammed.

"Explain away," I encouraged.

"I wanted to tell you when you got here."

"I'm here."

Mohammed was practised. I would not throw him off. Guidebook warnings about fuel surprises notwithstanding, I thought it would have been proper to note this in one of his e-mail responses to my questions about cost components. Not wanting to care, I asked, "How much?"

"Seven hundred and thirty."

I cared. "U.S.?" I asked hopefully.

"Euro."

"Quite a jump in travel costs," I posed.

"We always charge fuel extra because we don't know the itinerary and it's expensive." He didn't even cringe. Humility was foreign to him. I wanted to get started on the road later that day or first thing the next morning. No fuel, no vehicle. No vehicle ...

With Mohammed there was always more. We bartered about what was included, what was not. Dennis, sage after a month of this, told me later that he had encountered several "extras" and simply paid in order to move along.

Mohammed said he could arrange a camel for riding in the desert, at my "addition," which I thought was fair. He had both hands in his trouser pockets, yet I felt them in mine. He outlined a routing, obviously profitable for him because others were involved, which reduced his costs while not reducing mine. I eliminated many of the guided days he proposed, deleted hotel stays and dickered on vehicles.

"I don't need the adventure of a four-by-four on paved roads, Mohammed. I've got a Jeep at home."

He relented with a cheaper vehicle for several days. "But you'll need a Land Cruiser north of Douentza or you'll never make it to Timbuktu."

Bamako had one bank machine, at the Banque Internationale pour le Commerce et l'Industrie au Mali, and we headed there to square the deal with cash. At BICIM there were only two customers ahead of me and we were soon finished, CFAs in my clenched hand. Mohammed's palm opened.

"You should take out more money," Mohammed said. His shiny face was both serious and smiling, a perilous business combination.

"I've got what I need," I replied sternly.

Mohammed talked and I was not listening as we walked the streets to find our car. We'd driven ten minutes into town and were on a bed of dust kicked high by cattle and mopeds. A driver pushed his horn to move people into storefronts stacked with rice sacks, welding supplies, fruits, and bicycle rims.

Back at the hotel, I poured coffee for each of us as Mohammed and I argued about my itinerary. We sorted costs by vehicle, by day, by guide — he repeated that "Gao is a must" for my trip and again I said, "No."

"I think eight or ten days hiking the Dogon will suit me fine," I told him, becoming more specific, perhaps because he disagreed. We quarrelled about this until I said, "Mohammed, it's my trip not yours." But the Dogon was left unresolved. Another key decision was whether to go to the festival, something Mohammed encouraged, and I wavered from my initial interest. It meant a more hurried routing to Timbuktu, about which I was not keen, but in exchange there would be the rare experience of participating in the Tuareg festivities.

Mohammed then said, "Each night, the hotel is seventy-five Euro."

"Is every hotel equal?" I asked.

"All are good hotels," he told me. "Especially this is important to arrange now for in Ségou, Douentza, and Timbuktu." Without having comparisons, I accepted his estimate. It was a mistake.

Irritatingly, he once more urged Gao, and I finally realized he had others making that trip, so my joining-in would offer a better profit margin. "I'm not going to Gao," I said, feeling silly that the decision was driven more by my desire for independence than by the attractiveness of the destination.

He sparred with me. "You don't know what you need. I do," he insisted.

"My money, my risk. I'll decide on the Dogon, and let you know," I said, and stood up as though to leave, then remembered it was his country, his vehicle, his contacts, and my need. I sat down and said, "Look Mohammed, let's sort this out and I'll be on my way."

Mohammed said that I must pay him in advance for all the accommodation, as he needed to secure the hotels. I tallied. He balked. He tallied. I balked. We shook hands — a dated gesture of trust. I said, "If I route this way, I can shift my air departure from Bamako back a day to make better my tight connection home through Dakar. That I like."

There was a faint smell to the deal with Mohammed. It was costing more than I was comfortable with, in circumstances that were slipping beyond my control. The goal of Timbuktu could not elude me. He took me for a slightly obsessed Western tourist masquerading as an independent traveller.

It was time to pay Mohammed using U.S. dollars and Euro bills from my money belt and the *seffe* cash I'd just withdrawn. He wanted the entire payment in *seffe*, and I felt I was in a set-up. The conversion of foreign currency at his own bank would take two days to process and provide a splinter less in the exchange rate. Mohammed yanked a cell phone from the desk clerk's hand and dialed nimbly. He barked quickly into the phone, then seemed caught off-guard by whomever he spoke with, and slowed down, nodding as he spoke in Bambara. Then he smiled, turned the phone off, and tossed it in the air to the clerk.

Fifteen minutes later a fat man arrived, a motorcycle clenched between his flabby thighs. His belly rested on the handlebars. The money-changer waddled our way, his pants low with pouches sewn onto the leggings. They bulged. A white shirt floated around him. Sitting on a chair that groaned, he opened a wallet that was fist-thick with *seffe* and U.S. dollars. From his purse he pulled a clump of Euros. He sulked at the negotiated rate when Mohammed announced it, shuffled his bills, and paid me with a feigned reluctance. In mock defeat, he buried his greedy chin in his shirt collar.

The front desk clerk passed a note to Mohammed, and I admired the Africa-shaped necklace he wore. Mohammed said immediately, "It is very rare. But I could have another made. Three hundred. Euro." On my trip I wanted to find something special for Janice, who, after all, had prompted this whole escapade to

Timbuktu. The clerk lifted the necklace over his head and gave it to me. I looked closely, considering this the perfect gift. Mali was outlined on the continent and the etching showed Bamako.

"Could it be made with the River Niger carved in? And show Timbuktu?"

"Yes, of course," promised Mohammed.

"I'm interested."

"You pay now and it will be ready when you return to Bamako."

"Three hundred?" I confirmed.

"Yes. For the gold."

I was thinking this a rather expensive piece for a clerk to be wearing. "Mohammed, why am I not liking this?"

It was as if I'd addressed the mud wall. "And the craftsman would be extra. For your design."

"No, thanks."

In the courtyard, Dennis was alone. A cluster of Malians was gathered nearby.

"How's my fellow adventurer?" I asked, strutting more comfortably.

"Ready for home. But I'll miss Mali," he said.

"If I'm lucky, I'll feel that way at the end of my journey," I responded.

"Hey, meet Zakarie," he said, introducing a twenty-ish man tucked away under a tree. "He was my guide in the Dogon. We were on the whole trip together."

Zak was a wisp of a man, light of weight and with powerful legs, from Dogon Country. We leaned into our first handshake. "Hello," I introduced myself. Zak's face spread into a disarming smile that made all of him seem bigger. There was something daring in his eyes. I felt immediate comfort with this young guide. Why do some people exude trust?

"Hi, *Rick*." He said my name for the first of a thousand times, and it was soft, somehow italicized, in a way I would hear only from him. We planted a friendship.

"He's solid. A fine guide," continued Dennis. "You'll not do better. Sure could find worse."

The three of us nattered about their trip, Dennis telling me that Zak spoke Dogon, of course, and also French and Bambara. He had decent English as well.

"We're all going to dinner. Come along," Dennis said. I realized that my first day in Mali had nearly passed.

A hunky black man arrived, boisterous in his greeting. "This is Mamadou. He's been my driver," said Dennis. Not twenty-five years old, Mamadou was tall, immediately gregarious, and wore his collared shirt open over his jeans, as a smock. We fumbled our handshake as he dropped a backpack, just our thumbs catching. People laughed. Both of us got serious in our second attempt at a greeting. He intentionally bunted my hand and then grasped around my fingers and slapped them together, completing the mime with a firm shake. He said my name, twisting it with his Bambara tongue, *"Wrick."*

At Zak's suggestion, Dennis and I agreed to a restaurant neither of us had heard about. Mamadou, grafted onto our group, drove us to our destination. In the back seat of the car, as we bumped along the roadway, Dennis provided a one-line synopsis of his trip: "Everyone knows Africa is hopeless. And everyone is wrong."

Along the main road, off on a potholed turnaway, was a lantern-lit patio. The open-air restaurant was busy, but a table was cleared in the centre where we could watch and be watched. Chicken and chips and ketchup of a sort seemed a safe order. Thinking that beer should wash away any cooking sins, I hedged my menu choice with that.

To Dennis I said, "Toss me on a local bus. I don't want to be organized."

"Fine," he said with a seasoned voice. "I hear that has charm."

"Understand me. I'm not wanting to be coddled." It was not a smart statement, nor informed. It was therapeutic, a wedging out of my reluctance about Mohammed's influence.

Dennis was practical and not condescending toward my naiveté. "You'll see people wasting a day, two days, waiting for local transport. If that's how you'd like to see Mali, it's your choice."

"From what I've seen of the *bussé*, they're a rickety ride," I acknowledged.

He went further: "And when you get on one, you suck exhaust for the entire trip."

"Loses the romance," I admitted.

"And that's before they break down."

I appreciated Dennis's willingness to educate the rookie, even being philosophical. "Never express ingratitude in Mali. Even the most fortunate Malian steps from air conditioning to stifling heat, has poor and envious relatives, and breathes noxious fumes in the cities."

I wondered how long his perspectives would stay with him once he returned to his home and job, particularly his shared observation: "Few people here have a complex notion of life. And we must learn from them."

Across the table Mamadou was animated, happy that one trip had ended, and eager for his next long drive. The man spoke seriously in Bambara with the genteel Zak, lobbying for the job as my driver. He gobbled his chips, and Zak's chips, and stared at mine. Zak, when our conversation lagged around him, fiddled with his cell phone. They bought phone time on street corners or doorsteps or from wandering merchants at a traffic light. The cardboard cards carried a code to be scratched as a lottery ticket might be in America. The uncovered numbers were punched in and used for the talking time purchased.

"Timbuktu takes effort, though less than you might think," Dennis encouraged. "We all like the lure."

I said, "You've spent a month exploring Mali. Did you find what you were looking for?"

"That's a question for every explorer," he smiled, as though the personal nature of the question meant it was as much for me to ponder in one month's time as to ask him now.

Dennis treated us to dinner, his remaining *seffe* being impossible to exchange outside of West Africa. As we drove back to the hotel he said to me, "Here, you go back in time, and it will change how you go forward in life."

Mohammed had an updated itinerary waiting for me at the hotel's front desk. He was suspiciously efficient. There was much I wanted to see, and I didn't have the luxury of having days evaporate in transportation delays. I saw Mohammed's helpful, if profitable, hand at work.

Dennis and I relaxed in wicker chairs on the hotel's covered patio. The area was barely lit. I smoked my pipe. The hotel was in a residential area, and neighbourhood laughter and evening television filtered through the walls. Dennis offered his insight about patience: "In Mali, no traveller has the same plan on Tuesday that he had on Monday."

His end-of-trip actual costs reflected what I now knew were likely to be mine, which replenished my self-confidence. Either that meant the charges to each of us were fair or, less charitably, that Mohammed had tagged us both as marks, thus making Dennis a poor precedent to compare myself with. I felt hustled by Mohammed's brisk talk about costs. Embarrassment fluttered about me like a soft breeze.

"You must stay ten days in Dogon. Must," Dennis said over coffee. "And take a cook."

"A cook?" I asked.

"Do you like food?"

"Yes," I smiled.

"Are you serious about eating?"

I wasn't sure where this was going. The conversation might be long, but none of the sentences were. "Reasonably. I like to know what I'm eating. Where it's been."

"Cheap guide, cheap food," he said.

This was among the best advice I got in Mali.

"Take a cook," he advised for the second time. "It is not much cost. You should do this especially for the Dogon. I've been here a month and have met too many travellers with food sicknesses."

A moody Mohammed appeared around a post on the patio and gave me my rebooked air ticket from Bamako to Dakar, several weeks away. "Here. You are set." It had the tone of cement, not of arrangements.

At the hotel desk was a hand-lettered sign with four names. "Dutch," grunted Mohammed proudly.

"Let me guess," I said, "They're going to the festival."

"Yes," he replied, as though I'd find that special.

Dennis saw my disappointment and said, "Some Frenchmen jet to Timbuktu for New Year's Eve."

"Vain," I smirked. I wanted to feel that *my* travels were different, that they were not travel as *others* experienced it. But then Mohammed cheerfully gave me his company's T-shirt. The last thing I wanted was a fucking T-shirt.

The largest country in West Africa, Mali, like all nations, is a fabrication of history. Ten million people are citizens under that name, dotted over 1.2 million square kilometres — an area twice the size of France, much of it vividly inhospitable. Mali's variable (if not uncommon) history of wars, invasions, and shifting commands led to nation-state status a little over forty years ago, the namesake of a once-great empire. Mali is an apt name, derived from a thirteenth-century Mandigo root word meaning "free." To achieve this connotation of a country, various tribes and nationalities endured the ebb and flow of defeats and dictatorships before settling on a common accord of suffering and optimism.

Trade, rather than knowledge, is the great motivator for exploration; greed and acquisition are more common human traits than altruism and sharing. Exploration first, followed by trade, followed again by travel and its economic moniker, tourism. Today in Mali there is little sign of the once-immense gold trade, and even less of the salt trade. No sign, thank all gods, of the slave trade (though there are rumours of Malian children being taken to other countries as forced labour). Ostrich feathers, once an item of value, along with ivory, have dropped from the export list. Today, countries trading with Mali receive cotton, coffee, gold, grains, and little else. It is joked that the culinary specialty of Mali is rice. Goat or sheep or cow are added to many dishes. Livestock, as a result, are more prominent in trade within the neighbourhood, a subsistence economy, than within or outside of the nation. Tourism, though, earns important foreign currency for Mali. Even a thoughtful government in this part of the world flirts with crippling foreign debts to sustain itself.

A door slamming in the hallway jerked me awake. I lay there. Midnight, an hour's sleep behind me. An unfamiliar anxiety undermined my practical side. The trip itinerary, costs and such ... the festival and what seemed to have become my own "rush to Timbuktu," contradicted my trip's purpose and ruffled my contentment. Somehow, along the way, my trip had morphed from adventure and unpredictability to entertainment and a program.

"This is serious sit-up stuff," I thought aloud. And I did sit up, pinning the pillow against the wall. Waking would be understandable if it had been induced by jet lag or resulted from indigestion, but neither was the case. I was addled with buyer's remorse.

I'd thought well of myself for travelling to Timbuktu. Had I let the trip become a trophy? In Asia, I'd shared a speakers' panel with Peter Greenberg, the American television commentator, where he had observed: "We live in a world of experiential one-upmanship." I'd added, "And, travel is the measure. It's become a necessary story to say 'I've been to ...' as though travel is an ornament that demonstrates one's relevance or sophistication." He'd condensed my thoughts: "Travel name-dropping." Was I ill with the sickness we had diagnosed?

In that night, I could not dispel the notion that one route over the next few weeks offered the novelty I sought, while the other, more structured, would not let my sense of accomplishment happen. The destiny I sought was proving elusive.

I wanted fresh air, and opened my door to find two Americans with their shoulders to the wall, smoking cigarettes. "Everything is expensive here," a thin one said in greeting.

"Old news," I said.

"Going to the festival?" he asked.

"Think so," I replied.

"Got a ride?" the second fellow asked, standing to make his pudginess less obvious.

"Think so."

"Can we come along?"

"Think so."

"Everyone's going to the festival," he said excitedly.

"Think so?"

They seemed far from home; raised in American schools.

The Festival in the Desert was a side story to me, fit for music enthusiasts who could do it justice. I felt oddly threatened. It had not originally been part of my plan to go to the festival, and try as I did, I could not make it mine. Obstinacy gave way to ambivalence; did I want to understand Malian culture, or did I want to understand myself?

My random plans were skewered, held together like a brochette; my quest had been eclipsed by a schedule. It had become "going to the festival" rather than going to Timbuktu, a *vacance* lacking the clarity of a journey. Timbuktu, my purpose, was relegated to gateway status, a place en route. Some journeys, it seemed, are about the destination!

I wrote Mohammed a respectful note that night, proposing rejigged travel arrangements. Skip the festival. Arrive in Timbuktu after it is over, the commotion passed, the people gone. I attached a freshly reworked itinerary, tallied my cost estimates, and left a column for his estimates. I even showed a "change fee" for his time and expenses.

My personal goal was to find a quest in travel again. My fear was that a crowded Timbuktu would lose any semblance of remoteness or worthy accomplishment. I envisioned the fabled city awash with more white people visiting it now than at any time in the past two centuries.

During the night I had awakened the clerk and had him arrange for Mohammed to meet me at 8:30 in the morning. At the appointed time I was in a comfy chair on the patio, tired but enthusiastic about my solution.

Mohammed arrived at the hotel as promised, and as he walked toward me, I overheard him talking to the Americans. One said, "But I didn't bring that much money." Sensing a limit to his ability to extract funds, Mohammed smoothed the situation with, "It's okay. It's okay." He then came to where I sat stirring powdered milk into a mug of Nescafé. I outlined my suggested alternative.

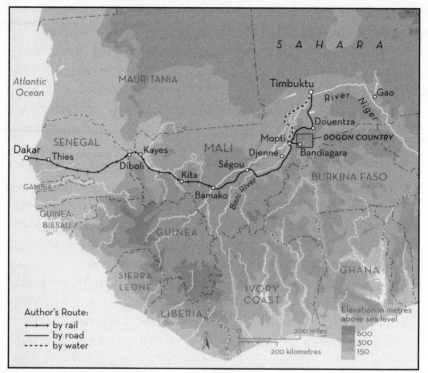

The author's travels through Senegal and Mali in West Africa.

Mohammed pursed his lips, making the skin of his chin firm, which scrunched the stubble of his goatee into a look that was reptilian. "If you change the route, you miss the festival. Then you arrive when the Dakar road race goes through Tombouctou. People. Planes. You'll not get a room."

I flinched. This dislocation was a feeling I'd not anticipated. I did not then realize that his claim was spurious. "You mean it'll be as crowded after the festival?" I was unhappy.

"Busier. Honest." Both were words without meaning to him, but I did not yet know that. It would be a week before the word "gullible" crossed my mind.

I could get my route changed, lose money, and still be among throngs in Timbuktu. Choice: music lovers or the racing crowd. "Crowd" dramatized the facts: either event would add only a few dozen people to Timbuktu, but that image washed over the one I'd harboured for half a year: only a dozen other visitors, the daily average, in Timbuktu at the same time as me.

There was a churlish twitch in the corner of Mohammed's mouth. "Rick, you make it difficult. The boat is difficult. It has gone."

"Gone?"

"Yes. This morning. The *pinasse* must be there to come back." Even though I'd become insensitive, there was a numbness about our dealings. Mohammed, I now learned, owned the *pinasse*. It had been, if he was to be believed, dispatched to Korioumé, where it would be available for my return.

My plans sidetracked, I opted for the festival and the necessary routing through Timbuktu, going there by land rather than by river. At least I had the solace of individual travel. Mohammed assured me that no one else would be with me except the driver and guide. A tad disenchanted, yet knowing it would be fun, I overlooked the truism: "The last temptation is the worst treason; to do the right thing for the wrong reason."

The time was fixed. On a certain day, I would be in Timbuktu.

I had yet to learn that Mohammed would transfer everyone he could along with a paying traveller. That might include a guide who was to meet you later, cooks, equipment, another driver, and other travellers he squeezed in, at their cost, and with no alleviation of yours. It was my fuel bill, the whole way.

Prearranging a driver/guide between Bamako and Timbuktu was a "must," I was told during my preparations by the one other person I knew who'd been there. Zak had accepted my invitation to guide, and was happy with the job. When I told Mohammed of my decision, he did not disagree. I pitched Mamadou as driver. We planned to motor 235 kilometres east to Ségou that day. We aimed to then drive northeast, via Mopti, to Douentza for the next evening. All this on a decent road. North from Douentza, by patchy roads and across two rivers, Timbuktu waited.

We were ready to leave. At least I was. Zak sat cross-legged on the ground nearby. He was speaking Bambara with an attractive young woman. Dennis had pointed her out the evening before and said she'd travelled with them as cook for much of the trip. He had recommended her. Zak called her "Nema." She eyed me sternly as though she might have to cook for this body, walk with this man in the desert, and put up with Western ways for a week or more in the Dogon. She flounced from one foot to the next and back during her appraisal. A grin slipped free, but not yet a smile.

"My name is Rick," I said. "Will you be my cook for the Dogon?"

Zak said yes on her behalf, and she berated him, claiming the right to state her own acceptance. She stood straight and was taller than him, fuller of form, with strong arms. She wore beige slacks and a cream-coloured smock that was wrapped loosely around her. A single-strand necklace hung around her neck, weighed down with a handful of punched pebbles, all white. Her face gleamed with healthy skin, and when she felt the time was right, her lips parted and big teeth of the whitest possible smile sealed the arrangement. Finally, she did an unexpected thing. She shook my hand. And she twisted my name to confirm, asking, *"Reek?"* And I said yes to what would become Nema's term for me.

"Zak, about the car."

"Yes, *Rick*. What?"

"Where is it?"

"A be na sonni," he told me. And then in English he clarified what I learned to be their answer for everything. "It will be here soon."

Mamadou was always loud, always talking, his face glistening as though the conversation were a physical workout. When he arrived with the vehicle, he immediately threw his arm over my shoulder and then pushed the back of my head in jest. He wore a baseball cap, and an aerosol can of lubricant stuck out of the pocket of his blue shirt. He mimicked our first clumsy handshake, letting it again deteriorate into attempts to batter one another's hands. He restarted it, slowed it down, guided our closed fists to a butt, opened my palm and his, curling all our fingers together. He thought his creation was the funniest thing imaginable. He added a back-hand to back-hand slap, twisted my fingers, and initiated a ritual that would signify our greeting many times in the coming weeks.

Nema, not needed for cooking that day, would be sent along in the car at the behest of Mohammed, through whom I would pay for her cooking in Dogon. Zak and Mamadou boarded the tattered Peugeot with Nema and me sitting in the back.

I was surprised by the trees through which the road was hewn. *"Balanzan,"* Zak called them. They bore fatty fruit. "We call it shea butter. They are shea trees." We passed by the picturesque village of Sanankoroba, giving us a small sense of what to expect en route as villages large and small drew close, then faded away from the roadway.

Afro-funk music pierced the car as Mamadou fiddled with the volume. His audio tape cassette was stuck. He pounded the dash, then found the proper pull, sprung it and pushed it back to load the deck. Eventually, a soothing sound emerged, but loudly. "Afel Bocoum," Zak said, with Malian pride.

Mamadou had zero English except for my name, and his conversation with me was in Bambara. As I mispronounced the tree name, he entered the fray, self-appointed teacher of Bambara.

"I ni sogoma," he said.

I searched his face for meaning. He repeated. I re-searched.

Villages like Sanankoroba stretch beside and away from the roadway between Bamako and Ségou.

Zak helped, "Hello. Means 'hello.'"

I spoke the word clumsily.

Mamadou said it slowly, flicking his lips.

I attempted it again.

"*I nice,*" Mamadou said, chuckling, his success apparent, my gratitude expected.

"Thank you," interpreted Zak. "I write for you." Then, "Say *owo.* Is word you need."

"And it means?"

"Yes."

I could imagine only trouble with this.

Nema reached across the back seat and removed my broad-rimmed hat from my lap, claiming it as hers. "*Mon chapeau,*" she postured with a dimpled grin, and pulled it taut over her bunned hair.

"*Owo,*" I kidded. Here began my weeks of struggling to reassert ownership of my hat.

Nema's black hair was streaked orange. Not everywhere, but with enough of a tinge to harmonize the unfathomable brown of her skin. She cast a mesh over this to hold the hair away from the fire and food while cooking. A gold earring dangled from her left lobe. That beady smile consistently pushed her face to round, making her eyes skimpy and her nose larger, and taking her lips to the brink of a pout. Her perturbed look (such as when she was tugging for control of my hat) pulled it all in. She could not but look beautiful. We travelled many miles together, starting with our misunderstanding in the back seat of that car. Malians are a casually, politely touching people. When Nema's hand landed on my arm or if she sat with her leg touching mine, it was nothing. Nothing but trust.

Zak, at his core, was avuncular. He voiced constant encouragement, unsolicited advice followed, and, in a mentoring manner, he repeated himself. I was not sure which one of us he was reassuring. His height barely crested my shoulders. But in most everything he did, he stood taller. In T-shirt, shorts, and the flip-floppiest of sandals, his lithe body could move anywhere, move anything. His calves and haunch and arms were all muscle. His training gym was the Dogon.

Zakarie, the guide; Rick, the author; Nema, the cook; and Mamadou, the driver.

Mamadou cranked the music up to hear it above the talk, which was in turn loud in order to be heard over the music, which he spun louder in a circus of sequences. The singer strained in a plaintive way, her voice more powerful than her words, as I didn't comprehend them.

Every day a traveller could see the things I saw for a first time: a donkey-fest of nine carts, each laden with market goods, firewood, and blackened pots; three Malian grandfathers making their own caravan on bicycles, with a high sack of trade wares on their backs, vegetable shoots springing from each pack's wrapping. Beyond the ensemble, a single man in brown clothing flowed from a village, a long pole slung over his shoulder in the fashion of an American hobo, a symbol for the ages. He approached a camel, its legs cracked at the knees, and touched the pole to the camel's thigh and backside. It rose desert true.

We were in a land vulnerable to drought and poor crops, and the road was not well travelled. The harmattan, which flogs this land during the rainy season, had left to recover from its own effects. Vegetation had died in its path. Structures strong on history were whittled by its breeze. Water supplies were blown to vapours or covered with sand.

Mamadou was an expert at driving on this Third World three-lane road. It was really two lanes which, when there was other traffic, had three active lanes: us, a passing vehicle, and the target. *Bâchés* belched along, local passengers, oblivious to the smells and the occasional Caucasian visibly choking in the transport's smoke.

Nearing Ségou, Nema insisted on "Salif Keita." Mamadou, who controlled the tape deck, declined. "Salif," Nema demanded. Her teeth were large, and it was impossible for her mouth to be angry without also looking like a smile. Mamadou responded sharply, refusing, saying "Super Khoumaissa." Nema let forth a tirade of Bambara streaked with vulgar terms, or so it seemed to me. Mamadou was adamant in his choice of music. Soon we were listening to Salif. Thus I learned that Mamadou, Zak, and I, even when we argued aggressively, deferred to Nema whenever she had a want.

In the distant Sahelian lands, a regal man appeared, his blue robe streaming with his gentle movements. He walked purposefully out of a cluster of trees, a staff in his right hand, crossed the road, and entered the desert that stretched over the horizon. From where? To where?

A donkey caravan trod the earth beside the pavement. Eleven carts in all, with cargos of rope and millet, and children with mothers in purple and red and green. More colours: a lighter red, an orange, two distinct greens and white in the clothing.

We arrived in the ancient Bambara dynasty's capital, Ségou. This is one quarter of the length of the River Niger. We eased off the blacktop onto dirt, around the potholes, and stopped in front of a home where there was a room for the night. This was one of the "hotel" charges on Mohammed's listing.

It was good to stretch our legs and not hear car sounds. A walk toward the river with Zak eased my morning's disillusion. Nothing troubled this young man, and his readiness to please was Malian to the core. We strolled through gardens tilled by happy people. Patches of vegetables covered a hundred acres. A Mali firefinch fluttered, disappeared and came back with a friend. It was my first night of dusk and bush, with mosquitoes at my ankles.

Zak commiserated with me about my itinerary woes. In Mali, one needs a great sense of the practical. Last night's missed sleep hadn't bothered me during the drive. What had worn on me was being taken advantage of by Mohammed. I had wished for distinct challenges in getting to Timbuktu. Patience seemed my only test thus far.

Around a bend and past a grove of trees was the River Niger, my first sighting of the majestic waters. The river was wider than I had imagined from reading Mungo Park. I squinted to filter out the sights and sounds of farmers as I watched the *pirogue* (a small boat traditionally used in West Africa) being poled along the river by a solitary man. It had been like this for his ancestors, for generations, and I thought: Mungo Park stood here.

We meandered along the shore, past the working farmers, and talked in French. As we walked, I noticed that everywhere was packaging and junk, acres of bags, the plastic planted and growing. Flapping wrappers substituted for flowers.

"*Un problème pour Mali,*" I raised, "*est le litter.*"

"Liter?" Zak asked, recognizing my poor French. His tolerance for my sloppy linguistic skills was notable.

"*Non.* 'Liter'" — I mimicked drinking from a container and shook my head. And then showed two fingers for two T's. "Litter. Garbage."

"Yes, *Rick.* We know."

Amid the garbage and the garden, the clouds slowed to grey, the sun did a purple bow and was gone. A donkey trotted past us, his breathing making a nose-whistle; a cyclist passed us in the dusk, and two ladies joined our trail, noticed the foreigner, and laughed pleasantries that I simultaneously didn't understand and did. No lights. No fear. Trust and confidence grew in the village garden.

I reaffirmed to Zak, "You are my guide for Dogon."

"You wish?"

A decision needed to be made. "And we will trek for ten days." It was significant. Mohammed had kept pressuring for Gao, less time for Dogon. Pricing drove his interests. I would tell him my decision. My heart wanted what I believed was needed: a long walk.

"*Inshallah,*" Zak said. It is their word. "If God be willing."

I'd originally thought to approach Timbuktu from the west, by river, earning my way with endurance as Mungo Park had. Then, returning to the city on camel from a night in the desert, as Gordon Laing had, I'd leave on four-by-four southward (unlike Laing). Now, I approached going north, closer to the last leg of René Caillié's route. This was not the journey I wanted, but it was the journey I had. How like life it was becoming.

On the porch, where we stayed that night, café at my elbow, I heard that the house was actually used for Mohammed's office, with a bedroom as a part of it. I felt my independence usurped again as Mohammed's charge for a hotel room did not reconcile. I unfolded the Mali map across a table, and turned my mind to other matters. Zak pinned two corners of the map with rocks, and we plotted the next day's drive.

"We leave Ségou at seven," said Zak, "Mopti for lunch." Mopti's market was famous. "And then to Douentza. Overnight there." Timbuktu awaited us the day after.

Zak hunched over the unfurled map and used my guidebook and compass to pin the other corners of the sprawled geography. He quizzed me about place names in French, and his face furrowed around my mispronunciations. His vocabulary was extensive, as was his patience with my lack of it. I aborted and abridged. I pointed to *Le Pays Dogon* and said to Zak, "When we leave the Dogon, I wish to speak French much better. We will speak French there all the time."

"Is good," he said, with a teacher's nod of approval.

Nema arrived with a boyfriend on his motorcycle. She wore my wide-brimmed hat and strode defiantly from the bike to the porch. "*Mon chapeau,*" she preened. It looked so fetching on her that I couldn't ask for it back. I resigned myself to wearing my baseball cap.

Nema, spirits high, said we needed to buy food for dinner and signalled me to sit behind her on the bike. She revved the engine, swerved precariously, and propelled us down the road, bouncing energetically. We rode: she carefree, I worried, her dress billowing, her beautiful brown breasts open to the air through the broad sleeves of her shirt. I gingerly clasped her hips for balance as we dodged potholes.

At the roadside, merchants squatted beside their treasures. Their open shutters displayed skimpy selections. Nema told me to pay for what we picked up — juice and lettuce, tomatoes, chunks of meat, and two cups of rice, which she poured into a plastic bag. She stuffed the other foods into the bag as well, and I carried it under one arm as I sat on the back of the motorcycle, the other arm holding on to my biker friend.

When we arrived back at the house, Nema's boyfriend had left, and she went to a neighbour's house to cook. Zak and Mamadou had gone their separate ways. I was alone. I welcomed the evening's coolness. Across the road a bent man scraped his feet along the ground, chickens at his toes. He spilt feed from a bag. I joined him and tossed handfuls in all directions. Followed by chickens, I sprinkled.

Shortly afterward, Nema produced plates of rice, veggies, and boiled goat parts. After Mamadou, Zak, and I had eaten, I hinted for my hat as Nema walked across the porch, vamped Malian style, and disappeared. I gathered up the dishes — mine the only one with leftovers — and stacked them on a side chair.

Inside, Mohammed's office was spacious, containing two desks, three makeshift posters, a computer, a couch, and two chairs. Across a hall, I found my bedroom. It was not intended for the discriminating traveller. It hadn't been cleaned in a long time, the sheets were filthy, the air was dank. I thought of trips I had made with Janice. In restaurants we had visited around the world, Janice moved from table to table until she was satisfied; at hotels in countless cities she moved from room to room until happy. Here, she wouldn't have changed rooms, she'd have changed countries.

At 7 a.m. I was up and anxious for the day's travels. The street was empty. No car. No one at all, in fact. Eventually I scrounged

Nescafé, milk, and some boiling water from the man who had let me feed his chickens. He now shared his freshly risen bread.

Near eight, Zak rounded the corner. He was looking for Mamadou, who thought to drop by about nine, on a motorcycle. No car. Two chickens hung upside down from his handlebars, squawking, shitting on their own faces.

Ten-ish, in the rusting Peugeot, gear loaded, we headed for Mopti. My intended solo journey continued with three people. We set our compass for the traveller's holy grail. "I am on the road to Timbuktu," I whispered to myself, echoing Laing's words.

William Makepeace Thackeray's poem "Timbuctoo" also came to mind.

> In Africa (a quarter of the world)
>   Men's skins are black, their hair is crisp and curled
>   And somewhere there, unknown to public view
>   A mighty city lies, called Timbuctoo.

Now, as sand swirled behind us, I wondered: How mighty will it be? Will I have the good fortune to make it there and return safely? Mungo Park died without seeing Timbuktu. Robert Adams, brought as a slave, didn't know where he'd been until he had left. Laing was killed after leaving. René Caillié's achievement brought him only derision when he first returned to Europe. Heinrich Barth spent over five years on his journey in West Africa, and reaching Timbuktu was the emotional centrepiece of his travels. There were so many possible outcomes.

At midday we stopped where a row of shacks sat in dirt a metre from the pavement. One shed stepped into another, all ingesting sand, their only common decor. This was Mali's version of a strip mall. Car parts rested beside bowls of fruit, adjacent to a stand tended by a lady offering bread. Next was a cupboard on a table, its shelves holding old liquor bottles filled with petrol, their glass a dull green. The shop fronts were not aligned. Dirt mixed with food. The long body of a cow hung over a fire to cook. Garbage blew among the wares.

Nema did not know the wise ways of a Western woman. She was wiser. At the roadside market, in the store, or standing against the open door of our car, men drifted by her, close. They touched her slender back and gazed at her bare legs. Graced with her smile, they stopped and waited for more. She ignored them. Instead, she went to a stall and returned with black ginger. She popped two of the candies in her mouth and tossed one each to Zak, Mamadou, and me.

Two hours down the road, Nema noticed a fire pit and commanded Mamadou to drive off the road, proceed down the potted slope, and stop at the butcher's kitchen. It was the only shack for miles, a *dibieterie*, Zak said. Barely a metre square, it had posts that angled against one another for mutual support to hold up a low, woven roof on which I hit my head. Wood branches stoked a fire draped with gutted goat. Nema selected and pointed and ordered and argued in Bambara. As the butcher hacked, Nema indicated yes, no, no, yes. At my suggestion, portions of the animal were tossed back on the coals.

A five-year-old girl in a yellow dress, streaked with grease and sand, held a metal pan for her father and stared at me. I gave her a pin with my country's red maple leaf flag on it. She turned and happily gave it to another youngster and then looked back to me, asking for one more, which I handed to her.

To avoid more gift giving, I wandered off toward the car and heard *"Reek"* close behind. I turned around and Nema shoved a piece of partially cooked meat into my mouth. I bit too quickly, catching two of her fingers in my teeth. "Like? Chew." Nema commanded. *Easy*, my stomach said. I relaxed my jaw and she forced the meat farther into my mouth. I held it with clenched teeth and Nema twisted a chunk loose. She put the torn-off piece in her own mouth and walked away. I ground and swallowed my portion. The cooked part of the meat was warm from the fire; the uncooked part seemed still warm from the animal's recent death.

The little girl trailed behind me. She'd given away the second pin and asked for yet another. She slowly drained my supply with her cleverness.

We motored past settlements too small to be villages. The people seemed permanently paused, their melon patches neglected. Zak said, "The places are deserted today. Some people go to burn bushes, some collect firewood." I considered the irony.

An adult goat and kid head-butted, playing at the lessons of life, and I wondered if I'd done enough of that with my children.

The Bani River was beside us on its way to meet the Niger at Mopti. We stopped and drank coffee with powdered milk at a shack and I delayed taking my daily malaria pills, remembering that they bind to dairy products and thus are less effective. Back in the car, I scratched my swollen eye where a mosquito had bitten me, the welting worried away. Finally, in spite of the coffee, I fell asleep to the road's rumble.

"I have broken my dentures," Nema said, waking me.

"What?"

"I have broken my dentures," she repeated, her diction perfect. She was reading from the *Lonely Planet French/English Dictionary* that she had found while rummaging through my pack.

Even when research had taught me about Timbuktu's relative accessibility, I nurtured the awe that others expressed about my quest. I'd said much about what had once been the rigorous challenge of reaching Timbuktu, but did not share the knowledge of how reachable it might be. I approached Timbuktu aware that I was safe, not alone, not far from medical assistance, and in no danger.

Often we drove fifteen kilometres before encountering another vehicle. Sacks of coal and wheat were stacked by the roadside, waiting for transport. In the middle of nowhere (now there's a trite Western phrase) there was a woman in bright yellow dress belted with an orange cloth. Her hair was couched in a pastel blue wrap. She sat with three small children beneath a tree. The country's economic woes did not show in her contented face or in the buoyant greens and reds of her children's clothing. Maybe they didn't know what the foreign debt was.

The city of Mopti has bustled for many centuries. We arrived on the outskirts of this river port after encountering the *frontière*, a shift in administrative regions marked by oil drums blocking the roadway. Dead tires stacked as a wall and a crossbar of defeated metal prevented passage. A guard stuck his head in the car's window and stared past Mamadou toward my face, then rolled the rims out

Salt, once valued pound for pound equivalent to gold when it traded in Timbuktu hundreds of years ago, is today still assembled in slabs for transport at the market in Mopti.

of our way. As Mopti began to take shape along the roadway, cattle and people crossed it at a leisurely pace and slowed our drive.

"Is there Internet?" I asked Zak.

"Yes. Is not reliable."

Intrigued with this world where "remote" may soon disappear as a concept, I decided to try connecting. A two-storey mud building, the second level a false front, had a sign, making good on the first half of Zak's answer.

"There?" I pointed.

"Only there," said Zak as Mamadou pumped the brakes and we stopped in a swirl of dust. My door opened with a creak and bumped against a motorcycle's handlebar propped on the ground. I stepped around it and walked into a shop crammed with crates and barrels and sacks and iron holders. No computer.

"May I use the Internet?" I asked a teenager, who was cinching tight a rope knot to hold a wooden box closed. He looked at me as though I'd ordered up the moon. Zak came in behind me and sorted things out, speaking Bambara.

Grinning in response to Zak, the shopkeeper shifted a dented container and carried away two boxes. A chair was positioned in front of a carpet that was draped over shelves. He lifted the rug to unveil a dead computer. He restrung an electrical wire from its service to the light bulb, dimming the shop further. Then he linked another cord and pressed a button, tapped the central processing unit repeatedly and spoke to Zak.

Zak relayed it to me, *"A be na sonni."*

Eventually I was able to e-mail my two sons that I was well and happy, Mopti-style.

After I helped restore the prized computer to its darkened storage, I stepped into the bright sun and stopped. What had I seen? I retreated into the shop and looked at the young man. He was wearing my hat! I pointed to it and he pointed to Nema outside and held it tight to his head. She'd given it to him. This was really crazy. I reached for it and he backed away, but I got a hold on the wide brim and tugged. It came with my hand, he having decided not to make a fuss while my face showed exactly the opposite. I walked into the street with the hat on *my* head. Nema yelled at me. *"Reek.* He's my friend."

"Lucky man, but he's not getting my hat," I said.

"Give it to him," she said, looking mean enough that I knew it was not a joke.

"Not a chance, Nema."

With her foot, she scuffed sand at my legs and made a grab for my hat. I raised both hands to hold the brim secure to my head and she jabbed me in the ribs. She left the hat, but took my pride.

It was another kilometre to the market. Swarms of merchants and itinerant buyers converged on the garbage pile that is their harbour, home to quick barter and discarded packaging. *Pirogues* conveyed goods from one place to another. Even the idle looked busy. Goats and cows and dogs dragged nourishment from the piles of litter.

If you saw a thousand people in Mali, no two would be dressed alike. Occasionally they would look similar, but only by chance. Absent was the Western commonality of fashion, similarity of suit and skirt, slacks and jacket. It seemed true, too, of their personalities. The individuality was intense, based on the struggle for life, the indifference to community judgment, and the fact that one ate and wore what was handy. The uniformity of poverty seemed to result in an absence of the ambition to conform in dress.

As I raised my camera for a memory shot of a *pinasse* that teetered under a heavy load, an ancient man yelled at me. He was robed in torn red, his brown body showing through the tears, his face covered in a stubble of blackish-grey on the cheeks that screamed. A beard hung below that. His eyes shouted the loudest.

"Non. Non." He was angry with me because my camera angle may have included him in the picture. At first I thought him foolish.

He rushed forward, still bellowing at me, and our faces were very close, our eyes unblinking. I respectfully lowered my camera.

My hand was open, motioned his way, and he reached out pre-emptively for control. He grabbed my hand to thwart picture-taking. Anger rose in his voice, and the market stilled at his shouting. His grip tightened. A bone crunched. I blinked.

I pointed to his black hand clasped in my white. It was to him immediately funny. He laughed. Although his grasp did not loosen, his mood did. I asked if Zak could take a picture of our joined hands.

"Oui. Oui." The man pushed his sleeve up a java-black arm to further the contrast. He danced a jig in the sand, holding on tight, blurring the photograph and crystallizing the memory.

Zak and Nema guided me to where they preferred lunch. We had a communal platter of chips and chicken. Sitting still, I was white prey for trinket sellers. One man appeared every ten minutes. When he asked in French if I knew the term "bargain," I said, to Zak's amusement, "No. Do you know Mohammed?"

We loaded a case of bottled water into the trunk of our car and left Mopti. As we drove, people hoed rows in the fields, preparing to plant. Pushcarts were tilted to the ground, their loads secured. In their shade, men rested.

As the sky darkened to a bronze-teal, cooking fires fuelled by millet husks lit our lonely road to Douentza.

We pulled off into a black nothing. First, a wall, then a gate appeared. A building emerged from the darkness. There was a large courtyard, a covered patio, and dusty trees. Two old Toyota Land Cruisers braced an open fire, the only light. It was my first *campement*, an outpost of sorts. It was only a place to sleep, where travellers gathered.

I hauled my bag toward the silhouette of a building. Zak switched on a solitary light bulb. He said, "*Rick?* Is okay?" I saw the cell-like walls with rotting paint and the lumpy mat on a little bed made of lashed branches. The closed window had protective metal flanges and the air smelled days old.

"Perfect," I said. I had not expected a Fairmont property. I slipped my pack to the concrete floor. Home, at least for now.

I made the room mine. I stuffed a pillow in the case from home and unfolded my sleeping bag on the bed. I placed Sean's gift of *L'Alchemist* and my baseball cap at the head of the bed. Then I found the open-air *douche* across the yard from my building, where it was separated from the toilet by a chest-high wall of dirt. The shower spewed cold water.

Travel in Mali was about perseverance, long drives, and dismay at my chambers. Like forest camping, it took only a short while for any night's lodging to become familiar.

A young Frenchman, his Burkina wife, and his parents sat near their fire and the Land Cruisers. Kevin was lean, sanded rough by years as a guide. New to Mali, he and his wife had been married for most of his five years in Burkina Faso. His parents had flown earlier in the day from Paris to Bamako to Timbuktu, where he had met their plane and driven directly to Douentza.

His father told me, "Many of my colleagues in Paris did not believe we were going to Timbuktu. They thought it does not exist."

"There's not much to show them in Timbuktu," said Kevin. "But now they've been there, and that makes a good story for them to take home." He knew Mali well and reminded me of the dangers for travellers. "Before '95, there were often Tuareg hijackings of four-by-fours," he recounted. "Not now. Not much, anyway." Kevin intended to stay in Mali to guide visitors. His knowledge of

European expectations would provide refreshing competition for the locals.

I was reading by the light of a candle when Mamadou and Zak returned from town, where they'd gone to pick up dinner, but carried nothing.

"Dinner?" I asked.

"Yes, I'll go now."

"Now? You just got back."

"Is close," Zak said.

"Let me go with you." We walked from the dark into the dark.

It was pitch dark outside the encampment; it was black as Zak. Across the road and down a hundred metres was a light and loud talking, but we walked the other way. A small flame glowed as we approached some chopping noises coming from a hut. A man was bending over the glow, cooking.

"Cow," Zak said. They'd bought meat in the village and left it with the roadside cook when they'd returned.

"Let it cook longer," I urged.

The man chopped and sorted the meat toward a meal. We wrapped it in slimy paper already greasy from use and thanked the cook.

At the encampment, we pulled chairs around a small table not far from Kevin's fire. Zak smiled as I carved part of the tough meat with the saw blade of my multi-pronged Leatherman. He picked the silver housing off the table, closed the greasy blade and opened the screwdriver attachment, laughing at the gizmo. He pried open six tools at once, nicking his finger with a sharp piece. He grinned widely. "Is great, *Rick*."

"Yup," I said. "Best thing since sliced bread."

He looked at me quizzically. "Sliced?"

Perhaps I should have said, "The best thing since pointed sticks."

Five feet from my coveted solitude, three villagers moved five tables from around the courtyard and into a group and found lanterns to place on them. A dozen glasses appeared. Kevin's family turned their chairs to face away.

Four trucks shuddered to a stop outside the gate, and in walked two men. One carried a television camera on his shoulder.

"Where's the liar who said we could drive from Bamako to Timbuktu in one day?" he snarled.

"At the bank," the other smirked.

I listened as the two mates sorted out a trip gone amiss. It was a BBC film crew, festival-bound on a documentary assignment. As their caravan of four-wheel drives invaded my peaceful setting, I could feel their exasperation. They looked at me and, with a *bonjour* and *bonsoir* on my part, presumed me French. Being British, they ignored me.

"No one showed on time," said the cameraman, setting it down.

"And the fuel was a surcharge," the short bloke added, whining, "can you believe it?"

They were colleagues travelling in separate vehicles, catching up on their complaining. A third sulked into the conversation. "God, I'd love a beer."

"There is no beer. I've already asked," said the disgruntled cameraman.

"It's been sixteen bloody hours. I'm exhausted," the first man moaned. His chums agreed.

Their dozen travelling companions assembled around the tables in hope of food and drink. Among them was an elegant woman of African descent and European bearing. Soon the patio became a setting for their documentary. A candle glowed on the woman's face as the camera ran. Now clearly a broadcaster, she had an upper-class accent and practised her lines for the London audience, speaking into the microphone.

"We started at six-thirty this morning," she began, her face tired, "and didn't dawdle. It's now ten o'clock at night and we're still nowhere-fucking-near Timbuktu."

On the third take she added, "And there's no room at this hotel."

I eased over to the director and suggested that the word "hotel" was stretching the concept some. They reshot the scene with, "And there's no room in this village."

In Mali, food was always ready. Fires were constant, and parts of animals were moved closer to the flame or farther away depending on the traffic and the time of day. Locals set dishes of rice and quick chicken on the BBCers table.

"There is beer," announced the *campement*'s man through an interpreter, "But it is warm."

"Warm? Hell, we're British," said a lanky fellow. "Crisis over."

I overheard them talk of plans to keep driving that night. "We're still a long way from Timbuktu," said the cameraman.

I was in and out of their conversations, and it was nothing for me to say, "In both of our countries, laws protect against tired drivers on the roads, even those who haven't gone sixteen hours, like yours."

"Bloody right," nodded the cameraman. "And none of us are keen for more road, except to get there."

Another, looking around at the ground they'd be sleeping on, said, "If it's six hours away, we can make that. Better than staying here." I offered my room to the elegant broadcaster, saying I could sleep outside. She thanked me but also wanted to be gone.

I knew it was none of my business, but I suggested they talk with the French guide who knew the route and they agreed.

"Kevin, these folks are thinking of driving to Timbuktu tonight," I said by way of introduction as we approached his fire.

"The river crossing you might prefer to do in daylight," he said. "It's your decision."

"How wide is the river?" one asked.

"The first one you drive through is not too far across, but the water will be up to your truck windows and probably wash in."

"The first one?" came the surprised response.

"The second river is the Niger. It has a ferry. If it's on this side, it'll take you across. If not, you'll have to wait till daylight."

"What would you do?" the cameraman asked, wiping a sweaty face that shone in the flame.

"I'd sleep here," said Kevin. "The bandits aren't out in the daytime."

Kevin's mother and father climbed the outside stairs of my building to where they'd sleep on the open roof. Kevin and his gorgeous wife slipped away to his tent. The BBC crew's boisterous talk did not reflect their tiredness and almost drowned out the muffled sounds of pleasure drifting from Kevin's tent.

A donkey squeal woke me, a novelty that would soon wear thin. The watch that was hooked to my pack glowed 6:40. They'd all be up, packed and waiting. I hurried, despite my intention never to hurry on this journey. Stuffed my bag. Outside, Mamadou, the only one of our crew who was visible, said, "*Wrick*, café?"

Where I'd tidied last night's leftovers, garbage was strewn and the pickings bare — the work of a four-legged nocturnal cleaning crew.

I hauled out my gear.

"No, the four-wheel drive not ready," Mamadou said in Bambara, then again in French, thinking it helpful as I shuffled my backpack. He motioned that I should leave it on the ground.

"Not ready? I thought we left at seven," I said.

"Wait," said a voice. It came from a weather-wrinkled traveller sitting on a wooden stool, with a steaming drink cupped in her hands. This was a woman my age, whose teeth, hair, and skin look uncared for. She was apparently a veteran of travel in that corner of the world.

"You're travelling on W ... A ... I ... T," she advised, enunciating each letter. "*West Africa International Time*. Get used to it."

I smiled and walked her way. "You sound patient," I suggested.

"Now. Not at the start. I've been here a month and lost my impatience in the back seat of a *bussé* my first week in Mali. If you hurry, you'll be the only one stressed out."

An hour later, Zak and Nema appeared, seemingly at odds with one another. Might it come from having shared quarters for their night's sleep?

The *campement*, Auberge Gorma, bordered a village of mud homes held close by wind and dust. When I asked Zak about our four-by-four, which had arrived at Mohammed's direction and was sitting unloaded, he said we were waiting for another one because it was safer to travel in pairs from here to Timbuktu.

"Where's the second four-by-four?" I asked. Silly me.

"*A be na sonni.*"

I strolled away. It could be hours.

I wandered through the village and sat down on the rubble of a dirt fence to scribble a note. Kids hounded me for my pen, "*Le bic, le bic,*" and when I gave the chipped *stylo* to one, there sprang a chorus for more: "*Un cadeau, un cadeau.*"

Chased away by their chattering, I found an empty street. At its edge, families were eating their first meal of the day. And, at its corner, the street widened where boys played soccer with a ripped ball that collapsed when kicked. Two big boys scored twice on their smaller competitors as I approached. I sided with the underdogs. A child passed the ball to a boy in pants too long for his legs, and he kicked the dead ball my way. I got dust. One of the big fellows leaped for the ball, but my leg was longer and I trapped the leather flat to the ground. Standing on the ball, I hip-checked him away, as he had done with the smaller kids. They cheered. The ball popped round and it was all mine. I've a move from my grade school days, and it always works on kids. It is a step across the ball and a back-of-my-heel kick the other way. Never fails. He blocked it. I rounded, showed him my back and put my feet to work. Quickly now, a fifty-four-year-old outmatched by the speed of youth, I kicked the deflated ball in front of me only far enough to keep it round and rolling. My team yelled. I was in front of the two tall boys and moving away, the floppy ball at my feet. It was not a short field. I was winded and needed to rest, but the little kids wanted me to score. I was being chased and could not give up. I slipped my instep below the broken ball and lifted it between two rocks that marked the goal posts. Cheers.

For fifteen minutes more I kicked and defended my nationhood. Mali won.

There was a chant of school lessons behind me, despite the many children skipping class. A hundred cattle in the foreground were moving toward us as if they were on a guided tour of the schoolyard. The recess bell rang and the kids, cows, and shepherd mingled.

I wound my way back to the *auberge*, where passing vehicles were leaving people of various colours and nationalities by the roadside. They hitched a ride with us — at a dear financial cost for their eagerness to get to the Festival au Desert; supply and demand set the price. Arbitrarily, seats were taken in both Land Cruisers, and I sensed Mohammed's opportunistic influence. Hands were shaken as we loaded. Monica, dark-haired and with deep, brown eyes, was from Portugal and in the company of a lanky lad, John, from the U.K. Helena, a child psychologist near retirement, came from Sweden, and beside her but of no common travels was a fellow Zak's age from Scotland, who had travelled with his dad across the Sahara by truck. The woman who earlier told me to W.A.I.T. slipped into the back of the vehicle and told folks how lucky we were to have a ride. "I've waited since ... whatever day that was ... three ago." Cheap and unreliable travel. "I could have left earlier, I was ready," she said, squeezing with others into the four-by-four's luggage area. "But ... no one ... goes north."

It was noon.

Our designated Toyota (there was a seemingly total absence of Land Rovers and a paucity of Jeeps; the Japanese trade with France being an early inroad to the colonies to provide reliable four-by-fours for the deserts, ensuring a ready supply of parts and cornered the market) absorbed each additional pack without budging. Its four doors were opened for the get-in, get-out rearrangement of passengers: strangers were apportioned a patch of seating, then told to move.

It is a Malian government goal to create passable road north from Douentza to Timbuktu. In our first hour we travelled over sparse clay pavement, where only a few years ago untamed ruts and sand drifts slowed movement. The "improved" road was a vehicle-and-a-half wide. When that patch of pseudo-pavement ended, our driver lugged the two front wheels with a wrench and we were in four-wheel drive.

Nema, tucked in the luggage area, was one of eight passengers jammed in the vehicle that Mohammed had reserved and priced for just me. I wondered if I would ever again see Mohammed and, if so, what insult would first come to mind: the sloppy rooms at unfair prices or his brazen crowding of the vehicles for his own profit? Or were there other surprises for me yet to come? Nema flirted across the back of the back seat, tapping a song on my arm as she sang. In Bambara she uttered a pleasing phrase I did not understand while she moved her hand along my bicep. Mamadou laughed so loud that we could barely hear Zak announce to everyone, "Nema says that if you stay in Mali she will take care of you." Her eyes averted our laughter and she did not smile. Then she bowed her head shyly and let the right corner eye open slightly to take in my appreciation and respectful decline.

We saw another four-by-four, its hood propped up, its travellers temporarily stranded. A second vehicle we passed was abandoned, its windows rolled up. By the time we reached the first river, we were alone. Slowly, Mamadou nosed our vehicle into the water. Rocking along the uneven waterbed, it made waves that sprayed into our windows. But, as we hoped, in five minutes, the Land Cruiser crawled up the riverbank, shedding muddy water and likely a few fish.

Two hours later, when we arrived at the bumpy road's end at the River Niger, we were no longer alone. Donkey-pulled flats, stationary four-by-fours, and a gathering of Malian merchants sat by the shore, waiting for the small boat to ferry them across. Children were strapped to the backs of a variety of hard-working mothers: porter moms, millet-pounding moms, here's-the-tit-suckling moms, cooking moms, and water-carrying moms. Our embarkation dock consisted of packed mud, wet, slippery, and humming with roaming people and defecating animals.

Any rig that was out of line was hollered at by the native drivers. Even when there was no apparent order, one must not jump the queue. Efficiency was not the goal, respect was.

I walked a few hundred metres down the shore to get away from the din. I squinted and used a tree to help fetter people and vehicles from my view. I was alone with the river. Some distance down river, at a place known as Bussa rapids, one of my heroes had died, killed by the Tuareg on his journey through these waters.

Mungo Park had not set out for pleasurable-though-adventurous travels as I had, yet he did hope for a change of pace, a break from his daily life as a country doctor in Edinburgh.

Mungo Park, the Scottish explorer, twice failed to reach "the great object of my search," Timbuktu, and died in late 1805 or early 1806 on the River Niger, either killed by the Tuareg ambush or drowned in the Bussa rapids.

Park's name became synonymous with West African exploration. His 1795 and 1805 travels provided essential practical and geographical knowledge to later explorers who participated in the rush to "discover" Timbuktu and begin beneficial trade with its residents. He initially travelled at the behest of the

African Association, whose directive was to identify the "rise and termination" of the River Niger. Other explorers would eventually place the facts before a European public that was hungry for grandiose stories: Timbuktu was about poverty, not prosperity; its streets were filled with sand, not gold; the homes there were drab.

Travelling these waters, Park misjudged both the river that made him famous, and its people. His belief held: he was about to determine the direction of the River Niger's flow, one of the century's great geographical riddles, on par with the question of the source of the Nile River. In London and Paris, academic debate on the route of the River Niger had narrowed to four views, none of them founded on first-hand accounts. Either it crossed Africa to join with the Nile, as many hoped for reasons of trade, or it flowed east to a vast inland sea, or it curled back on itself to empty in the Atlantic, or it meandered south to meld with the Congo River. Vast patches of contemporary maps of Africa were blank, and the theories were a mixture of false hopes and tall tales. Even Africans told Park that the river ran "to the world's end," a place he may have felt he'd already found.

On the final stretch of his second journey in Africa, Park's boat was a craft cobbled together from two canoes, damaged during his desert crossing, bolstered with local wood and secured with lashing. The Niger was, however, too great a river for that poor a boat.

In a self-indulgent gesture, only a few days before attempting passage through these waters, Park had dispatched a courier to London, hoping to make his reputation. In his journal he declared, "I shall set sail to the East, with the fixed resolution to discover the termination of the Niger or perish in the attempt. I have heard nothing that I can depend on respecting the remote course of this mighty stream."

Park had arrived in Africa well prepared for his second attempt to reach Timbuktu, and boasting an impressive accompaniment of forty Europeans, including thirty militia. Now, burnt by the sun, humbled by blisters from the sand in their shoes, and diminished by sand blizzards and disease during the desert crossing, the party had been reduced to four soldiers, three servants, and a guide. The crew was ill-prepared to defend itself as it neared Timbuktu. The desert experiences had blinded Park to diplomacy and accounted for his reckless firing at Tuaregs. That action forced him to abandon the overland journey to Timbuktu, "the great object of my search," and kept him on the fateful river.

The journey outmatched the man. Bitter, the Tuareg awaited Park's passage through the River Niger's narrows, several days' river-journey from where I stood. There, they attacked. Park's surviving guide and the victorious Tuaregs told the story of a tattered boat, its fateful travellers, and the River Niger's swallowing of the mighty Mungo Park.

The dilapidated ferry rolled to our side of the River Niger, its flange scraping on the water. It rammed aground and disgorged a two-wheeled rig, four donkeys, and six men. Ready. Half a dozen four-by-fours and as many donkey-drawn carts scampered on and weighed it down. We clambered aboard. Thousands of tiny birds swooped around us in an undulating cloud that then swirled above us and off to the horizon. Our overloaded ferry was ready to head in their direction. Its steel ramp was pulled loose from the mud dock. We were on the Niger.

Half an hour later, we crashed ashore at Korioumé, wedging into the soft mud of the riverbank. Bustling began on-board, stopping while the ferry adjusted its landing platform, and then starting all over again. Vehicles spilled from the ferry in a rush for solid ground. Donkeys whined at the disorder. Feeling safer outside our vehicle, I walked off the ferry, down the metal flange, and into the mud. Hawkers rushed the boat and nearly reversed the tide of disembarkation. In the bizarreness of it all, darkness fell.

In the style of Mali travel, we waited around in the afterglow of the temporary market that had appeared for the ferry's arrival. Three new bags were tossed on the top of our truck and roped tight. Then two Malians were shoved in our midst as we wedged back into the Land Cruiser.

Our two Land Cruisers rode through the port's chaos and alongside trees in swampy water. Then we drove in the desert for seventeen kilometres on the *Route de Kabara*.

Heinrich Barth, following the same path in the daytime, found his arrival in Timbuktu disappointing. "We approached the town, but its dark masses of clay not being illuminated by bright sunshine, for the sky was thickly overcast and the atmosphere filled with sand, were scarcely to be distinguished from the sand and rubbish heaped all round." René Caillié's sentiments, on arriving at sunset, however, reflected what I felt approaching the great city. "I entered Timbuktu the mysterious and I could hardly control my joy."

FIVE

Among the Tuareg

Upon our nighttime arrival at the hotel in Timbuktu, Zak had announced: "We leave at seven." I'd come to realize that this was code for "We wake up in the morning."

At eight Zak surfaced, showered and ready for the desert dust.

"Ready to go," he announced. Ever the optimist.

"Glad you are," I said, slowly finishing my coffee.

"*Rick*, where's your pack?"

"*A be na sonni,*" I replied.

Since our Toyota was not actually there, I had time to explore the setting in the early daylight. We were on the outskirts of Timbuktu, and our hotel was built of sandstone. The desert was at our doorstep. I had walked alone on a side road last evening, but it was very dark and I could barely see the Sahara. Now, in the morning, it was clear that we were at the edge of an expanse that went on forever. I walked back to the hotel an hour later and was still early for departure.

When the four-by-four finally arrived at the hotel, I tossed my pack on the roof rack, strapped it down, and climbed in. With Mamadou at the wheel, we drove along the Route de Kabara into Timbuktu until the pavement ended and then churned sand at the Place de l'Indépendence. Our vehicle fought the stream of Malians, pushcarts, and animals that is the Boulevard Askia Mohammed. Mamadou steered the Land Cruiser into a gathering of young merchants in front of the weary Hotel Colombe, stopping only when they jumped aside. The bags and backpacks on the stairs represented eight fellow travellers who looked anxious about the day's preparations. Two Toyotas raced from a side street and angle parked with only a foot of space between them, a most inconvenient position for loading.

There was no apparent sequence in the decision-making that followed. Most likely the purpose was to identify all those going to the festival and to get us into two trucks for the trip. I lazed in the centre seat of one vehicle, avoiding the sun, and over the course of half an hour had four different seatmates. This all before the drive began. A pandering child told me his name was Jimmy Carter. "That American president visited Africa. I gave him a present. The name, my friends then made for me."

The Hotel Colombe was on the fringe of Timbuktu's Old City, its buildings low, sad, and uninviting. The nearby Petit Marché was crowded with sellers of produce, ladies weaving blankets, and pots of boiling meat. In the bustle, another Land Cruiser arrived and from it jumped slim John, whom I'd met while leaving Douentza. He worked with a British tour operator who had used Mohammed's services in the past, and travelled with Monica, his roommate's girlfriend. Neither of them could resist the lure of Timbuktu when Mohammed invited them, at their own expense, to ride along with his paying guests on a familiarization trip. They had been all set to see Gao, as Mohammed had promised, but that had changed "because Mohammed's paying client decided not to go to Gao," John explained.

"We're staying at the L'Auberge Amana," Monica said. Her eyes wobbled to indicate its stature.

"Café?" John asked, looking around for somewhere that might serve coffee.

"There's a place," I pointed over his shoulder. A sign was tacked on the awning: *Poulet d'Or*. It was fifty metres from us, and as we strolled over, we walked through the breath of an open oven, its fire bright. On the street's shoulder, a lady used a flat pan to remove humps of bread from the oven and slipped them onto a tray beside the stove. We purchased two loaves, breaking pieces from them and eating as we walked. The garnish of sand was subtle. The Poulet d'Or had a few chairs and we commandeered them, found a waiter, and ordered coffee. Soon the café was full of the people who had been crammed into vehicles at Korioumé, had driven here late last evening and dispersed to various accommodations. We had all found each other again.

"Timbuktu. Can you believe it?" said Monica, pouring the hot water into the mugs of powdered coffee we were preparing. "A month ago I thought it was a made-up name."

When we sauntered back to the hotel, the throng of locals had grown threefold, many of them children. Two more trucks had arrived.

"It's ten o'clock," John said as bags were secured in the back of a four-by-four, then jettisoned and stacked in the dirt. But it was of no consequence what the time was. I looked down at the timepiece that hung uselessly on the epaulet of my backpack. It struck me that I had erred in bringing a watch to, of all places, Mali. I unhooked its O-ring, unzipped my pack, and stuffed the chronometer deep inside. Out of sight. Away. Gone for the rest of the trip.

The ritual of loading and unloading luggage continued for a while. Then, without warning, everyone scrambled for a seat and we were off. In minutes, Timbuktu was behind us and the desert was all we could see. The tracks took us many miles in the first hour. Then the tracks disappeared and the desert shimmered. Where once camel caravans known as *Azalai* had ruled the dunes, a fleet of five trucks was now trying to keep in file over rough terrain.

The road became merely a suggestion. When one four-by-four struggled, the others passed, leaving it. When one stalled right in front of us, Mamadou created an alternate route in the sand beside it. But we slipped on one sharp turn and heard the ominous spinning of all four wheels. We were stuck.

Everyone in the Land Cruiser jumped to the ground to lighten the load. Two weeks earlier I had used my hands to scuff snow from under the wheels of a friend's Jeep that had got stuck in Canadian mountains. Now, I carved armfuls of sand from behind the Land Cruiser's wheels to achieve the same effect. We pushed and the vehicle lurched forward.

We continued toward Essakane. Our vehicle's shocks abdicated. It was an atrocious experience, and I loved it. These hours, as we bore northwest, were among my most memorable experiences of the land — vast, faraway, uncertain. It was what I'd long envisioned Timbuktu to be. The rough passage rekindled my zeal for travel. I no longer felt a rush to discover Mali, nor to force my plans.

Hours of jostling followed as drivers and guides raged in debating on where Essakane might actually be. Directional disagreements revolved around opinions, not knowledge. It was not that we were lost; rather, no one knew where we were going. And this in a land where a compass error can mean slow death.

We stalled in a hollow of sand. Not stuck this time, our engine was overheated. The hood was raised, the hatch opened. It was a call for help, but no other vehicle was in sight, so we sat on the dunes for an hour. While the engine cooled, however, the travellers' temperatures rose. Mamadou and another Malian yelled at one another about the cause of the overheated engine and who was to blame. No matter; soon we were off in a bolt of enthusiasm and renewed confidence. We crested a sandbank and saw tents lining

En route through the Sahara to the oasis Essakane, a breakdown means there is little to do until another four-by-four passes by, hopefully that day.

the horizon. Essakane. At the moment of its appearance, as if it were a mirage, the four-by-four slowed, lulled, lost momentum, and sank. A few of us picked up our day packs and left the Malians shouting at one another as we set out toward the oasis, half a kilometre away.

An hour later, our gear arrived. Only when it was stacked next to the Land Cruiser was the skimpiness of some travellers' preparations evident. They'd heard that tents would be provided at the festival and were surprised to see broad frames of tree branches being tarped with camel skins. There, lying on the hard sand, they would try to sleep — open to the swirls of dust and bugs, with not even a blanket to cover themselves. I silently thanked Mohammed for his advice as I shook my nylon tent from its sack and sprang its metal ribs. It was up in a few minutes, providing a private space. The netting, designed to protect against mosquitoes, instead sifted wind-blown sand into my sleeping space.

We were in a large dip between dunes, a dozen tents sprawled between open desert and two Tuareg camps, their placement a shelter against the breeze. Along a ridge of sand, five hundred metres away, the festival's stage had been built in a desert amphitheatre carved by wind and time.

Near where I pitched my tent, a Tuareg man grabbed a squealing goat by the horns and pulled it away from the flock. It bayed. The flock bayed in unison. In front of me, out of sight of the flock, the Tuareg unsheathed a long knife. The chosen goat yelped pitifully to its friends. They replied, almost screeching, knowing. The man yanked the goat's head back, stretched its neck. A single bay of resignation followed. Among the flock, friend to friend to friend, the baying moved in fear. Slice. Silence. The sawing sound of further slicing. Bays from the flock. Then that stopped, too.

The group's food was being prepared by Nema and another Malian woman, who took Nema's instruction while barking back at her. It was Nema's manner to assert and direct, and the other woman's to sound strong in defiance while acquiescing. They worked on a makeshift counter carved into the sand and covered with a cloth.

This was where we would eat for the next few days. Large pots were loaded before being set over heat: chicken meat was unwrapped, picked apart, thrown in the pot; the paper wrapping was dropped on the ground. The cooks opened tins of peas, emptied them on the meat, and tossed the cans under a bush. They poured a sack of couscous into a canister bubbling over the fire and set water to boil in another pot — a hint to relax with pre-dinner coffee.

The ground suddenly shook, and a thundering in the distance came closer as fifty warriors on camelback galloped from a stand of trees. "No!" a woman shouted. The camels charged single file along the narrow space between me and my tent. I froze. Hooves pounded around me. They kicked sand in my face but I could not look away, and they knocked me back. Finally it was over and the last passing Tuareg slowed, glanced my way, and smiled. Then he whipped his camel and caught up with the herd.

We abandoned dinner and ran to the festival grounds. A hundred strong now, the camel riders were a formidable sight. There was nowhere to hide: if these warriors attacked you in the desert, would you dart to the next dune? Startled by their hard arrival, even the Tuareg spectators at the festival were in awe. The men on camels rode away, climbing the horizon as the sun set red. They slowed, swerved around as one and pounced back at us, yelling and flying across the desert with raging colours and frightening beauty.

Their riveting prelude completed, the camels came to rest and their riders dismounted as music blared to open the festival. The swirl of excitement was quickly quelled as drums, amplified with speakers, primed the audience and then stopped, the silence filled by politicians who postured with their event-opening comments, celebrities who read poetry, and organizers who spoke in earnest Tamacheq.

Dusk descended and drifted into night. I walked away from the stage and up the amphitheatre's hillock of sand as desert music rocked the gathering of three hundred Tuareg and guests in front of the stage. The rhythm of the *djembe* drum produced a haunting tranquility.

Essakane is without any supplies, facilities, or expertise suitable for a festival of any kind. It offers only splendid remoteness. The equipment used here had made the trek from Timbuktu and, before that, Bamako. This explained the leanness of the structures, the appearance of the generators, and the price of Coca-Cola. The festival's intention was to be one of the *grandes festes*, and it succeeded, with variations. One writer called it "Woodstock in the Desert." The performances were traditional, easing the logistics. The light and sound and staging were funded by Germany, but despite that country's engineering efficiency, power outages were frequent.

On the slope of the dunes were two-dozen stanchions: wire mesh tubes a metre high, half a metre wide, and filled with coals. As the evening progressed and temperatures cooled, the stanchions were lit to shed warmth within a five-metre radius. Many of those people gathering before the stage also took to the acres of sandy slopes, in clusters near the fires. Seeking to be alone, I drifted a further hundred metres from them, stopping atop a solitary dune and beneath stars that seemed as bright as the kliegs.

The musicians' chanting and singing appeared to be effortless. Their words were lost in shocking melodies or tucked behind haunting drums. The unfamiliar French accents of some of the entertainers, along with the Tuareg's singing in Tamacheq, made it difficult for me to discern if Tinariwen or Afel Bocoum was on stage. Names like Takumbawt and Kel Amazagh meant little to me, except that they were Malian. But I cherished their music in the same way as I had been captivated with Ali Farka Toure when first I heard the wonder of his music back home, for now I was at the music's source.

An Essakane family was gathered near me, and close to them three men sat talking and smoking. We were a small cluster, far from the others. The night got colder and I lay down on the firm sand, nestled in my jacket and with my baseball cap pulled down over my eyes. I shivered and shunted from side to side against the breeze. It was as hard to feel warm as it was to feel solitary.

Into this peripheral gang, appearing slowly over the dark brown sand, rose a man in a blue turban. He stood full height atop the dune, a silhouette of power and intrigue. After a moment's hesitation, he walked down the dune and came to sit beside me. His attention was riveted by the music, and it was half an hour before he spoke.

"I am Tabel," he introduced. "I am Tuareg."

"I am Rick," I replied. "I am not."

He kind of laughed. "Dutch?"

"No. Canadian."

"Ah. Far away. I, too, live far away. I live in the desert." He gestured over his shoulder where nothing and everything was far away. "There."

"I want to go 'there,'" I said, with the shifting of my head.

"You should ride my camel," he said.

"Tomorrow?" I asked, and it was a confirmation. We shook hands. Tabel was the first Tuareg I met face to face. He was a herdsman. His family lived as nomads; their provenance was sand.

The Tuareg captivate. They reflect the glamour of the desert — desolate, dangerous, and remote. Feared defenders of their territory, they have dispatched Moors, Arabs, British, and French with equanimity. Those around Timbuktu are the Kel Tademaket tribes. Travelling through their lands in 1825, Gordon Laing feared them: "I shall consider myself as fortunate if I get through their territories with the loss of half my baggage."

The region the Tuareg tribes cover is vast, and their contacts with each other are rare except to protect the trade routes. René Caillié was the first European to fully cross the expanse of Tuareg lands, traversing the Sahara to Morocco after his success in reaching Timbuktu. Caillié's view was that they "roam about ... and behave in the most arbitrary way, making the inhabitants give them provisions and other property — in fact, seizing whatever they can get their hands on ..."

It is said that the Tuareg later taunted the colonizing French soldiers as cowards for using rifles. Their camel charges against these invaders, with shiny sabers held high, were repulsed repeatedly by the French, who rode into Timbuktu in 1893.

The word *Tuareg* is not their own; its origin is Arabic, from the eleventh century, denoting a classification based on religious criteria for pagans. Northern Mali's Tuareg ancestors were

Berbers, though the younger people today often prefer to speak Arabic. Indeed, some Tuareg call themselves Tamacheq, after their language. Fergus Fleming's book *The Sword and the Cross* explains: "The term Tuareg (or Touareg) is currently used in the West to describe a person, a group, their language and their script. The correct declension is: I am Targui, we are Tuareg, we speak Tamacheq and we write Tinifar."

They have lighter-coloured skin than other Malians do and, as a result, are sometimes called "whites" by their countrymen. They are also known as "Blue men," as a result of their ever-present blue veils and turbans. These distinctive dirt protectors, dyed a dark indigo, transfer their colour, via sweat, to the Tuaregs' faces.

Jeremy Keenan's book *The Tuareg* focuses mostly on those inhabitants of the Ahaggar region of Algeria and the Sahara in northwest Mali. (The Tuareg also inhabit Libya, Niger, and Burkina Faso; Mali may be home to 500,000.) Keenan wrote for all Tuareg when he said, "After sixty years of 'protection' under French colonial rule, from 1902 to 1962, they have been obliged, as it were, to enter the twentieth century, but without grace and dignity, and perhaps that is the sadness of it all." Keenan observes: "They have not at any time formed a single politically united kingdom, state or federation, but comprise several major groups which seem to correspond to politically autonomous units or federations."

Their feudal society sufficed until their nomadic lifestyle, clashing with modern times, fell victim to the droughts of the 1970s and 1980s. In the Tuareg rebellion of 1990, the freedom movement concentrated on the desert north of Timbuktu, an area known as Azaouad. Thousands of Tuaregs had returned from their years in Algeria and Libya, where they'd migrated when times became economically tough. These repatriated Malians had a combination of political irreverence and military savvy. Weapons were available. The goal became one of establishing an independent status for their race. They wanted an autonomous territory within Mali, one to which the Tuaregs of Mauritania and Niger would also move.

Mali's standing army fell under attack from the Tuareg. It responded vigorously, and the ensuing deaths, economic

Once feared by every explorer, and known as the Blue Men of Africa, the Tuareg today host "the most remote festival in the world."

disruption, and world interest forced a resolution. The peace negotiations, brokered by France, Algeria, and Mauritania, resulted in the National Pact in April 1992. This peace accord did not appease a number of side groups, whose splintering kept the revolt alive. Their banditry continued unabated, and civil war threatened. For years, this pocket of Africa had the attention the world gives only to locations of violent uprisings. Eventually, the killings stopped. With nothing to be gained from continued strife, all sides agreed to make the National Pact meaningful and to implement its guidelines. On March 27, 1996, the Tuareg revolt ended (others would say "culminated"), though final agreements with some holdout rebels were still three years away. The peace pact was celebrated with a burning of weapons in Timbuktu at the Flame of Peace.

The Tuaregs' future has always been one of "today." Tamacheq does not possess a word for tomorrow.

The Essakane oasis rested in pre-dawn tranquility. As I woke, light breezes barely creased the camel hides that were draped over the tent frames.

The Arab traveller Ibn Battutah visited Timbuktu in 1353 and wrote of the Tuareg as "the most perfectly beautiful of women."

The sound of deep spitting startled me. The Tuareg too were up. They expelled phlegm from their throats as though it was esophagus-driven. I thought, I must remember to wear sandals when I step outside the tent.

The prospect of the morning exhilarated me. I sat up in my tent and looked through the flap. The sun was low in the sky, glowing orange, the desert sky making it more so. Only I and the Tuareg were awake. Absentmindedly, I moved the night's deposit of sand particles around in my mouth, inadvertently grinding them with my teeth.

A few metres from my tent an old Tuareg tended an embryonic campfire. His presence softened the desert's fierce beauty. He pulled unburned branch ends from the fire's edge and placed them in the flames. The wood would soon become cooking embers. Nothing sat above the fire, though a teapot rested ready next to it. Its warmth and smell comforted me. I felt that only once in my life would I see this: a Tuareg performing the rituals of fire-making in the light of the rising sun.

That people take photographs of such a moment rather than cherishing the gift has long seemed rash to me, though I prepared to do the same. I forsook the moment to preserve it. Stepping out of my tent, I intentionally alerted the old man by the fire. I squatted and indicated that I wanted to photograph him and the sky. He whispered in reply, but I didn't understand. I pointed again, and he whispered once more. Then he adjusted his shawl and seemed to accept my invitation. One photo. Pleased and impressed, I took my camera, framed the instant and pressed.

Nothing. I adjusted and clicked again. Nothing. I inspected the camera and concluded the battery was dead. No matter. Tuaregs have centuries of patience, and my other camera was in the same bag. Grabbing it, I repeated my actions. Nothing happened. At this point the old man surely thought I'd taken half a dozen pictures, more than my request for "just one." When I popped the camera back, a canister of rewound film sat passively in the hold. I held it open to show him, by way of naive explanation on my part. He looked at the camera, at me, and then, with utter indifference, added more wood to the fire and invited me to join him.

Here, sitting with my back to the camel-skin tents and beside a crackling fire, I had my first Tuareg tea. Centuries of tradition required that the elderly man pour tea in a high arc. His right hand stretched a thin stream of tea half a metre toward a tiny cup on a tray. He offered me the filled teacup. I accepted and lifted the hot cup from the serving tray. The cup had pressed many lips before mine. I sipped, sitting cross-legged in the cool morning. He firmly poured a second cup. There are three pours to a serving of Tuareg tea, each separate, and with a purpose. The first drink was "strong against the desert's harshness," the second was said to be "cut with warmth and sweetness." The third was "pleasant" and completing. I sipped each cup, sensing the tradition, and accepting it as a privilege. I felt I should bow. Especially when I was not offered a fourth cup. (It is said that if you are given a fourth pour, you are not really welcome.)

I walked away from the camp, past camel saddles piled under a tree, and, beside them, Tuareg blankets taken from their tents and folded after use. My sandals sifted sand, making calluses on the balls of my feet. Sacks of grain were arranged under a tree to provide a windbreak for two men tending a fire of saplings. One of them sewed repairs on a tarp. They nodded to me. The women were

Everyone has special attire for the festivities at the oasis.

elsewhere that morning, tending kids, doing chores; gossiping, one hopes.

Essakane did not offer the romantic image commonly found in books, where weary travellers come upon an oasis sheltered by greenery beside a broad pond, and camels are secured nearby. It was dust-haunted, distinguished by square buildings with missing boards and flapping metal siding in need of a nail. Water, pumped from beneath a shed, was shared among the villagers. The Sahara is a timeless tableau; with winds, it sculpts itself by breezing litter into corners, drying green to brown and covering where and what it will.

The brief beauty of the morning had passed.

Solomon, young, British, and believing that school should never interfere with one's education, was part of Mohammed's crew. I suspected foreign-aid funding had been found to keep the lad busy. He could walk in ankle-twisting sand and still pull off a swagger. I had breakfast in the common area with a Dutch couple, amid the piles of past meals' refuse and the next meal's preparation, and listened to Solomon's pronouncement.

"I've bought a goat head," he boasted. "Two thousand seffe. Good eating." And in the way of repeating a lesson he'd been told as though he already possessed the knowledge, Solomon said, "Paid too much. Didn't get the legs."

"I'm inexperienced, but somehow the legs seem where to start," I offered.

"At the least, shouldn't they come along with the head?" the Dutch man suggested.

"The head's the trophy," said Solomon.

Surprisingly, Mohammed arrived at camp, having scrounged the last empty seat on a Bamako to Timbuktu flight and then having driven to Essakane under cover of night. He strode about as a cattle rancher on the range might. To me, he suggested going for a camel ride, and my hesitation about that day or the next seemed silly to him. "You've got nothing to do here; you'll be bored." He was at his best when the going was good.

"I've made arrangements," I replied.

Mohammed scowled. "Troublecane," Only Mamadou laughed. "Not *Essa*kane. *Trouble*cane." He worried about his burden — that of organizing people. Even he had been asked to repay the entrance fee when he arrived. The earlier payment had apparently gone astray.

His quick temper showed. "Security is lax. People do not pay, and they come anyway," he complained. I did not see how the festival organizers could gate the desert. Mohammed's slender body tried to shrug, but his shoulders didn't quite do it.

"Artists do not show. Performers are promised but are not here."

His eyes said he had a plan for me, and some profit for him. I pre-empted the attack: "Last night I met a fellow and promised to ride his camel," I said. "Tabel."

"Yes, he is my friend. Tabel has a camel. You must go."

"Tabel is *my* friend," I countered.

He ignored my pretension. "Others are going," he told me. He stood lean, hunched with the pressures of his life. His pant cuffs were frayed, and through his sandals I could see that his toenails needed clipping.

I retorted, "I will go later. I will go alone." I did not want him to organize my life.

"Yes. No. Those Americans are going for only one hour. You go a different route. Until late afternoon."

"Café first." I stalled, trying in my mind to reconcile my commitment with Tabel. I walked toward the dwindling fire and found Nescafé, powdered milk, and boiling water. Plunks of donut-like cakes were frying in fat over the fire: tasty, doughy. I was suspicious of the contents, the history of the fat, and the potentially mouth-scorching temperature, yet I was hungry. Eat. Ouch. Drink. Ouch. A lump of semi-dissolved powder caught my teeth in the last scalding swig of coffee.

I retrieved a full bottle of water, two power bars, a knife, and sunscreen from my tent. I grabbed my brimmed hat from next to the cookstove, while Nema tended the fire. A young Tuareg tugged my sleeve. "Camel."

Walking over a dune, I asked in French, "How old are you?"

"Eleven," he replied, proud of his role, that of which I was not too certain. My guide? We walked a few hundred metres to where the camels sat on their curious three-part legs, knees bent beneath them, their ankles oddly not extended.

As I prepared to mount, Tabel came around a corner with the charming Portuguese woman, Monica, walking beside him. He said, "She is going with you." My solo trips always seemed to include a surprise companion.

Monica was thrilled to be a part of the adventure. We each bought a blue *cheches*, the Tuareg turban. Tabel wrapped mine around my head and neck. Monica spent ten minutes learning to do it herself and tugged hers into place. She stuck my sunglasses through the cloth of my turban, pressed them snugly, and, after rubbing suntan lotion on her nose, smeared it on mine. We mounted our camels. With a shout, the guide trotted away and our two camels trailed into the world's largest expanse of sand. *Sahara* means ocean, and, where it flounders, *Sahel* means shore.

Tabel had informed us that, "Allah removed all unneeded life — animals, and people too — from the desert, to make a place for him to walk in peace ... and so the Sahara is called the Garden of Allah. If you get lost, remain calm. The desert is calm." I would try to remember this.

We traversed *ergs*, plains that shift with weather, to the great openness. Monica was as silent as the desert. My camel made not a sound. The sky was empty. The wind, *alizé*, was gentler than the worrisome *harmattan*.

The ubiquitous sun, purveyor of heatstroke, skin cancer, and exhaustion, also made for a continuously dry mouth. Turbans sheltered our throats and noses from tiny, swirling particles of dust. My feet cramped one over the other against the camel's neck. I straddled the dromedary's hump, the stiff leather seat grinding against my crotch.

There is only the broadest of schedules in the desert and they relate to seasons, generations, possibly centuries. After a morning of searing heat, we stopped near trees but did not use their shelter. We spread a blanket under the open sun. From a saddle pouch, the guide offered us food and we sampled. Our own packs had granola bars, which were a treat for him.

A weathered man approached, as if coming from nowhere. He believed it our good fortune that he found us, as he had wonderful pieces of silver, all of his own tooling. Sitting on what seemed at that moment to be the sanded centre of the universe, I bought Janice a Tuareg wedding band. In appreciation, the man gave me a fist-sized rock as a gift. Using sign language, he indicated it was for milling pepper and softening meat. Nothing was rushed. He smoked his pipe and offered it to me. I puffed, unsure from the taste if I smoked tobacco or sand. My elbow leaned in the earth and with my free hand I reached into my pack and gave him a clump of good tobacco. It was then I realized I was sitting among red ants (Africa! Red Ants!) and bolted upright.

I tossed the old man his pipe to hold while I brushed off the ants.

"Pests. Pests," I said, not knowing the term in French nor Berber.

When I turned around, the merchant was walking toward the desert's horizon. In the botched farewell, who forgot to thank whom?

The scorching heat sapped our energy as we remounted and rode through the miles of uncharted desert between us and the oasis. The camels picked their way around small rocks strewn on the broad path, the distribution work of flood waters. In the belligerent heat, with our throats parched, we travelled along the forlorn, would-be-waterway. It led to the traveller's salvation: Essakane.

The guide did not touch his *guerbas* all day. "Water," he stated, his one necessary word of English. He took *my* water, avoiding his goatskin container. With my bottle in hand, he washed his mouth, swirled, spat it out, and sucked more from the bottle mouth. Then he handed the bottle back to me.

Here, the great desert sculpts new stories each day, changing landscape and lives with its winds and dangers. Being parched was a reminder of perils others encountered in their travels through that unforgiving land. With the sun penetrating my shirt, I thought of the unwilling traveller Robert Adams. The American pressed across these lands on foot, and when he weakened, his captors draped him across a camel.

A New Yorker, born in America and of Afro-American decent, twenty-five-year-old Adams (originally named Benjamin Rose) was the first non-African, non-Arab to see Timbuktu. It was 1811. His misfortune was to be on *The Charles*, a ship wrecked off the coast of Mauritania.

Thrashing ashore after their shipwreck, the terrified Americans, unconfident even with solid earth beneath their feet, found themselves in a strange, hostile land without their weapons, which had been abandoned on the ship. All who sailed the Atlantic off West Africa had heard of the terrible Moors and would have preferred to cast their fate with roiling seas.

Their first morning on the harsh shores dawned with the threat of heat. From the horizon came a greater scare: Forty armed Moors, whose fishing camp was nearby. They surrounded the frightened men and stripped them naked. From Mauritania, the American sailors were sold into slavery, in a reversal of that time's terrible trend.

The unforgiving sun blistered the sailors' skin and dehydrated their bodies and souls. The sand gouged the blisters, and the sun baked the sailors' scabs as they walked without any protection

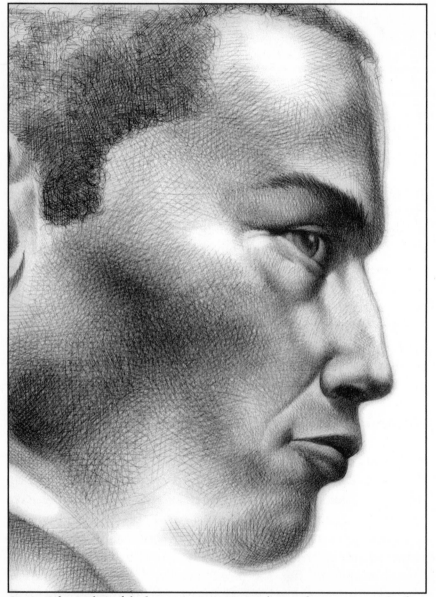

In 1811 Robert Adams (also known as Benjamin Rose), an Afro-American sailor from New York, was shipwrecked, captured, and taken as a slave to Timbuktu, about which he later mused covered "as much ground as Lisbon," a perspective that brought his other observations into disrepute.

from the elements. Eventually they were force-marched in the direction of slave-trading marketplaces and desert transfer points, where most of them were sold to northbound nomads. Adams and a Portuguese mate, however, were traded separately from the rest and taken eastward.

It is said that such journeys require the ability to judge where you are by the colour of the sand, to know direction by the sand's different tastes. The *alizé* wind brought a comparative cool to the desert during the dry season when Adams and his captors moved forever east through the haze. For nourishment they caught the urine of camels in their cupped hands, and drank it.

Four months after *The Charles* gave way to the sea, a bitter and resigned but living Adams arrived in Timbuktu without any preconceptions of what the French call *La Mystérieuse*. He stayed there from February until June, that month marking one year since his departure from the United States.

Adams knew nothing of the reputed power of the city or of its rumoured wealth. Not one thing there impressed him. He did not see the mosques for which Timbuktu was famed. In his wanderings, he estimated the size of the city to be similar to that of Lisbon, which then would have been two hundred and fifty thousand people. He qualified this: "As the houses are not built in streets, or with any regularity, its population, compared with that of European towns, is by no means in proportion to its size." The arrival of small caravans ensured that Adams saw all types of trade goods, from tobacco to ostrich feathers, muskets, swords and skins, grains, and ivory. Slaves were profitably sold in Timbuktu, and that would continue to be Adams's fate. Traded to a northbound caravan, resold to yet other slave traders, he was eventually rescued by the British consul in Algiers. He recuperated in North Africa and worked a passage first to Greece and then to England.

Living without work on the London streets while trying to return to the United States, Adams was recognized by a dockworker he'd once known and who had heard stories of his being in Timbuktu. Word of mouth connected the destitute Adams with merchants interested in African trade; the rumour of his journey through Timbuktu was both tempting and hard to believe.

In 1814 the Committee of the Company of Merchants Trading to Africa, also known as the African Committee, interviewed Adams extensively and then published his story as *The Narrative of Robert Adams*. This itinerant slave's account of Timbuktu was such a contrast to the expectations of both European authorities and the public that they dismissed his narrative. He was called a fake, his travel accounts were questioned. How could this illiterate and inarticulate man have reached Timbuktu? In support, the committee provided a qualifying statement in the *Narrative*: "Notwithstanding, therefore, the alleged splendour of its court, polish of its inhabitants, and other symptoms of refinement which some modern accounts (or speculations), founded on native reports, have taught us to look for, we are disposed to receive the humbler descriptions of Adams as approaching with much greater probability the truth. And here, we may remark, the relative rank of Timbuctoo amongst the cities of central Africa, and its present importance with reference to European objects, appears to us to be considerably overrated."

Desert day's end.

Monica walked out of a clump of scrub brush and across a flattened dune toward the camp.

"Rick, the shower. You must." She grinned. "Wonderful."

"Shower?" There'd been talk of a public facility strewn with unpleasantries and hooked to a gravity-fed, low-pressure hose from a tank.

"Tell them I sent you. Two men and a trailer."

Towel in hand, I went, oblivious to the obvious: I'd just had a woman tell me to go take a shower after we'd spent a day together. I found the truck tucked beneath a tree. There, three men just sat in wait. Nothing else happened. There was no one I recognized. I babbled on about a shower in my poor French and much depleted English and showed my coins.

"A place. Water hose," a sulky one said in French. "Over." They all pointed to the rumoured messy place.

It was not a ruse; Monica had emerged too clean for this to be a trick. I sulked and turned to leave.

"Wrick!" It was Mamadou, calling from around a corner. He appeared and spoke to them, and the quietest man eventually said, with his hands, that I should go behind the camel skin. There, I found a shower head, a tap, a glint of privacy.

Drenched, albeit not in a cascade, I scrubbed and felt revitalized. And indebted. "Many thanks," I said, and offered them money. They would not take it. This was strange to me, given the value I'd just received. Mamadou smiled at their kindness, knowing his intervention had been a favour to me.

Walking back to our camp, I noticed Solomon and Nema hunched over the fire. They peered into a pot of thick, reddish stew. In it floated a skull, bare of flesh.

"Let me guess," I ventured.

"The goat head," Solomon boasted and he held high his saucy, bloodied fingers. "Quite the delight. Sorry you missed it."

"Me, too."

"Not much left, but you're welcome." He tipped the pot my way. I saw he'd been gazing at the entrails.

I shook my head. "How was it?"

"The eyes tasted different than the brains," he said.

"Did they pop like a grape?" I asked.

"Eyes soft. Brains stringy," said Nema, smiling, with red goop around her lips.

It's been said that the Japanese dine with their eyes, such is their reverence for food presentation and culinary display. Here they would blink.

Abruptly there appeared the red gold of a desert sunset. A final flare, and then it was dark. In the sudden change of colour, it seemed as much that the sand had set as the sun. A dozen of us sat on the slope of the dune that tilted toward the cook's area. Various languages from around the world spoke both of the difficulties of travelling here and of the uncertainties of getting home. We dined on couscous and grilled goat meat.

"If they wish Europeans to travel with them, they must stop throwing garbage where we eat," Monica asserted as the dinner was ending. The cooks had vanished, leaving garbage — wrappers and empty cans, used boxes and plastic bags, dribbles of food scraps strewn among discarded bones — a scene that was becoming an increasingly prevalent feature of camp life.

"It's not acceptable," Helena echoed. "I told Mohammed. It's terrible how they spoil the setting."

Monica said, "Maybe we can persuade Mohammed to commit his company to producing less garbage and training his staff. That'd give him a positive image."

Mohammed and commitment: it was a combination I'd not thought of.

Monica stood up and found a cardboard box. "First, we clean this place and put the box of garbage in Mohammed's Land Cruiser." She stuffed clumps of plastic into the box. One of the Americans picked up tin cans. Helena pulled broken glass from under a tree and started piling up empty water bottles. "I will not have them leave a mess in my name."

"*Non. Non!*" Mamadou saw us cleaning and didn't like it.

"Mamadou, it's okay," I told him. But it was not. To him it was as though guests had arrived at an American home and, seeing dirty dishes in the kitchen, had begun to wash up. It was offensive.

My broad-brimmed hat covered my face as I dozed that evening. I was lying on the open dune near the fire, and the festival's music played in the distance.

"Are you leaving Sunday or Monday?" asked a French girl, lifting my hat.

"Monday," I said with more confidence than I felt.

"Our trouble," she claimed, "is that these Americans leave tomorrow, and Mohammed arranged our ride in the same four-by-four. Now we'll end up with three days in Bamako, which we don't want."

"Everything gets rearranged," the plump American complained.

Then, angrily, the French girl murmured: "It's never what you expect."

"Speaking of change, see the box over there?" I wanted to change the subject. "Others have a plan to make Mohammed more environmentally responsible."

The short American scowled. "They've got other things to work on first."

"Such as?" the French girl inquired.

"Trust. Being honest about what you pay for."

The Americans stood together. The French girl shifted her pack, took out a flat hat and leaned against the bulky case. Putting the hat on, she frowned. "I told Mohammed how much I make, my rent, but it's not helping. I pay and don't get what I was promised. How can they do that?" She kicked the sand.

The desert calm made my sleep that night feel long. I awoke refreshed before everyone but the Tuareg. I walked out of the camp and toward the capes of sand.

A cooking fire was being readied by a Tuareg who had risen before me. It was cool and I bent over the flames, motioning with my hands. "May I?" The man replied in Tamacheq, and it sounded welcoming. I warmed my hands and added some small twigs to his fire. Another Tuareg walked over and chose a few glowing coals, which he took away to start his own fire. Then the first man placed camel dung over his fire, and both the smell and the warmth made me want to stay. A Land Cruiser rut that curved near the fire pit formed a comfortable perch, away from the sellers of jewellery and camel-leather-sheathed knives, so I took it as mine for the morning.

I craved the solitude.

Within an hour, a German fellow wearing a pink hat and a gold earring walked by. He had a beard that aged him and he looked down at me through wire-rimmed glasses with a broken frame. "I'm tired. Only six hours' sleep in last two days."

"Why?" I asked.

"Festival. Music. We dance. We make joke. Then it is five. Sleep only till nine."

"*Fatigue,*" I said in festival parlance.

"I did it when I was young. Then, family. Now, I do it again."

"It is good," I replied.

"I will do it until I die. You can't get enough." The philosopher walked on. He was immediately challenged by a galloping camel, which almost collided with him and passed only a metre from me.

When the dust had settled, Nema came by with a small cup and knelt at the skirt of the wheel rut. "Tea," she stated in her own way, one that never asked. The drink was sweet, almost thick. She squatted before me and shifted her dress discreetly to cover her knees, sitting picture perfect as she poured.

Soon Tabel appeared.

"I leave for the desert tonight," he said.

Slowly he took bracelets out of his sash, then two attractively crafted necklaces, one made of beads with a silver pendant. The other was a totem he described as symbolizing "north, south, my village, and animals passing."

He let me dig in his satchel to choose a chain with desert agates cut oblong. Pieces of ebony were painted with curly designs. There were silver balls on the chain as well. He told me, "The Tuareg have three prices. The Tuareg price. The price you want to pay. And the price we agree."

He wrapped his wares and, still squatting, asked: "Do you have any clothing for my family?"

With three weeks of travel remaining, I was unable to oblige. "No. I am sorry."

Solomon crept into view, sneaking away from the camp. "Goathead," I called, saying the nickname for my amusement, not his. "How's that head in your tummy?"

"Not well, not well," he said and kept creeping toward a bush in a sphincter-tightening walk.

I rose from the ridge of the rut and a hundred flies left me.

Mamadou held a pot from the fire toward me as I walked into camp. "Café, *Wrick?*" The morning's empty cans were stacked behind him. Not a wrapper in sight. I spooned powdered milk from a smudged container, scooped coffee and sand from an opened jar, and found the least dirty sugar cube in the box.

The festival would be over that night. Goathead soon appeared before us, seemingly cleansed and with colour returning to his face.

"All the vehicles leave when the last act is over," he said, clearing his throat as part of the sentence. He paused for air, swallowed hard and continued. "Probably two-thirty."

"Leave?" exclaimed Helena. "I travelled eight thousand miles for three nights at this festival. I'm not leaving."

There was a hush. "You must see the market at Djenné," said Mohammed, who had a tendency to appear on every possible miscue. "You must leave."

"Scoundrel," one of them said.

"I've never heard of Djenné till now. I'm staying here," Helena protested. Mohammed backed off, but it was a feint.

The murmuring subsided. Of course we must leave. He who owns the trucks sets the time.

Walking near the festival's production setup for the finale, I heard a call. "Canada." The BBC cameraman was arranging his tripod on a precarious perch. He looked tired, happy it was the last evening, and ready for home. Our meeting in Douentza four nights before seemed to have occurred long ago, perhaps even during another trip.

"How was your midnight drive to Timbuktu?" I asked, recalling that they had been gone when I woke in Douentza.

"Difficult," he admitted, putting down his camera and sitting on the deck. His legs dangled. "We had to abandon two of the four-by-fours."

"What sort of troubles?"

"Mechanical," he answered. "The radiator gave. The other had a crankshaft break. We piled into the two remaining four-by-fours and got here at about the same time as if we'd stayed and slept the night in that hovel."

"Lucky it worked out." I coughed.

"Stories to tell the grandkids," he said.

With a wave, I left him to finish the setup and started to climb the long dune. My legs were gaining strength from all the "up the dune, down the dune" walking I'd been doing in the past two days. My voice was taking on a rasp from the late-night cold. The dusk turned to dark. The stanchions, which had provided heat during the first night, were now burned out, and fewer people sat on the large dune that swept the length of the desert-made amphitheatre. Most fans crowded for warmth and a better vantage point near the stage.

The Malian singer Ali Farka Toure defines Mali in the world of music. In anticipation of coming here, his voice often accompanied my drives to and from work the previous fall as I tried to acclimatize myself to Malian culture. His appearance that evening had been staged early so that the documentary crew could get its film footage and make an early exit before the rest of us.

Midway during Ali's performance, the power failed. The stage lighting disappeared and the musical instruments faded away. The desert night went bone cold. You could not see for looking. Groans could be heard throughout the crowd. But the blackout was not to be one of the quickly fixed power outages that are common in the desert; the electrician had pulled the plug. The technicians had not been paid. It was a flawless strategy; the power of power. Malian folk hero on stage. No pay, no lights, no music. The organizers rallied and paid cash. Ali rocked.

At two-thirty, sleepy, cold, and tired, a dozen of us were at the appointed place, the location where we'd been told to gather if we wanted a ride to Timbuktu. Two four-by-fours and our packs were where we'd left them before the evening's performance. The drivers were asleep and our gear lay open, there for whomever the night might have brought. We roused the drivers.

The implacable Mohammed had left Essakane earlier in the evening. Two people unknown to me tried to sort out who was to go where in the overbooked vehicles. They yelled at the drivers. Everyone fumbled in the dark. Talk was fast and urgent, but it didn't seem to speed the organization of the trip.

Seated beside the driver sulked an ill Goathead, who, as paid help had sat himself in the finest seat in a vehicle, while I paid full price simply to ensure transportation. It was to be for me, my guide, and my driver: that was it, Mohammed had said. Meanwhile, in the back seat I was wedged against the right-hand door, with Nema pressed next to me, the Swiss lady angled tight by her, and Zak's slenderness crammed into the other door. In the cargo area, stuffed among the extra bags that wouldn't fit on the roof rack, were the French girl and her two male friends. Perhaps I should have felt grateful to have avoided their predicament, but I didn't. I felt cheated.

Other four-by-fours attempted to leave, but few actually departed in the disorganized dark; paying passengers were slow to show up.

We lurched into the night to find dawn. We crossed routes without ruts or tracks, in a land once called *Beled-es-Sudan*, "Land of the Blacks." Our road was without light except for that provided by our own vehicle's headlights. The other four-by-four disappeared on a different route, so we sidled on alone in a southerly direction, perhaps not without aim but certainly without confidence. We reconnected with the other vehicle in a near accident while coming over the rise of a dune. We stopped and everyone jumped out of the Land Cruisers while the drivers shouted at one another and finally determined to continue on together.

We travelled at high speed, hurtling through deep dips and up steep dunes. One vehicle or the other frequently stalled, and often all the passengers got out and pushed beneath a sky of patchy cloud and patchier stars. After one long pause in which we were stuck in the sand, the second four-by-four departed on its own, leaving us stranded. It occurred to me that a compass would have been a good idea.

Our driver, worried that driving too slow might sink our four-by-four, raced whenever a semi-hard surface appeared, skirted less sure ground, and skidded on bends. We careened around corners when he reconsidered the direction in mid-turn. Not surprisingly, sleep did not come easily to the passengers, but our slunk heads indicated our attempt. Suddenly, a swift yank left and slammed brakes brought my side of the vehicle unimaginably close to the ground. Only the balancing weight of other passengers prevented a teetering crash.

Finally, and against all reason, we arrived in Timbuktu. As we stepped out of the vehicle in the dawn, one passenger started to cry with relief. Another comforted her and cursed the forced night drive in frightening circumstances. "It is dangerous enough in the daytime," he said. "Why the hell a rushed drive in the middle of the night? Now we need to pay for a morning's hotel room."

I was too exhausted to join their conversation.

Zak sighed, "I not think we'd live. Honest. Seem we have terrible accident. Many times almost hit road."

SIX

The Forbidden City

IT SURPRISED ME HOW REACHABLE TIMBUKTU was. I'd been willing to put up with sporadic travel and delays, to accept cramped and stuffy spaces, to be hot to the point of suffocation, to adjust to communication gaffes, to accept "price surprises," and even to eat sand. None of this was easy for anyone. Nevertheless, "the Forbidden City" was, after all, accessible.

I early awoke on top of the bed, still wearing my clothes. This was exactly where I'd crashed two hours earlier. No one else would be awake yet. I owned the day. I stepped out of my room and into the hallway. Zak was already up.

"Mohammed wants to meet you," he said.

"Why?"

"I don't know. He sent me."

"Here?"

"No, at the Bouctou Hotel."

"When?"

"Now," sighed Zak.

"Is there a car?"

"Yes."

"A driver?"

"Yes."

"Gas?"

"*Rick.* Let's go."

I had taken a day — one day only — in the middle of my life and set it aside for Timbuktu. This was that day and its evening and the night.

The Bouctou Hotel, low and unassuming as a sand dune, seemed to attract litter into piles wherever people sat or squatted. An irascible Mohammed, determined to remain aloof from the scattered groups around him, leaned alone against a tree, where my Land Cruiser stopped just short of his scowl.

"Rick!" he shouted at my open window, commanding the scene and muting the hubbub of conversation. I shoved the vehicle's door open and swung my feet to the ground. I was a titch taller than him; his eyes were darker. He held the advantage. "The boat must leave today at three," he smiled.

"Nope." I said this quickly, and noticed that the bystanders gasped that someone would dare disagree with this forceful Arab. The air quickened.

"It would be good," he continued with self-serving self-assurance. "You have lots of time in Timbuktu. Then the *pinasse* can leave."

In the ensuing silence, he knew that I knew that this change was necessary to make a related itinerary work for him. The River Niger could wait. I said nothing. People looked away. Zak scraped the sand with the heel of his sandal. Then, all eyes turned toward Mohammed.

Finally.

"Rick?" It was sharp, the way he flung it.

"It's not going to happen, Mohammed." I breathed for the crowd. "The boat leaves tomorrow."

Tagged with labels such as "The Town of 333 Saints," Timbuktu no longer receives accolades. Those who call it home do not share the foreigner's fascination. The city's mystique is powerful only until you arrive. I'd like to pretend it's different, but it isn't.

Nothing prepares the naive visitor for the absence of intrigue quite like the question Malians consistently ask when they find out that one is travelling to Timbuktu: "Why?"

UNESCO's list of World Heritage Sites grew in 1988 with the designation of Timbuktu and the specific inclusion of its three

Once rumoured to have "streets paved in gold," the reality of Timbuktu has always been mud homes that fight the relentless assault of the Sahara Desert's sand.

mosques, of which the Djinguereber Mosque, built in 1325, is the most prominent. Its reputation rests on its history and its current state of disrepair, as well as for its periodic acceptance of visitors. The Sankoré Mosque, part of a school, attended by 25,000 university students at its peak in the sixteenth century, is also notable. Its colonnades and courtyard were rebuilt in 1582, though it was first constructed a century earlier, and the mosque is cited as "unique earthen architecture." The Sidi Yahia Mosque, which takes its name from one of Timbuktu's saints, is in the best condition of the three, but non-Muslims are denied entry. All three mosques, however, are crumbling away. In Timbuktu, the restoration of monuments is a continuous process, and the drift of earth among them relentless. Timbuktu, once the "Pearl of Africa," also has the dubious distinction of being on the United Nations' List of World Heritage Sites in Danger.

Surviving there to this day are homes of the three earliest European explorers to reach the fabled city and live among its inhabitants. Each feared for his personal safety and was eager to return to Europe and relate his achievements. In the nearly two hundred years since then, the mud houses of Laing, Caillié, and Barth have been, as they were before the arrival of their historic guests, shelter for residents of Timbuktu. And they remain intact, despite the desert's continued attempts to erode them.

Scuffed by history, Mali benignly accepts its diminished status. The Malian Empire is no more, and the country vies with Bangladesh as the world's poorest nation. Desertification is Timbuktu's greatest threat; Mali's nemesis, the Sahara — with 7 million square kilometres of sand — assaults every man-made structure. The Sahara gave birth to Timbuktu. Now its sands are trying to bury it with a persistence more treacherous than the heat's.

Endangered, too, are the rarest of writings — pieces of history-on-paper that form one of the world's great treasures — the Timbuktu manuscripts. Many crumble at the touch of a well-meaning hand; others wither simply because of their exposure to air. Without them, we will know immeasurably less about a glorious time for Africa, some six hundred years ago. The manuscripts provide a portrait of life, of religion and science, of law and architecture, and of a society that thrived like none other at that time. Before leaving on my journey, while researching Timbuktu's fourteenth-century history and its extensive libraries, I was disheartened to read about thousands of ancient manuscript pages that today lay tattered and unattended in mud homes and deserted buildings. Images of ancient books and furled pages falling apart for lack of care provided a powerful incentive for visiting Timbuktu. My newly gained awareness of their existence, and their peril, infused my journey with a worthy purpose: to find the manuscripts and find a way to help with their preservation.

Once known as "The Eyes of the Desert," old Timbuktu was quite the sight. In 1933, William Seabrook wrote, "It is, I believe, the only city in the whole wide world which has none of the banal blessings, or curses, of what we choose to call 'white civilization.'" Old Timbuktu, the inner part of the city, was innocuous and compact, its walkways the now-trampled swells of desert. Few markings or signs designated its streets or paths.

Travellers and travel books said it would be wise for a visitor to hire a local guide, if only to rid oneself of pestering youngsters. I asked Zak to come with me that morning. We walked away from the Bouctou Hotel's drabness to a wider dirt road and along its rim into the old city, a district neglected by charm.

The Djinguereber Mosque was an exceptional find, though it does not loom physically as it does historically. To imagine that it had once been a centre of learning, filled with fervent adherents and peopled night and day with scholars as well as those in prayer, paints a picture of a vast house of worship. But we found it was not much over twice the height of the other buildings in the neighbourhood of the Place de l'Indépendence, off the Boulevard Askia Mohammed, and that it had a modest entrance. Centuries earlier, Leo Africanus wrote, "There is a most stately temple to be seen." In those days it must have been more impactful on its surroundings.

Caillié had noted another reality in his journal: "I visited the great mosque on the west side of town. The walls are in bad repair, their facing being damaged by rain. Several buttresses are raised against the walls to support them. I ascended the tower, though its staircase is almost demolished." Since 1325, when the poet and architect Es Saheli created this unique design, Timbuktu's most important mosque has needed constant reworking and repair. Wooden support beams poke through its slanting walls, acting as stabilizers for the wall and for mudding crews. Though Mansa Musa directed its construction upon his return from Mecca, it was Saheli, brought from Egypt, who created the striking pyramid base that now defines Timbuktu, Djenné, and Mali generally in photographs. Musa also encouraged broader belief in the tenets of Islam, and building libraries and universities known as *madrasas*, most of them no longer in existence.

Non-Muslims are generally not invited into mosques, so when the opportunity arose to enter this one, we took it. The caretaker waited inside the house of prayer, his mood as solemn as the dusty light.

Quiet. The caretaker gestured to me to shed my leather thongs. Streams of sunlight were the only other intruders as he showed Zak and me along the passage where prayers were uttered.

Timbuktu's Great Mosque, Djinguereber, is recognized as a World Heritage Site by the United Nations.

He indicated privacy hollows, fortified by wood and carved mud, where worshippers made penance.

We entered three inner courts. Rows of pillars, twenty-five in all, stood in an east-to-west alignment. Zak whispered the translation as we walked. "Islam too has pillars. Five. Primary belief, 'Is no god but Allah,' and Mohammed *his* prophet."

"Second, Muslims face Mecca and pray. Must at daybreak, noon, mid-afternoon, sunset. Again nightfall."

"And they give alms," I added, happy to contribute.

Walking within the mosque, with no one else about, the austere expanse made it seem less a place of worship and more a magic hall where, when I stopped and let Zak drift on, I could imagine a throng of prayer-makers, hear the shout of calm from the Imam and, in my own way, feel compelled to kneel and give thanks.

"Another, Ramadan," Zak said, no longer repeating the caretaker's words, and only then noticing me pondering prayer behind him. But I'd heard, and nodded, so he continued. "Commemorates first revelation to Mohammed. Muslims fast. One month. Dawn to dusk."

"And Mecca," I added, to complete the fifth pillar of their faith.

"Yes," Zak said. "Every Muslim. Pilgrimage. If they afford. If healthy."

Religion has long been a travel motivator: the seeing of sites, the paying of tributes, homage given to deities or a pilgrimage. Faith led to travel as surely as a current carries water. If you are fortunate, you travel with two religions: your own and that of your host, from whom you learn. Many people travel to learn the rituals of other religions rather than to comprehend the beliefs underlying these rituals.

"Zak," I asked, "do you believe in God?"

"Yes," he said. He did not elaborate.

The caretaker left us alone, and we ascended the mosque's stairs to the roof. The architect Es Saheli had invented the mud brick, a revolutionary technique in a land where previously mud and weeds were slapped on wood frames. The stability of this brick, augmented by upgrades over the centuries, accounted for the sturdiness of the stairs. Caillié too had climbed those stairs, two centuries ago.

Throughout old Timbuktu, narrow, shallow ditches line the centre of every street. We strolled with one eye to the ground and noticed the locals stepping carefully to avoid dipping a foot into those sewers. It meant we were not able to fully appreciate the buildings that bordered the walkways.

Leo Africanus's memories of Timbuktu inspired centuries of envy. "Here are many shops of artificers and merchants, and especially of such as weave linen and cotton cloth." We did not find that splendour; rather, we witnessed the eking out of a life.

I asked Zak, "What does everyone do here?"

"They sell." It was true. Everyone sold. I wanted the guy who sold haircuts.

But the shops were not defined. Nothing said, "Come in ..." Nothing on the streets recognized the visitor or the need for rest, or refreshment. Residents set a pot of still-cooking food on the bunting of their homes, or used a table to promote their wares: fried fish, individual cigarettes, old tools. Bread was stacked three loaves high and four deep on a rickety chair in front of the flat-sided mud house where it was baked. I bought one and handed half to Zak.

Children played tag, the world's most affordable game. Centuries have transformed the personality of Timbuktu and her people. Africanus noted, "The inhabitants are people of a gentle and cheerful disposition." He continued with something I'd not noticed, that they "spend a great part of the night in singing and dancing." Those were the days, my friend ...

The sun dictated that we hide. Zak and I dawdled over fried chicken, smoked tomatoes, and what tasted like sawdust at the Poulet d'Or. Sheltered from the midday heat, we snoozed a little in our straight-back chairs. My thoughts drifted to the morning's conversation with Mohammed, in which I'd challenged him. He was unkind, arrogant. "Police, your embassy, these people can do nothing to me." I did not agree, but it was his country. I asked him, "What if a traveller wrote about you? It might not be favourable."

He was contemptuous. "People can write whatever they want. It is nothing. I have no care for it." He acknowledged that the hotels and transport were not as he'd portrayed them and agreed to reimburse me: "I'll do that." I scribbled an address on a piece of paper and handed it to him. He said, "I will look at everything and wire money Western Union to Janice. You and me can then meet in Ségou on the twenty-sixth."

Mohammed might still shirk his responsibilities, but I did not want that possibility to colour my mood, to spoil my lunchtime rest, or to detract from further adventures in Timbuktu.

I sensed that my greatest discoveries were ahead of us that hot afternoon. Hidden down old roads were the places that Laing, Caillié, and Barth had temporarily called home; I had to find them. More poignantly, there was my immediate need to find even a portion of the Timbuktu manuscripts. I knew that within this old city, centuries of neglect had allowed a wealth of literary and scientific writings to age, deteriorate, and disappear. Would this day provide a way for me to help reverse that trend, to be a part of recovering and saving these documents?

Lunch was over, and so was my reverie. "Zak," I said, "let's go find the manuscripts."

We headed out to search for the *bibliothèque*. For thirty minutes we stepped carefully around garbage, urine, and feces on the streets of Timbuktu. The scene did not reconcile with Caillié's description: "The streets are clean, and sufficiently wide to permit three horsemen to pass abreast." After we had walked into the same empty square for the third time, I was becoming exasperated.

"Zak, do you know where the *bibliothèque* is?"

"Here," he said with a guide's overconfidence. He led us into yet another alley, and for ten minutes I followed. We circled nicely. Then the same deserted surroundings appeared.

"Zak, have you ever been to the *bibliothèque?*"

"No." He sulked, unwilling to admit defeat.

"Do you know if there is one?"

"No."

I had thought that patience was my strong suit, but it was running low. Near us was a dilapidated warehouse. Its loading platform gave us some shade. "Zak, sit down," I said. "Listen."

He cast his eyes at the ground.

"There are a few things that are going to happen here," I began. He listened as a child would under reprimand. "One, we're going to find Laing's house. Two, Caillié's home. Three, Barth's place. They say it's a museum." I trumped that many fingers in front of him. "Then we're going to find the *bibliothèque*." I flipped a fourth finger to catch up. "Zak, if we don't, you get to tell Mohammed that I'm staying tomorrow in Timbuktu."

In 1826 Alexander Gordon Laing, the British major, was the first European to reach Timbuktu and wrote that "it has completely met my expectations." He was attacked and killed by his protectors upon leaving thirty-five days later.

He nodded, the fear of Mohammed evident on his face, and then he smiled, up for the alternative task of helping me find these places.

"And," I added, my full hand flat, the count clear: "We'll find the centre where I can get my passport stamped."

"I don't know where that is," he confessed.

One of the demons of travel is hesitation. "Let's ask," I suggested.

"No, we'll find it." (I read that there's scientific proof that males of our species don't ask for directions. This was proved by the fact it takes a thousand sperm to find and fertilize one egg.)

I spotted a boy watching us nearby, and asked him. He looked halfway down the street, at a bend, and there it was: Gordon Laing's place. His guidance to Caillié's home was clear, and his directions to Barth's sounded unimpeachable. I should have hired a local guide.

Laing's house was before us. A crooked *Mission Culturelle* plaque was stuck to the middle of a mud wall, and, to my delight, a carved Moorish door was lodged open.

In this alcove of time there was silence. This building had been Laing's home for most of his stay in 1826. Now owned by a local, it did not seek passers-by. As I stood before it, there was no one in view to ask if I might enter, so I did under the pretense of obtaining that permission. The mud walls did not differentiate this building from other homes; neither did the height of its ceiling nor its crowded passageway set it apart. It did have a notable street presence accented from the second storey by two Moorish windows of carved wood.

"The Timbuctoo Mission," as Laing's expedition was officially known, reflected its leader's ambition. It offered the journey he sought and the fame he craved. Laing complained in his writings from the desert that he was continuously pressed for money by those he'd hired and already paid. He wrote that one intransigent chief "insisted I should go no further if I did not pay." Death was common in these parts, and robbery convenient. Threats, putrid food, hostilities, and ransom requests were impediments long registered by Africans, Arabs, and the few Europeans who'd ventured this far.

Laing arrived at Timbuktu in a terrible state, destitute after being attacked in the desert by Tuareg, shot in the side with a musket ball, slashed on his upper leg, crippled by a knife thrust that sliced his ear and cut his face. His companions fled, and the explorer was left for dead. The rest of the caravan's merchants were unharmed. They patched him up as well as they could, lashed him to his camel with rope, and let him trail the caravan. They believed he would soon die.

Laing survived the one-thousand-kilometre trek to Timbuktu. With what energy he could muster, and despite the squalid surroundings, he sent optimistic dispatches with native couriers accompanying the northbound caravans. Once he was settled in Timbuktu his wounds healed slowly, and meals of fish and bread helped his recovery.

Only one of Laing's letters from Timbuktu arrived in Tripoli at that time. He wrote of Timbuktu that the city had "completely met" his expectations. I chose to believe that Laing had penned that line within the walls where I stood. Those words contrasted with his later accounts portraying "bitter disappointment" with Timbuktu. He was under constant pressure from the Fulan sultan to leave, though he had freedom of movement about the town. He sketched a city plan of Timbuktu and spent his time "searching the records in the town, which are abundant."

This man, the first European to knowingly stay in Timbuktu, spent five weeks in the city before receiving permission to leave. A few days out of Timbuktu, heading for Europe, Laing was attacked by his African protectors. Using his own turban, they strangled the man who loved Africa and decapitated him. His remains were left uncovered in the desert. Birds, insects, and sand had their way with him. Laing's servant, who survived the attack, over the next two years made his way to Tripoli, where he reportedly delivered some of Laing's letters and told of his murder. The explorer's journals, which are thought to have been exceptional records of observation and history, were, however, missing. Often presumed to still exist, no trace of these artifacts has yet been uncovered.

Laing's former home in Timbuktu was on a street corner and was two storeys high. The house appeared vacant on the lower level; not abandoned, just not in use. Finding no one to give me permission to enter, I walked up a narrow stairway to the second floor. A shaft of sun picked its way through an ornamental window frame and cast an eerie pall on the room's three-metre-by-four-metre space. There was a complete absence of furniture or any evidence of occupation. Out of all of the potential ghosts of Timbuktu's European explorers, Laing's was the most likely to stay in the vicinity. I imagined the two of us sharing a moment in that dank space, separated by 178 years, and I envisioned him writing his last journal notes in this room: "I fear I shall be involved in much trouble after leaving Timbuktu."

Finding René Caillié's house was exhilarating. It stood (if this can be said of an often re-mudded structure, 174 years after his visit) to the west of the fifteenth-century Sidi Yahia Mosque. The building, still lived in, was not set for visitors. I was more in awe of the man than the structure, yet it was a Mecca-like destination for me.

Caillié has been called "one of the oddest figures in the history of travel." He departed for Timbuktu (calling it "the mysterious city which was the object of all my curiosity") full of ambition and a sense of adventure, and was unknown to the other prominent competitors seeking the glory of first arriving in the fabled city. He travelled without official sanction, having been refused support for his "preposterous" plan. He studied the Koran, learned to speak Arabic, and presented himself, convincingly, as an Egyptian born of Arab parents. In that guise, he ventured through hostile land, attired as an Arab.

No one responded to my asking, in French, "Is anyone home?" Zak, bemused, offered up Bambara's version of the phrase. The door was ajar and I sensed it bid me enter. For the moments I spent in Caillié's former home, I was a tourist in history, not a traveller in the present. With a deferential nod to the past, I walked into the open part of the house and replicated a two-century-old sliver of time, feeling like an imposter.

While I travelled far beyond the bounds of my own skimpy knowledge, Caillié travelled with an understanding of places and lands far beyond that of his contemporaries, even beyond that of the local guides who passed him on to more local locals when he journeyed across their territory. He battled scurvy and deprivation. His urge to be self-sufficient was at the heart of his explorations. On camel, with the assumed name of Abdallahi, the twenty-seven-year-old son of a French baker approached Timbuktu from the port of Kabara, now Korioumé, riding north under the watchful Tuareg. "My idea of the city's grandeur and wealth did not correspond with the mass of mud houses, surrounded by arid plains of jaundiced

Today one can still see the homes once used by explorers Alexander Gordon Laing, René-August Caillié, and Heinrich Barth. Each is marked with a plaque, such as this one on Caillié's. Only Barth's residence is open for travellers to visit.

white sands," he observed. "I looked around and found that the sight before me did not answer my expectations. I had formed a totally different idea of the grandeur and wealth of Timbuctoo."

When he arrived in 1828, Caillié heard details of Laing's desert misfortunes, his arrival in the city and his death, and he discovered that the explorer had lived in the house behind his only two years earlier. Caillié continued to avoid arousing suspicion of his Christianity. His host, Sheikh Al Bekây, provided sanctuary, freedom of movement, and food while Caillié rested in Timbuktu. Caillié's candour still resonates: "I cannot help contemplating with astonishment the extraordinary city before me, created solely by the wants of commerce, and destitute of every resource except what its accidental position as a place of exchange affords." He resolved to leave the city.

His desire to leave Timbuktu, however, exceeded the willingness of his hosts to let him go. It was Caillié's goal to travel to Morocco to make the outside world aware of his amazing accomplishments. His efforts to persuade his hosts to allow his departure became increasingly assertive, and he was eventually given leave. Four days' travel away from that Timbuktu house, en route to Tangiers, Caillié's caravan stopped near the camp where Laing was killed. There, the Moors showed him confirmation of that terrible deed.

René Caillié was the first European to return safely home from Timbuktu. He received the Société de Géographie de France award of ten thousand francs, offered in 1826 to the first European to reach Timbuktu and return safely. It was an award he'd heard of in Freetown, Sierra Leone, and of which he'd said: "Dead or alive, it shall be mine ..." In addition, France's King Charles X made him Chevalier of the Legion of Honour.

Caillié's residence in *La Mystérieuse* had been short, his observations picaresque, and the eventual telling of his rediscovery reliant on jotted memories and scrupulously kept notations, secretly scribbled after excusing himself from the company of others, requesting time for quiet meditation. Although his writings covered his entire travels, they were not able to persuade a skeptical world that Timbuktu was without the charm and stature

René-August Caillié, the French explorer, has been called "one of the oddest figures in the history of travel." He arrived in Timbuktu in 1828, disguised as an Arab, and became the first European to return safely home after that accomplishment.

created by legend. Controversy would swirl around Caillié's book, *Travels Through Central Africa to Timbuctoo*, which appeared in both France and England in 1830. But public acclaim continually fought with scholarly disdain. As Brian Gardner noted, "René Caillié's book did little to stop the Timbuctoo Rush."

The Tuareg Halis jests with the leather bucket at the alleged "well of Bouctou," from where originated the world's greatest travel name.

Circling the Sidi Yahia Mosque, I inadvertently found Bouctou's well. My guess is that most visitors don't find it, and don't bother to believe that the propitious well is even marked. Yet that hole in the ground at my feet was the origin of the name *Timbuktu*.

I politely shooed Zak away. I wished to be alone in my travel fantasy. The two keepers of the place, oblivious to my presence, talked in their sleep. The Ethnographic Museum encircled its namesake "Tin," the Berber language's grammatical kin to "well." A recent construction, it showcased Tuareg and Songhai artifacts of music and costume. Standing over the well of the woman whose name became the byword for remote, I stared into the hole, its shallow depth blocked by mud. At the end of a rope swung a camel-skin bucket that dropped from a wooden winch, itself secured by tree branch props. I looked within the well and sensed Bouctou contemplating her distorted navel.

Zak sloughed along a block away and waved to me. Bolstered by our logistical success in matching a street name with an explorer's home, it made sense to Zak that we chance Barth's Lane to find the house of the man who finally convinced skeptics that Timbuktu's fame was founded on exaggerated claims.

Sweating and covered with a day's dust, we stopped outside the home of Heinrich Barth, to the northeast east side of the Sidi Yahia Mosque. I breathed deeply. Barth's stay in Timbuktu was the signature piece in his five-year crossing of the Sahara. If there was a hint that Timbuktu might have a tourism future, this house was it: we paid an entrance fee. Pictures on the walls had descriptions in English, French, and German. Barth's maps and sketches were displayed. Framing was elusive, but some of the documents were protected behind glass, where the heat had melded them to the surface. A pamphlet on Barth's exploits was for sale. Was the furniture his? Did he slouch in that corner, surrounded by curious and untrusting observers looking on in silence? Did the tall German feel the urge to hunch over, given the lowness of the ceiling, as I did? Was the air as tight in his lungs as it felt in mine?

Barth arrived in Timbuktu with a debilitating fever and recuperated as a guest in this house, close to Sheikh Al Bekây. He stayed here for the first month, during which the competing authority, the local chief, who challenged the sheikh for power over the Christian, made many attempts to expel Barth. Among other reasons, it was suspected that he was Laing's son. The result of this competition between two conflicting and influential local rulers was that Barth was unable to move freely about the city. Sheikh Al Bekây eventually moved him to an encampment in the desert, from where Barth, on occasions, visited Timbuktu's mosques and spent hours among the townspeople and visiting the "lively markets." But political pressure mounted for this symbol of foreign intrusion, the infidel, to leave. It culminated in a late-night conference between the sheikh, the Tuareg, and the Fulani. The Fulani gained control over Barth and held him for two months in another camp while he tried to resolve the compromises that kept him from departing.

He remained a total of six months, a stay that resulted in the most thorough European-recorded observations of Timbuktu, including notes on the city's commerce and customs. Barth undertook language and vocabulary documentation, and wrote of tribes, place names, and daily habits.

His restricted movement meant that he had time for letter writing. Halfway through his visit he wrote, "You will have heard, I think, of my happy arrival in this ill-famed place." And, predating today's urban anti-smoking bylaws, he noted, "Amongst other things they have smoking a capital crime, so that even in Timbuctoo, except near the house of Al Bekây, a man smoking is in great danger ..."

His prolonged absence, and the African rumour trade, resulted in an erroneous report of Barth's death in Berlin. His obituary was published, and all hope of knowing his whereabouts disappeared. He was still 2,700 kilometres from safety. Sheikh Al Bekây, whose father had protected Laing in Timbuktu, travelled with Barth along the River Niger's north shore for weeks to ensure his safety. Finally, in September 1855, five years and five months after his journey began, Barth wrote from his north African camp: "I set out on my last march on the African soil in order to enter the town of Tripoli."

London and the world responded excitedly to Barth's triumph. Oxford bestowed an honorary degree on him, the Geographical Society of Paris awarded its Gold Medal, and Queen Victoria presented the Order of Bath. Heinrich Barth became president of the Berlin Geographical Society. But his five-volume work, *Travels in North and Central Africa*, although popularly received, disappointed its readers. Barth's reputation as a scholar and scientist was strong enough that his portrayal of Timbuktu as a mundane and dilapidated backwater was believed. He validated Caillié's descriptions of Timbuktu's unimportance in modern African trade. Barth's great achievement was that the public and politicians finally accepted the truth about Timbuktu. The myths of the "City of Majesty" began to lose their duel with reality.

We dawdled in the dust, letting our accomplishments settle in with satisfaction. "Thanks," I said to Zak, who had recovered his confidence.

In a narrow street, above the doorway of a building, hung a faded sign, tinged with mud that had been whipped high in the rains and dried by the wind: *Bibliothèque Manuscrits — Al-Wangari.* Feeling euphoric, I pointed to it and smiled at Zak. Just then, a blue robe appeared on the path, seemingly brought by the breeze. It came closer to reveal a tailored fit on the lanky frame of a scholar.

Ahmed al-Hadj grinned in greeting and unlocked the door to the library. He was pleased that I should enter it. The first two rooms were empty and I immediately remembered a photograph of a similar setting with stacks of crumpling sheets and broken books browned with dust and weather, poorly stored and in ruin. Then the man opened another locked door and we entered a larger, mud-walled room with furniture. A ceiling fan started when the electric switch went up. Immediately, I breathed air that had the aroma of old paper.

The keeper of the library, magisterial in his movement, went behind his makeshift desk and motioned for me to sit on a wooden chair with a woven brace. Zak, not used to the setting, shyly bridged the language gulf.

"My father was Imam at the mosque. His father before him. Our family values the old writings." The seated man leaned his chest forward on the desk, his palms open in the air, not far from either side of his face as though to narrow my eyes on his own. Then he gestured toward a bookcase along the wall. "These manuscripts, these books, I save for them, for my family. And for

In 1853 Heinrich Barth, the German explorer, wrote of his "happy arrival in this ill-famed place." Tough, stubborn, and said to have been "more clever than intelligent," he returned safely to Europe.

Africa." He was a man of letters saving historic writings for those who could not read.

I wanted to touch the pages, feel an ancient book, open history.

"There are many manuscripts in Timbuktu. It is important that they be kept," he said, not smiling. "But first they must be found." Most endangered were the unregistered, unknown sheets of paper stashed in closets or loosely stacked writings without bindings, without containers, a sheaf held only with a wrap of tired leather.

A wooden case full of books relied on the wall for support and stood beside two unmatched sets of shelving. Glass doors housed rather than protected the bindings and papers. The wall beside me had a larger case of shelves that sagged under the weight of a hundred volumes. Each shelf displayed pastel bookbindings. A bundle of papers was neatly stacked in an opened drawer. This trove of literary riches was merely a fragment of the challenge. I felt both encouraged and helpless; at once a believer that something was being done to rescue the manuscripts while also feeling that these efforts were woefully insufficient.

"It is difficult to protect these," Ahmed al-Hadj said through Zak. His left arm's wave covered a tiny portion of the "Timbuktu manuscripts" I'd heard about. "My family wrote on astrology," he explained, carefully lifting an old book from the collection and passing it to me. "Now, I wish to save everything." I took heart from his reassurance, yet struggled to comprehend his perspective. "But it is not possible," he said of the dilemma.

This man in blue stared as though gauging trust in my eyes. He rose slowly, and walked to a mud alcove behind his desk to share a secret. He concentrated on me, his long arms carrying a burnt-wood box. He set it on the ground at my feet, where he knelt, the smoothed earth not dirtying his robe. He pried loose the top, shifted it off, and the carbon smudged his pink palms. The chest held eight damaged books and he removed one of the more intact volumes, its leather cover charred and flaking, and passed it to me.

"The Koran," Ahmed al-Hadj whispered. I cradled it in my arms as Zak interpreted with reverence: "It is from the twelfth century."

It would be hard to find the soul of Timbuktu, but the search, I thought, might begin in this room.

He showed me another book and, through Zak, described how the paper withered from dampness during the rainy season. "These

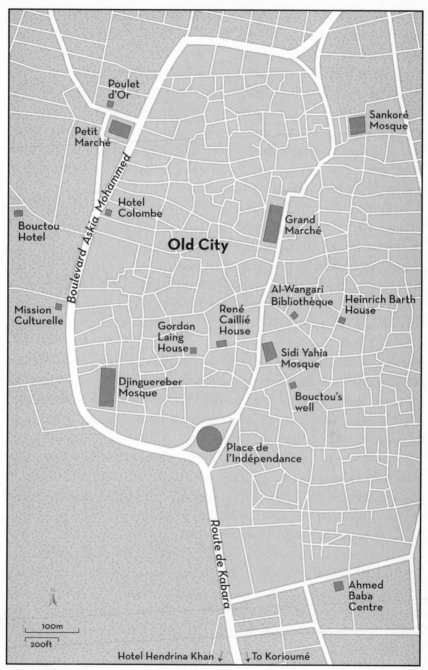

The jumbled maze of streets in Timbuktu's Old City, circa 2008.

books — many, many — were not properly stored." When I asked how he found this particular book, he said, "There was a home hurt in the rains. This was in it."

A pamphlet, dry and curled, rested on his desk. He pointed to it but did not lift it, telling Zak, "I cannot let him touch this one. The binding had bugs." When I asked where they went, he replied that they were shaken out. He went to a small pile of individual colophons, single sheets of history, and said of them, "Need more room for storage." It was not a complaint. A recent acquisition, papers without binding, was piled in studied disarray with no place to file them properly yet or to protect them from changes in temperature or humidity. They left a mark on the mind as would a stand of old-growth forest, a cove of pristine water, or the glimpse of an endangered species. I felt that this might be why I had come to Timbuktu; to assist, to make things better, to help save these precious manuscripts. I felt embarrassingly "Western": the only way to help immediately in this place seemed to be with cash. And I gave. He accepted. It was not his wish; it was his need.

There are 700,000 manuscripts in Timbuktu. Their discovery has been called "the greatest archeological find since the Dead Sea scrolls." Included in the cache are Moorish books with bug-riddled bindings, Islamic pamphlets covered with sand, ninth-century treatises baked by time, and scholarly pages a phase away from dust.

These literary remnants are mostly from Timbuktu's glorious fifteenth century, tucked untidily between Africa's Muslim encounter and the rancour of European exploration. They are the evidences of a proud, if not widely known, heritage.

Ignorance impeded their preservation over the centuries, and continued lack of awareness facilitated their slow disappearance — the loss of history's book one page at a time. Were they housed together, collected in temperature-controlled rooms, and catalogued from Arabic to Tuareg to Zahara, these manuscripts would be esteemed one of the world's bibliographic miracles. They are considered less a treasure only because of their scattered and deteriorating condition.

Such was the commerce of writing in Timbuktu that the city's trade routes in the fourteenth and fifteenth centuries became known as the Ink Road, a tribute to more than the manuscripts that made their way along them. Respected *marabouts* (religious teachers) and scholars were regarded as "ambassadors of peace" for their acumen in negotiations and Koran-based dispute resolution, not only in Timbuktu but in Gao, on the River Niger, and in Djenné. With their scholarship and mediation skills, they were respected as the ideal adjudicators. Sought when arbitration was required, they travelled the routes, figuratively and literally, of parchment and peace.

When Askia the Great ruled Mali in 1468, after his Songhai defeated the Tuareg, his rule was built upon Timbuktu's strengths in trade. The city then became the epicentre of learning and Islamic education. Arab scholars wrote and collected books and created large libraries in its universities and synagogues. The vast collections of writings were maintained, protected, and revered. They sustained a learned society and a community of understanding. Thus the phrase "Timbuktu trades in gold, salt, and *ink*."

In Timbuktu's golden age, sophisticated travellers would arrive with books known to be rare. During this period, manuscript-collecting was popular in Timbuktu, and caravans were forcibly detained while their written works were copied by hand by students at the universities. Texts from distant universities were often borrowed, studied, and copied. Timbuktu's libraries grew. At the same time, the city's private libraries flourished with copies of written contracts, religious books, legal texts, and letters. The marginalia of the day recorded everything from wedding plans to the previous night's shooting stars, providing a fascinating insight into the culture's everyday concerns.

Seeing those manuscripts today causes dismay. Often they lie in the homes of those who cannot read, and who perhaps do not know of the treasures they possess. Or the documents are crammed into the forgotten corners of mud buildings. Individual manuscript pages have been sold to travellers for food, thus disappearing from their family, from Timbuktu, from the public domain.

The protected manuscript collections that do exist, dating from as early as the second century, have prevented a cornerstone of Africa's history from sifting through careless hands. That

700,000 manuscripts have survived largely untended is astonishing. International travellers make their plans for Mali, browse a few websites, arrive, sightsee, and depart, oblivious to this literary conundrum: a wealth of historic manuscripts almost accidentally still available. But time is not a friend of these writings; the annual rains bring damaging humidity, the books in dry storage harbour insects, words erode.

In the race against time to save these irreplaceable treasures, Mali has attracted serious attention, irregular assistance, and modest funds from Norway, South Africa (where a major business consortium plans a new library to house hundreds of thousands of the manuscripts), the United States, and Spain. There is no small amount of controversy in the salvage work, with competing claims of authority and confusing mandates.

The Ahmed Baba Centre, named for the fifteenth-century scholar, stores nineteen thousand manuscripts that range from philosophy, mathematics, and Islamic law to geography and the sciences. This is the written history of Africans in Africa. It is of them, by them. Not the French, the British, or the Portuguese.

Restoration teams face a fascinating dilemma in deciding how to protect the brittle pages. Their work barely makes a dent in one of the desert's greatest challenges. "Rare book boxes" have been designed to house those manuscripts beyond reclamation. Repair

and restoration work is risky, too. Sometimes turning a page makes more dust than sense. The key to preserving the knowledge, if not the documents, is to transfer the words to another technology. Microfilming has been problematic, because the

Extraordinary efforts are underway to preserve Timbuktu's centuries-old manuscripts from further deterioration. Funding and expertise are provided by Norway, Germany, the United States, and South Africa, yet the demanding task outstretches the available resources.

ubiquitous sand tends to erase key data components. And the supply of electricity is sporadic.

The U.S.-based Timbuktu Educational Foundation* was created in 2000 for "the sole purpose of preserving, restoring, and disseminating the important intellectual contributions of the early African scholars from the famous Timbuktu University of Mali, West Africa." Those noble objectives for Timbuktu's disintegrating heritage are farsighted yet time-pressured. The foundation proposes to "translate and publish the manuscripts of Timbuktu" and "restore the historical buildings which house the University of Timbuktu," which they intend to "reopen with its classical methods of teaching." It also wants to open a branch of the University of Timbuktu in a major city in the United States with "the ancient, classical architecture of Timbuktu's great universities." There, it will recreate the famed Timbuktu "Circle of Knowledge," the sharing of complex decision-making through the intergenerational training of scholars who mentor professors who, in turn, study with Imams. The scholars deliberate contentious matters together and, in this flow of information, learn and decide. When their deliberations are complete they make a decision, perhaps issue a fatwa. Given these aims, it is understandable that the Malian government, mindful of the co-operation it needs from other well-intentioned groups, made the foundation "the legal custodians and caretakers of the manuscripts."

Musa Balde, of Oakland, California, is president of the Timbuktu Educational Foundation. He warns that "this entire African intellectual legacy is on the verge of being lost." While many of the volumes and decaying materials have been identified through the main universities of Timbuktu, Jingere Ber, Sankoré, and Sidi Yahia, much more work must be done. Balde has launched the foundation's Preserve-a-Manuscript program, setting a fundraising goal of one hundred U.S. dollars for each artifact that remains from the time when "Timbuktu flourished as the greatest academic and commercial centre in Africa."

---

*The Timbuktu Educational Foundation appears to have ceased programs sometime around 2010. See afterword for this story.

Meanwhile, in this antiquarian gold mine, the sheets curl and crack where the ink has set. Documents of a dozen warped pages are filled with hundreds of broken words. Africa is known as a land with a rich oral tradition, infused with song and dance; this trove of manuscripts establishes it as a continent with rich traditions in literature as well.

We emerged from the dilapidated Old City onto a wider street, which made the area feel new, that is, less than a hundred years old.

"Zak, had you ever been to Barth's home before?"

"No."

"To Caillié's?"

"No."

"To Laing's?"

"Yes, but only stand outside."

We stopped at a home that sold woven baskets. On its porch a pot of fish parts was at a boil. Farther along, a chair held dirty bottles filled with gas oil, each bottle holding just the amount needed to top up one of the motorcycles that were so common on this roadway. Zak stopped to buy a single cigarette, and we asked the boy selling it whether there was another *bibliothèque* nearby. Zak lit his smoke, puffed, and listened to the explanation as the boy pointed to a nearby building.

We left the dust-packed road and entered a courtyard thirty metres along. Inside, we found half a dozen one-storey buildings that looked to be residences. A colonnade appeared, and there was a raised walkway made of mortar. A sign hung around the corner: *Salle des manuscrits*. That was it. We woke the man we took to be the custodian. He said the man we wanted was bathing.

Apparently not. Djibril Doucouré sauntered toward us with such fresh enthusiasm that I felt as if I were the first to visit his library. The man was *Chef de Division Restauration & Conservation des manuscrits a l'Institut Ahmed Baba de Tombouctou*. He knew of Western interest in the manuscripts, corresponded with university students in Canada and the United States and, as he showed us to his rooms, was evidently proud of the manuscripts and books he had assembled as part of the preservation effort. Hundreds of protected volumes lined the walls. These books were intimates of his. Doucouré removed a bedsheet covering the glass display case in the middle of the room. In the case, a dozen books lay opened and labeled. "Islamique en 601/1204" was indicative of their ages. The Koran rested in two treasured copies respectively indicating both Muslim and Christian dates, 639 and 1241.

"These titles, they are about *pharmacie*," Doucouré explained, gingerly holding two aged books. "The spines, they crack because of heat." The temperature had created dry wrinkles, and both books were torn.

"May I?" I asked, extending my hands. Doucouré placed a book many hundreds of years old across my wrists.

"This one, it is on *optics*." He pointed to an illustration of a conical sphere with lines running through it and measurements indicating magnification. Arab calligraphy is among the most beautiful to be found, and it radiated here as well, though this book's lines ended with aborted words, as page edges were worn away by heat and humidity.

When Doucouré showed us a side room, we discussed the limited project funds he had. The library was large and cool and had sturdy shelves. The books were well racked, and I saw titles dealing with history and chemistry and mathematics. I thought if more Westerners visited, more would leave money. More Timbuktu manuscripts would be saved.

My Timbuktu day was ending. There was an office here that stamped international passports with an imperial-looking blotch. But it needed to be searched out, and soon.

I turned to Zak. "Shouldn't we hurry?"

"Why?" he replied.

"It will close at five."

"At five?"

"At five o'clock."

"*Rick,*" he stated. "Is Timbuktu. Nothing closes at five."

We picked up a couple of bottles of mineral water, a Diago for me, and Roc Vert for Zak. At a visitors' room in a courtyard behind a sign for *Mission Culturelle*, there were a few brochures in French and, more curiously for a non-country, the presumption of a passport stamp: *Tombouctou*. It marked more than my travel document, it marked an accomplishment. Each year fewer than five thousand travellers (Europeans, Arabs, North Americans) — an average of thirteen a day — make their way to Timbuktu. To have been one of them was satisfying. It pleased me nearly as much not to have seen even one of the other twelve visitors that day.

The day turned to night. Zak and I separated, him returning to the hotel. In the dust that shouldered the Route de Kabara, a yellowed building boasted of access to the Internet, a commercial courtesy of MaliNet. I'd read warnings that in Mali such signs, like those proclaiming VISA cards, were often meant as intentions, not facts. Inside was a table with computers, three of which apparently were functioning, others anticipating such a day.

The one I chose booted slowly. After all, this was the end of the world; I had to manage my expectations. French keyboards were understandably *de rigueur*. The uniqueness of this one lay in its individual keys. Each character on the keyboard was handwritten on paper, using different pens and pencils, implying that such "fixes" had been made over time. These pieces of paper were secured to the keys with Scotch tape, the heat making "secured" a tentative concept here. Two tags were on the floor. After three reboots, I was ready and sent my mother and father a brief e-mail: "Have arrived healthy and safe. Dad, I'm in Timbuktu and going to get my hair cut."

I left the Internet room. Outside, it was dark; a dim light bulb hung from a cable beside a merchant's doorway ten metres away. In beleaguered French I negotiated access to the shop's telephone. It was kept under lock and key in a wooden box. The merchant twisted the key and pulled hard on a sand-encrusted bolt. The phone was old, but in Timbuktu, what isn't? To ensure that I'd not misjudged the agreed cost, I placed *seffe* on the table and the shopkeeper gave me change, though he set it to the side in a gesture I understood to mean "In case it is more." I telephoned Janice with all the emotion of far-off love and, after three rings, reached the answering machine, on which I left a historically placed romantic message.

The occasional flickering light from a shop or candles in streetside homes lit my way back to the hotel. Periodically, a vehicle drove by, a dog barked. People scuttled along. The sand at my ankles slowed a walk that was already unhurried. Then it was quiet.

I found the barber's tiny shack at the roadside, marked by a hand-lettered sign that leaned against the outside wall and displayed the word *coiffeur*. When I poked my head in the open doorway, the barber was midway through a child's haircut. At the sight of me, he jettisoned the local and cleared the chair below an electric bulb. I waved my willingness to wait, but three other kids had gathered behind me as I walked in. I was not an inconvenience; I was the evening's entertainment.

At the British Library, I had browsed through *Zigzag to Timbuktu*, a 1963 travel story by Nicholas Bennett, who said, "I had always thought of Timbuktu as the most remote place in the world; that's why I wanted to go there." Another of his observations came to mind as I sat in the barbershop beneath the barber's sharp clippers. "The children, and this was a thing I had noticed in Timbuktu, had a strange kind of haircut. Half the head is shaved at one time, and it's not until the shaven half has grown again that they have the other half shaved off." I'd watched for this "Timbuktu hairstyle" and wondered if that was the origin of my dad's saying. Nothing I saw validated that, and I was not concerned about a strange trimming of my locks.

Too late, I realized that all the five faces looking at me in the barber's chair were below closely trimmed pates. This awareness was confirmed by the mirror. I couldn't remember my dad ever coming home with this hairstyle until he went bald.

In the deep dark, I overshot the lane that led off the road to my hotel and instead walked on for a kilometre in increasingly unfamiliar territory. Occasionally I passed the huts of street merchants. At one, I was flirtatiously asked by a young woman for *un cadeau* and she touched my pack. Then there were three, and to each I presented my country's flag on a pin. Their giggles were genuine, and in trade they offered me meat they had cooked for the evening meal. It tasted of grit and grease and reminded me that I was hungry. Their men joined us, and in French I asked about the way to a nearby hotel. They said there was none. They sent me away from the light and companionable warmth of their fire and into the night, alone. I was barely able to see. Then three goats suddenly jumped across the road, startling me with the reminder of my vulnerability. I passed large mounds of dark dirt that were actually mud homes, and finally found the narrow road that led into incredible darkness. At its end I stopped and stood at the edge of the Sahara, where the hotel Hendrina Khan was tucked into the sand.

I had spent a day rummaging through history to find some simple truths. Timbuktu is not an imaginary place, it is an embellished one. Its legends neither sought nor needed my sanction. Timbuktu is more a passage than a destination; more a pilgrimage than a journey. I thought, let the Timbuktu myth be.

Timbuktu does not long to be loved; it shrugged at my arrival. It did not judge my entry; it would as soon have let me pass. My coming meant nothing; it never would. Timbuktu is of consequence to me, not me to it.

No one is drawn to Timbuktu by today's realities. All come with knowing illusions. Timbuktu's aura will not crumble like its buildings. I felt, with René Caillié, "Still, though I cannot account for the impressions, there was something imposing in the aspect of a great city raised in the midst of sands."

The spell of Timbuktu would remain on the Niger's shore when I left Korioumé the next morning, it would not follow me on the river. If there was a sadness in my discovery, it was this: there is no quest for Timbuktu.

SEVEN

The Strong Brown God

I AWOKE, CONSCIOUS OF THE FACT THAT THIS was my last morning in Timbuktu, my once unattainable goal. We would drive along Route de Kabara back to the River Niger's port at Korioumé.

The disorganization that accompanied any Mohammed-instigated movement had become commonplace and no longer seemed worth noting. Zak had been emphatic the previous evening that we must leave at seven the next morning. I saw him through the steam of my coffee mug in the breakfast room at the hotel. I spread jam on a French roll as my knife grazed grains of sand.

"Ready?" I asked.

"No."

"It's seven," I reminded him.

"I must find the Netherlands."

"North of the France," I offered. He didn't respond to my humour.

"They were in Essakane. Man and woman. They're on boat with you."

"Are they here?"

"No."

René Caillié's tardiness nearly caused him to be left behind when it came time for him to leave Timbuktu: "To regain the caravan, which had already proceeded to a considerable distance, I was obliged, as well as three slaves who had also remained behind, to run a whole mile through the sand. This effort fatigued me so much that, on reaching the caravan, I fell down in a state of insensibility."

My sunrise wandering took me away from the small hotel to a place where a young Malian couple held hands as they watched their five-year-old pig-tailed daughter walk away from them unwillingly. She rounded plaintively to Mom and Dad. They stoically watched her shuffle down the lonely dirt road and smiled at one another when she turned her back to them. She shouldered a tiny pack in a journey shared by fortunate children everywhere: the journey to school.

When the girl veered into the schoolyard, the road I was walking on ended. I walked out of Timbuktu and into the desert. I walked past time, away from pleas for gifts or Bic pens, left behind the laughing women, ignored an angry dog — the first I'd feared — and past homes tattered and secure. I wanted to be alone.

Almost immediately, though, a small clatter of children appeared with that monotonous request: *"Un petit cadeau, un petit cadeau, un petit cadeau ..."* Like the cawing of a crow.

The near distance was strewn with wind-blown trash. The dunes seemed hard and unwelcoming; the desert's breezes will one day cover parts of this mess with forgiving sand, leaving only plastic protrusions flapping in the wind as evidence of the hidden garbage.

There are many ways to leave Timbuktu. Heinrich Barth's words echoed in my mind: "It seems not quite impossible, after all, that I shall finally leave this town, of which I am greatly tired. May the Merciful God grant me a safe return; my way is a long and difficult one."

A couple from Belgium, leaving later that day and travelling south on the northern route I'd taken overland to Timbuktu, encountered the feared roadside bandits. Their four-by-four was halted, and a gun was placed muzzle-tight to each of their heads. They were forced to the ground, where a boot firmly pressed their shoulders into the sand. Money was taken, lives were spared, the four-by-four was disabled, and they, their guide, and driver were left stranded. They were more fortunate than those whose vehicles are stolen; at least they had shelter until they were rescued by a Land Cruiser following the same tracks a few hours later.

Gordon Laing, upon leaving Timbuktu, travelled as self-assured as we did; or so he wished to be perceived. "I have little time at present to say more than that my prospects are bright and expectations sanguine. I do not calculate upon the most trifling future difficulties between me and my return." Two days later he was strangled by Tuaregs using his own turban-styled *cheches*.

Timbuktu is on the Great Bend of the River Niger, where it arcs and then flows southeast. We planned to motor against its current, heading west. I would travel on West Africa's majestic artery of life for three days.

I recognized the "Netherlands" from the festival and, with their arrival, began the loading, unloading, and reloading of luggage atop the four-by-four. We retraced the Route de Kabara in the early morning light, our vehicle crowded with others hitching a ride.

Robert was lean, browned from a trip to Cuba not long before. He had tousled black hair longer than the heat agreed with, and much of it hung over his forehead. His face sported honest eyes and a ready smile. He was fifty-three, though he looked younger, and owned a record shop in Holland. He had the weight of a vegetarian without any beer-aided plump; not fit, but travel-thin. I liked this man; he could fix things like sand-stuck cameras and zipper-snagged sleeping bags.

Anke had a long face that smiled, eyes and mouth as one, whenever she made eye contact or spoke, even when the conversation was about a problem. Her teeth had a charming and determined stance. Her hair, auburn in morning's light, was long and hung from an ever-wrapped bandana, an abbreviated turban. She was maybe in her mid-thirties, with a very pretty body, and without a trace of such self-knowledge. Confident. Jewellery dangled from both of Anke's wrists. Half a dozen pieces of Tuareg silver wrapped around one wrist; leather with spots of silver encircled the other. Four rings over two hands. A silver bauble hung around her neck, which was entwined with an ebony-and-bone necklace, and she wore dangly earrings.

Korioumé was a constant market, as boats arrived a day late or half a day early, only to pack up and leave half a day before travellers expected. All docking was informal: a beachhead here, a sloped bank over there. Three *pinasse* floated offshore, one departed with black people, black bags, and black boxes as its motor puffed black smoke. It was a commercial vessel first, and, when loaded with its trade cargo of sacks and crates, people were allowed to wedge themselves where there was an angled opening. Another *pinasse* was almost loaded, and the few white travellers would pile on soon, taking the best spots; the locals would follow. At the foot of the embankment where the Land Cruiser had dropped us was a clean *pinasse*, fifteen metres long, canopied with woven reeds and bobbing in the wake of a departing boat. It had a motor, a young captain, and a younger deckhand. It was ours.

The port of Korioumé used to be closer to Timbuktu, and the river's tributaries, size, and impact have been subjects of dispute.

The most common transport on the River Niger: this idle pinasse *will soon be overloaded with gear, goods, passengers, and animals.*

The River Niger swells during the rains, confusing its chroniclers. Robert Adams, the disputed storyteller, told of the river being wide, without a current. In his recollection it flowed near Timbuktu. In justification of his apparent error (or as evidence against those who charged him with distortion), it is said that the river may indeed have been unusually wide during a period of that year. René Caillié, when in Timbuktu, wrote: "I am inclined to think that formerly the river flowed close to Timbuctoo." This observation would have been based on the dry markings of a riverbed, perhaps. The river was unusually low during Caillié's visit, as it had been unusually high during Adam's stay.

One could spend a lifetime on the River Niger, and many people do, but not in travelling its length of 4,200 kilometres. People live near the river's inlets and bays, many of them within the Great Niger Delta, through which we would travel. The river's source is in Guinea; its mouth is in Nigeria, at the Gulf of Guinea. Mali is one of four host countries for this life-giving river, a path of commerce and communication, and a source of food and nurturing.

A bush taxi arrived carrying its clustered passengers — Malians and other travellers already aching from the short ride. They made last-minute arrangements for river travel. The journey downstream to Gao was said to be beautiful, and several cargo *pinasse* would head there throughout the day. The provisioning was basic – hand over some *seffe*, find a spot, inhale the unfiltered smells, and perch among the packed crates, straw bags, and locals. Food of indeterminable origin was passed from the back to the front of the boat. Take what you need, spill the rest back into the container. Pass it along.

On the COMANAV (Compagnie Malienne de Navigation) steamers, food travelled vertically, from the top deck to lower decks, its variety, warmth, and cleanliness diminishing at each level. So did the cost of the travel quarters and the price of food.

Two travellers approached our captain to see if the boat had room for more passengers. Zak, who had got us this far, asked if I minded these riverboat travellers. I was playing open-air *baby foot*, a twisty game of stickmen on metal bars in an arena box placed atop a table. I'd just beaten one dockworker on his coffee break and was plunging to defeat at the hands of an eleven-year-old as I listened to Zak's question.

"Zak, it's not for me to say. It is the river." Later, as he pushed our *pinasse* into the river, Zak explained: "They offered too little. They're on cargo *pinasse*." Yet we had others, two women, hardy Netherlanders, as well, who were willing to pay. My River Niger would reverberate Dutch for three days.

Jose neared my age. Earrings hung from both her lobes and a stud adorned the left flank of her nose, and she seemed to amble when she talked. She was without pretense to style, had a warmly harsh voice, wore a black dress, and wrapped a cloth around her head. The turban changed colour daily. Her energy was in her talk. Her cheeks were generous in their smile and flesh. There was much infectious goodwill in this woman.

Ona completed the European contingent. Once a striking woman with an open-mouthed grin that must have been irresistible; a one-time great beauty, she was now in that period's afterglow. She was the quiet one, tinkering with her camera and

Open-air baby foot is a twisty game of stickmen on metal bars in an arena box placed on a table atop the sand.

pack of lenses, the last to speak in Dutch or around the fire, content in the steadiness of a non-frivolous life. The sun had not browned her skin. Her hair was dark and wound within a green turban that she would wear during the whole journey. No loose ends.

"*Eric. Eric.*" I rounded. Jose looked at me. The name she gave me stuck for the rest of the river journey. "*Eric*, tell us about you."

Me? I was the khaki-shirted, scruffy-booted guy with thin beige pants hosed into socks, comfortably dated and irrelevant. I had the paunch common among my generation; my body had surrendered to gravity and the calendar. Atkins had tried to help me lose the pounds, but I'd raced it back into shape with wine and culinary delights. I craved earthly pleasures, cringed at the double chin, and admitted much of what I'd like to be, I was not. Would I ever be? Buoyed by successes, nothing singular had intrigued me of late. Then, this distantly inspired dream of Mali. Here I was.

We had all, except Anke, exceeded the average life expectancy of the people through whose land we travelled. Not that fifty-year-old men were absent, but our lives had the blessing of that age: no significant deterioration of health or mobility. What was more, we each carried a backpack, a camera, all manner of goods whose price exceeded the average annual income of our Malian hosts. Yet our arrival was not unwelcome, was not considered an intrusion. Malians didn't envy us being there. They envied us at home. Robert observed, "Many people leave here, countries like this, and come to Amsterdam. They work very hard there, live uncomfortably, and have more material goods, but less life."

Our *pinasse* was not a common sight on these waters, and many of the villagers we passed shied away from us. But half a day out, some of them waved. Five children stood on shore as we slowed, and others in the distance stopped their play. As we beached our boat on the muddy bank, the adults stopped work, laid their tools down, and rested. Ten, fifteen, now thirty children joined us at the shore, stepping into the water to get closer, shouting "*Ça va, ça va.*" Anke and Jose sat on the *pinasse* roof next to a dozen sun-drying fish, and the kids yelled mostly to them. I was close to the rail and in the shadow, while Robert continued to read. It was noisy and colourful and mostly happy, save for small children who cried at our strangeness.

Tiny hands tentatively reached out to me. They stretched from kids who had waded into the river next to our boat. I held out my flat palm for them to press. One did, then splashed away. A girl with a handless arm watched her friends. She was unconfident. I extended one of my hands her way, but it was still out of reach. Now, three young hands boldly touched mine. I rose from the boat's bench seat to the hull's ledge and squatted, hunched over, beneath the canopy. All went still until I stopped this movement.

Then the cry of *"Ça va"* sounded again, like a chorus of cicadas in the night. I threw my legs to the water's edge and all the noise ceased. Silence. Two small children teased their hands toward me, suspended in fear. I touched each hand with mine, and they stayed. I pretended to use them to pull myself out of the boat, through the water and up to shore. They played along. I rose. Tall. White. Big. Kids scurried back behind the protection of their parents' orange or blue skirts.

The cicadas started singing again.

Suddenly it was a palm-fest. My white hands to their black hands, extended from everywhere. Parents brought babies and held the child's hand out. I touched. Kids brought their little brothers and sisters, crying for retreat, within forced reach. Everyone wanted to touch the white guy.

On the canopy, the cameras of Anke and Ona clicked repeatedly, recording the rare event.

It was easy for me to walk up the sandy shore to the four older men who stood there and greeted me with a handshake. All were tall, all thin. Their bright robes draped with a classical elegance, each a different colour — a red, a blue, two shades of green. We talked in pidgin French, and all knew this to be a fine day.

The kids had now half-circled me and I was theirs again. We played the hand game. A mother shouted a phrase in Bambara and clapped. Astonishingly, thirty children joined her in unison. And clap they did, keeping at it, with no sign of stopping. They giggled and clapped. I started to clap.

An impromptu dance lesson is provided by young Malians along the River Niger.

Two three-year-olds graced the village shore. I was well past noticing the children's runny noses and sores and saw only friendly faces. One little girl swung her blue-skirted hips back and forth and there was a new rhythm in the crowd's clapping, a hurried pace. She had a rhythmic hip, step, clap that was a wonderful move to watch. Hip, step, clap ... parents laughed. Hip, step, clap ... kids laughed. Together, she and I danced to her lead. I am at my best on a dance floor with a country and western heel-toe; such moves tend to dig a hole in the sand. But my little partner was a star, pounding the ground with confident swirls as the beat crested. She towed my hand and I followed in a clumsy imitation of her natural gift. Everyone howled with laughter, both on shore and on board.

As I boarded the *pinasse*, Robert said, "They say you come to Mali to learn how to laugh."

"You could go on tour, *Eric*," Jose laughed as we were waved away by people who had done much to earn this bellyful of happiness. "You could do shows on this river."

"Big White Guy On Tour," Ona said, and we all laughed at our good fortune.

The boat travelled two hours farther on the river and motored on the southern side of a marshy isle, low and consisting mostly of pods of weeds that separated us from another route. Across that route crept a slope that led to the most beautiful mosque tower. Not one person strolled on that distant shore; the town was deserted. We, the passengers, decided to go there. The boat's captain said no, pointing kilometres down the Niger, and saying in French, "That is where we will go for lunch," with practised confidence. He worked for Mohammed.

The captain's name was Nanaga, which was spelled out for me on paper with a squiggle I did not recognize. "It is a letter you do not have," I was told. This reminded me of the name of a book publishing company I and some associates once owned, using the Inuit word *Nunaga*, meaning "my land, my country." I thought of the captain's country. He co-owned the boat in heaven knows what type of partnership with Mohammed, which earned my appreciation, if not respect. The longest journey he'd ever made was from his home in Mopti to Niamey, capital of Niger, a twenty-one-day voyage on the river. He was thin and smiley, wore leopard-patterned trousers, and was short of hair. He checked on us, his charges, often, in both Bambara and French, knowing that our comfort was for his attention.

He repeated that we were not going to stop here, that we would go farther downriver.

"It's our boat," Anke said, just this side of mutiny.

"We wish to go there," Jose stated, determined to see the village.

"The other village is better," Nanaga countered in French. It was unwarranted.

"We wish to see this one," Anke injected. Decisive move, that.

"There is nothing here," Nanaga replied, looking at me to make a decision his way.

"Good. Then let's go," I said.

He turned the boat around. It listed to port in a hesitant curve, as though to stall, until Jose repeated: "Let's go." The captain retraced half an hour of channel time and navigated around the island to cross the stretch of water.

As we approached, we saw children hiding near a tree. Nanaga beached the *pinasse* in a muddy stop. Our first impression of beauty was the shy kids running away. Then they snuck back to shore to watch from behind slender trees with few branches. They did not seek gifts or complicate our arrival. A novelty had landed in their village, and they were skeptical. A solitary man in sun-orange robes trod through the mud with a confident walk, but his green eyes did not reflect the friendliness we had met at our previous stop. An elder. Another skeptic. Not all visitors are good.

Politely, we tucked our cameras out of sight and extended open hands. Three children retreated into the walled walkways of their village. We followed rather than advanced, aware that they were nervous.

A bolder boy came to me. *"Ça va."*

"Ça va," I replied.

"Bonjour."

"Bonjour."

He chuckled at my pronunciation and ran away to the giggles of four girls. They now jostled near us, no longer feeling it necessary to flee. Their village took us in through its walks and to the base of its banco mosque, with a tower ten metres high. The children stayed beyond the reach of photographs.

We walked around a corner of high mud walls that hid any warning of our arrival. Where the path opened to a home's courtyard, we saw two girls about to leave. They balanced large metal pans on their heads, stuffed with utensils and cups and bowls of all sizes as they headed to the river to wash up after lunch. Their eyes widened in surprise at seeing me, and fright took over. One gasped and fastened her grip on the teetering pile atop her head. The other's mouth would not open to let her cry escape. Unbalanced, the pots, cutlery, and plastic glasses tumbled from her head as she ran away.

Parental protection appeared immediately. Seeing the cause of the girls' fear, the adults laughed. A small, skinny face poked through the group of older villagers. I smiled at the child I'd startled but she stared back, crying.

A woman standing near me reached for my hand and raised it to show her friends. Another came and tried the clasp, the contrast of black and white hands a wonder to them. The little girl I'd frightened came forward and touched my palm in a dart of her hand, then giddily walked away, her face seeming more weathered than those of the older women, lacking their shine.

Their village was home to about three hundred people. Its buildings were freshly covered with a new coat of mud. Their walls were sturdy, and the yards had a prosperous expanse. Opened doors let us see a way of life that was slow, unselfish, and contented. Where one path met a larger walkway to bend left, women sat with their gathered wood, a donkey, and their children beside the day's food. A sweet-looking young mother rose from nursing a baby, her generous breasts swinging gently as she strapped her baby to her back, using her long gown to secure the child to herself.

Anke and I walked well behind the others, not talking. We both felt that the secluded village was an extraordinary find. I finally said, "This is what my mind wanted Timbuktu to be."

"I think that is true," Anke replied.

We stopped at an open gate where a toddler cried as he stumbled across the ground, his feet wrapped in plastic green thongs. Watery eyes, beseeching hands, and a tender bellow moved in our direction then turned away. His brother lifted him up and carried the tear-runny face to us in a friendly display. We knelt to the boys' level.

"His eyes," Anke said, seeing their red and mucked corners.

"And nose," I replied, not from any need to mention it, because the scabs were as obvious to us as they were welcome to the flies.

I walked along the wall, away from Anke, to photograph her and the boys. I saw in her the desire to help overwhelmed by reality.

We walked on. A dozen kids snickered at us and pushed one another about, not touching anything but our sensitivities.

"They will remember this day," I said, "and talk about it later."

"It will be party talk," Anke said. "The day the white clowns came to Africa."

We found the men of the village constructing a new building. One said to Robert, in French, "Is there news?" There was none we knew of. We'd been away from news.

I lost my travel companions in the labyrinth of village paths and moved with the tide of children, now loyal to me — the Pied Piper who must soon leave. Fifteen children followed me with shy handshakes and peek-a-boo looks.

When our path merged with the others, the youngsters stayed close in a jumble of happiness. Each in turn slipped a hand into one of ours, forming the fabric of memories. Near the shore where our boat bobbed, the old man in the long orange robes waited. As we passed, he touched my hand lightly — not to shake, not to greet, but to know.

Aboard the *pinasse*, I said to Ona, "They need a doctor to visit once a month with medications."

"It is all they seem to require," she said.

Back on the shore, the children waved and jumped.

We drifted alone on "The Nile of the Negroes." Children rushed to the riverbank as we slipped by the village of Diré. Later, whether passing a large village or small village, the novelty of whites on a boat was enough reason to gather. Boats working on the river were busy enterprises, and the children pulled on their nets with one hand and waved with the other. The more isolated children, the ones who tended cattle or goats, were the most reluctant to wave.

"His eyes." Anke told the others of the youngster we'd seen, and the image of an insidious plight haunted me. River blindness crawls from behind the eye. First the parasite strikes old Africans. Eventually it invades the children who lead their blind elders by hand. Fewer villagers are able to work in order to support those without sight. Many infected people sit out their remaining days, which become years. Left with too many blind, too few seeing, the village economy falters. It is unsustainable. The last to see watch the village disappear.

Everyone knows of AIDS. Who has not heard of malaria? But river blindness, this little-known river-bred pandemic, persists as well, seldom noticed outside Africa. Mali knows the worm all too well. It is *oncho*, their abbreviated word for the calmly named intruder: *onchocerciasis*. River blindness.

It manifests itself in empty villages, abandoned cattle, and lost peoples. The disease is peripatetic. It moves with ease via savannah flies. The flies bite an infected person, get under their skin, pick up larvae, and pass it along. Itching precedes. Scratching proceeds. Children with the scratch, elders with the snowy white eyes in a land that does not know snow, are ashamed. Often their only recourse is begging; anything that can be done while stationary — so they can scratch. Suicide is an option; madness is understandable.

The scourge of thirty countries as recently as a decade ago, the debilitating disease has now been eradicated in nearly half these nations. But it survives in the other half, and it is feared that, borne by the wind, river blindness will find a new home elsewhere in Africa.

The outside world has a remarkable tolerance for the plight of Africa. Its "problems" often meet with indifference. But we're not ignorant. The stories are known.

In the past, prospective travellers would read of river blindness as an occasional health hazard. Older books pointed to it as a reason for avoiding certain territories. But seldom is the tale of its eradication told. The story of the fight against this pan-African epidemic came my way through the research of journalist Don Cayo.

In 1972, a development-minded Robert MacNamara, head of the World Bank after years as Richard Nixon's much-derided secretary of defence, identified a social hurdle to economic progress and to meeting the Bank's mandate to reduce poverty in parts of Africa. "We'd be wasting our time unless we were prepared to deal with *onchocerciasis* first," MacNamara told Cayo.

With scientific determination, a long-term commitment, the backing of the World Health Organization (WHO) and several supportive countries, a program of spraying marshes was begun. A decade after MacNamara's first visit to blinded villagers and deserted villages, his efforts were catapulted by Merck Pharmaceuticals' drug Mectizan, which impedes the spread of the larvae in the host body. It could prevent *oncho*'s start in others.

The story revolves around a business decision that makes cynics swallow a little less sharply. No one could afford the drug. Not donor countries, not local governments, nor the WHO or the World Bank. So, "Merck decided to give it away," said Cayo. Let me repeat that: Merck decided to give it away, "for as long as it takes."

The company receives a U.S. tax deduction for its donation, but this means squat to the villager whose body harbours adult worms. It is nothing. The drug is everything. Try to measure this gift to a child whose eyes will see her through parenthood, who captures the daily setting of the sun's glow, who loves her grandmother's smile.

On a continent where a man's cruelest predator is often his fellow man, a network of volunteers in thirty countries distributes this hope, this solution. Trained with little more than the ability to calculate doses based on age and weight, these people are saving villages, restoring nations, and winning the war against one of Africa's smallest and mightiest enemies.

Motoring against the Niger's current, our *pinasse* approached another village. We were thirty metres from shore. Fifty people clustered; children ran into the water, mothers carried babies, old men pointed. They waved. All of them could see us.

We pulled into a village with no dock, drifting close to where a young woman in a yellow dress stood on shore with a basket full of bread on her head. I motioned her over, and she held out a warm loaf to me. I leaned over and took it. Several more women came forward to sell other wares as I passed the loaves to Robert, and he to the others. We bargained happily.

A spirit slipped to the water's edge nearby, her white undergarment showing through a pale orange dress. She and the dress flowed as one, and silver jewellery hung effortlessly from her ears. Her hair was tied back tight with a dark orange cloth that had the effect of emphasizing her long forehead, which slipped in a long shine all the way to her eyes. Below that, her face was angular and spectacular, the pot she carried unnoticed until she lifted it full from the river and placed it on her head in a graceful arc that bent my eye. She slipped from the water's shallows and moved into her village. Robert looked at me and nodded.

Our boat travelled on. Cool air breezed over the stowed baggage. The river's surface spread like green gauze around islands with grassy edges.

Sugary stars eased the darkness while I considered my circumstances. Lying prone on the boat's roof, "considered" might be better understood as "took the stars into account."

Robert, Jose, and Anke climbed on top of the boat's thatch cover, as though we drifted in one large wicker chair. The Niger's shore, far from us, was invisible. Venus was reflected in the water and traced a line to our *pinasse*.

"I have not seen a plane in the sky, not for over a week," said Anke.

"It is good that way," said Jose, "We travel, and I'm happy at that, but travellers have a lot to answer for."

We did not at first follow her thinking. "Planes," she continued, "they spoil the air, if my English is right."

Right it was.

Anke told us. "There is a proposal to allot each of us on earth one plane ride of a set distance, perhaps equal to once around the world. One per lifetime."

"Impossible," said Jose. "Good, but impossible."

"Westerners would use that distance quickly and need a larger allotment," said Anke, not hearing Jose's response. "Others, like millions in Mali, would never use a mile, not one airstep. Their stipend would be for sale, to their benefit and our cost."

Robert sketched details. "The EU proposes to tax airfares and to use the revenues to offset developing country debts. Is that what you mean?"

"No," Anke told us. "It is about people repairing the carbon dioxide damage they generate by flying. You pay, and it is not much. The money goes to replenish your part." It sounds simple. Perhaps it is. "Otherwise," she determined, "there are limits to the travel."

"They call it 'carbon neutral,'" I said. "It is not about poverty reduction, or foreign aid. This is to plant trees, through paying CO_2 credits. It's an offset." Travel causes a wobble in the ecosystem. The world has less and less patience for any industry's misbehaviours. People matter. The travel industry stands shoulder to shoulder with other icons of commerce, such as the oil industry, forestry, mining, and fishing in their responsibility. But corporate amnesia and individual denial cannot withstand public calls for accountability forever.

Anke closed our midnight conversation atop the *pinasse* by summarizing our guilt. "Why should travellers from rich countries have all the fun?"

Our morning began when Captain Nanaga was ready to sail. The moon was still shining as the sky lightened to various shades of blue. Acres of treeless cracked mud rolled away from the shore that had been our camp. The beauty of the morning grasped my heart. Nanaga lit a fire in the hull's pit to heat water. Sitting astride the *pinasse's* starboard frame, I removed my shaving gear from the pack and prepared to shave. I squeezed lather into my palm and was about to apply it.

"May I do that, *Eric?*" asked Jose from her perch on a bench. "I'd like to."

"Sure," I said, handing over the utensils as she settled in across from me. "Here's my kit, take your time." And I moved away.

"No. On you," she said.

"On me what?" I asked.

"I'll do this *on you*," she repeated.

"You shave me?"

"Yes, I'd like to," she offered.

"Hmmm."

She lured me to her parlour farther down the boat's rim where it abutted the wooden plank she shared with Ono. I reached over the side of the boat, scooped a handful of river water and wet my face. Before I could do anything more, Jose took over.

She moved the lather around my chin and cheeks with her hand. She talked to my face, as though I was not present. "I have an entire shaving kit at home," she told my nose. "I bought it when I saw how beautiful one is. Often I look at it but it has never been used." Her hand glided east across the stubble and crossed back over, pressing against the whiskers. She smoothed the lather, slapped hard in a

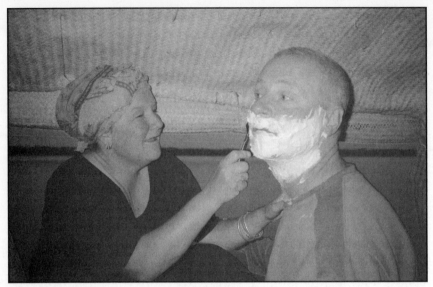

Jose, aboard the pinasse, *takes command of the author's shaving kit.*

couple of places to tauten the skin, and then placed the sharp razor against my jaw. She carved away as the boat rocked to and fro. A wind brought waves to the bow, jostling her hand and the blade into a stroke one might use to peel an orange.

"There. Nice," she said, practising her approach. She took her coffee cup to scoop up river water and splashed it on my cheek to clear the remaining lather, soaking my shirt in the process.

Now Jose became serious. She fully lathered my face, picked up the blade again, and then launched into a concert of strokes. Whip, slice, whip.

She leaned over the side of the boat to rinse the razor in the river and to freshen its sharpness. Quickly, the razor was at my face in a sideways stroke over the upper lip. Whiskers fell. I squinted and pursed my lips to tense the skin she was shaving. She slashed the razor into the river again to rid it of foam. Her eyes narrowed in concentration. Stroke, slice, side stroke, slice, upstroke, slice. Soon enough she was through.

"What time is the massage?" I asked.

Within the hour, we docked near a village where selling and buying made an attractive song. People thronged to market as birds flock to a carcass. They were through it and of it and with it, and then left only sheltered stalls as bones. Early morning was the busiest time of day, packed with both river transients and land-based sellers. I found a bag of peanuts and shelled and ate them as I walked past a Singer sewing machine that would be a valuable antique back home. The original paint gleamed and the black gloss on the housing evoked a memory of my grandmother. I saw her face and missed her. Pantaloons were being made by a man who twirled the handle wheel and guided material through the stitching. He pumped his feet to bob the needle. The tailor called out a promise that anything in my size could be done quickly.

Narrow stores stocked whatever the market did not. A store owner tried to charge a child fifty *seffe* more for a cigarette because he thought the youngster's purchase was for me — a foreigner's surcharge.

The town looked prosperous, as trees sparkled green hope through the dust. Clothes dried in the breeze, and wide roads divided uneven rows of homes and stores. Everywhere children laughed. Men cast sand blocks into cement. One woman swept the dirt street, which struck me as odd.

Chairs with plastic seats woven of rainbow strips danced against the ground's brown. Beside them were mattresses of uncommon colour combinations. I felt the lure of this brilliant setting and hoisted my camera.

"Photograph?" I asked the men sitting in the dirt across from the mattresses.

"Euro," one demanded. I put the camera away. He retracted in French and I sloughed off his words. As I passed, ignoring him, he retracted with, "Apology. Apology." His words trailed my disappointment.

Guitar music drifted from behind a wall, and I went in search of its source. Five young men, the youngest of whom strummed, picked up the beat. The strummer's friend leaned over and tapped the dome of the guitar with both hands to add rhythm. They were off with delightful music that I recognized from the festival sessions.

"I see I have a visitor," said a lady's voice in English behind me. She introduced herself and I missed the name, but I caught "from

Ireland." She was a seasoned traveller and had been lounging in the mud-walled room behind her, where it was dark. *"Eric,"* I said by way of self-introduction to the shabby lady.

Her right hand and its cigarette pointed toward the musicians. "I had to kick them out of my room so I could get dressed."

Not sure exactly where that was headed, I said, "They're very good."

"They have their own group with Afel Bocoum. That one," she pointed to the guitarist, "is his brother. They played at Essakane."

"Apparently Ali Farka Toure lives here," I said.

"He owns the town," she asserted. The music continued. "This is Niafounké."

I asked, "Do you live here?"

"My fourth trip. They say of Mali, 'First you open your heart, then you open your wallet.'"

"I can see that."

"Now I spend my time trying to get other people to open their wallets." She asked where we had stayed the previous night, and I described our shore camp. "In a *campement?*"

"No, on the dry mud shore," I said.

"In the open?" she asked in awe.

"Very," I said.

She was surprised. "No scorpions?"

"I didn't notice any."

"And no crocodiles?"

I began to reconsider my plans for the coming night's camp.

The musicians' singing was strong and moving. The Irish woman said, "Of course, they'd be thrilled if you left them something, but I didn't say that."

I pointed to *seffe* left pinned below my water bottle, which was lying on the ground.

"Very nice," she said. And then she asked where I was going next, to which I replied the Dogon. She warned, "There was a young Dogon girl who I watched boil water for a European trekker. Then she thought it too hot so she added fresh cold water from her well as she served it. He got sick. Be careful."

A shopfront ten minutes farther on displayed a Coca-Cola sign and had a fridge just inside the shade. I was prepared to pay whatever it cost, but the price was hardly anything. I'd found that when I bought something, this was also the best time to take a picture without creating resentment. While I waited for the Coke and took a picture, the store owner offered me sweet tea. I noticed there was no clean side to the small glass. I sipped.

Returning to the boat, Jose saw me and held high a wrapped prize from the market: "Peanut butter. For breakfast." It was a hand-packed ball, the colour of river mud.

"And this," said Ona, holding three loaves of still-warm bread. I split them open and used the knife to spread the peanut butter, wanting only for a garnish. And then Robert brandished a clutch of bananas.

We drifted. Villages that at first conveyed a sense of orderliness mocked it on closer scrutiny. The river also masked realities. We saw a hippo, its eyes floating on the surface of the water. The most feared of African animals, it is the killer of more people in Africa than any other creature except man.

Caillié on the Niger wrote, "The immense monotonous plains on all sides fatigue the eye of the traveller." I found the vistas more satisfying then he had; such may be the least of the differences between my four weeks and his two years in West Africa. Some newly appearing structures on the riverbank, back of the high-water marks, began to look like earthen sculptures, metres high, phallic-like, and oddly bent. We hypothesized religious icons, star guides, or sexual barometers. Later we discovered they were anthills.

Fishers lay their nets close to grassy shallows of this inland delta. Herons watched and benefited. A passing transport, fifty metres long, motored along the river with people wedged over and under goods of all sorts: baobab ropes, cans of grain, firewood. Our boat nudged toward a *pirogue*, its poles still and the hull stable in the eddies. Fish flipped around inside the boat; carp, capitaine, catfish. Our captain wanted a larger fish than anything on offer. Another *pirogue* hauled its nets aboard for our inspection.

"*Poulet yassa,*" the cook offered, watching a few fish gulp for water.

Robert explained, "Nile perch."

The captain spied dinner in the net, and coins changed hands.

Boats are generally poled from place to place, yet with the wind up, laundry or old packing cloths provide sails for speedier transport.

Across the water, the shores rose on both sides toward sandy hills. North was flat land, as far as I could see. South, in the distance, was a village. Gripping the rudder of a passing *pirogue* was a boy with a man's job, a yellow cloth draped over his head and neck. His family trusted him. Amid the sacks and household wares one young woman cooked, another nursed. At the bow, against the comfort of a rolled pad, rested the father, his bushy hair the colour of steel wool, with a patron's calm.

We pulled beside a broken vessel, its motor mute. We gained two new mates. A man joined us, holding a piece of iron and determined to get a mechanical fix at the next village. The other new passenger, a woman draped with a black blanket with red squares sewn on, was heading to Mopti to look for work. Before we left the captain said in French, "They want us to take him to the next village and her to Mopti. Is that okay?" We glanced at each other, puzzled at the oddness of the question. Robert replied, "It is not our decision. This is the river. Of course."

Four *pirogue* aligned near the riverbank, two boatmen in each, all young. This was the village's evening crew. They poled to position and, in a symphony of movement, cast four nets in sequence, bowed to the wind and lowered them onto the water with billows that would sink and capture surprised fish.

Our curious group flowed by; the fishermen and their families watched the oddity that was us. One slim girl, perhaps sixteen, stood at the end of a village, a blue-green skirt wrapped around her hips and a tiny string laced between her breasts, revealing a silver necklace, reminiscent of a page from *National Geographic* of fifty years ago.

My thoughts bore backward as I considered how best to go forward. My recent speeches to travel industry gatherings around the world had been concerned with tourism's economic and social impacts. In some places, particularly in developing countries, tourism has gone from good to bad to downright ugly. Changes in the behaviour of travellers as well as businesses are absolutely necessary if tourism is to be respected as an industry. In short: good hosts deserve good guests.

Tourism, both as an industry and as individual entrepreneurial practices, has not yet fully faced the media scrutiny that will surely come its way — as that scrutiny came to forestry, mining, oil exploration, and the fisheries on the world stage. The travel industry faces an increasingly skeptical public demanding to know about its

Young families would rush to the shore to greet our passing pinasse.

impacts, both visible and hidden, and of benefits true and false. We must all travel more wisely, be more respectful of what we take as well as what we leave.

The critiques of tourism are relatively new. Their intensity and sophistication will increase. Perhaps most notable is concern about environmentally responsible tourism, which seeks to minimize the footprint of mass tourism. Also important are cultural and heritage preservation in the face of a stampede of tourists. And, of course, the demeaning trend toward generic travel destinations. Most people don't have a compelling reason to be somewhere else. They are where they are for a good reason. What if, one day, people find there is no reason to travel? Access and envy are the twin enemies of local autonomy and indigenous integrity. In these areas, Africa can both teach and learn.

With difficulty in the darkness, the captain traced shore for a kilometre before finding a grassless opening. The boat grounded. Only then did a flashlight appear. A dried and withered embankment was our camp.

It was dead quiet. Robert started a fire for warmth and cooking. He blew the flame around twigs and branches deposited by the river, dried by the sun, and collected by Anke and I. The boatman, meanwhile, moved away from us. He knelt facing east toward Mecca, and we heard his prayers.

There was no strategy or method to setting up camp. Robert and Anke announced that they'd sleep on the boat. I pulled a ground sheet from my pack, took my sleeping bag under my arm, stepped off the boat, and splashed into the river, filling my boots with a swirl of mud and water. The captain tossed mattresses from the boat's benches to the shore. Ona took one, Jose another. A hexagon of mats formed around the bright fire.

It soon became cold, and I moved near the fire. I looked in the pot as the captain lifted the lid. A fish head was on a slow boil. Often, say with fish head over rice, I found it easier to eat in the dark.

The next morning we awoke to the clatter of dishes being washed in the river. The African lady travelling with us had chosen to sleep far away from us, as though we'd mind her being near. Did she eat? I could not tell; she had spent the night without the warmth of fire or companionship. I wondered what she thought about crocodiles.

That day was the *African Queen* day. We travelled the Niger Delta, as our river's great inland lake is known — little coves, wide and narrow channels, and a maze of island-riddled waterways. Here, the Niger was so broad it swallowed perspective.

"Europeans live for tomorrow," Robert said as we set off, continuing his river-borne philosophizing. "Africans live for today." It was too much of a generalization, but struck the right juxtaposition of a possession-needy Western society with one that struggled for sustenance. Cattle and horses stood motionless on the riverbank. Fields stretched against the sun. Irrigation ditches were dry, their foreign-gifted pumps silent.

Most Malians rely on the River Niger, and live close to it. Thirty kilometres wide here, the river that day was indeed a lake: Lake Débo. Murky channels entered and left it; fish places. We sidled next to a *pirogue*, its fish held high in promotion. The captain steered our boat away in a bargaining ploy. Offered a lower price, he returned. "Not just the head," I pleaded, knowing it would be boiled for lunch.

One village seemed deserted as we approached. Low piles of rubble lay along the riverbank. After the first grouping of foundations, the walls became taller but were still incomplete. They were not being built; they were crumbling. But newer walls were being added on the other side of this small place: it became apparent to us that the village was evolving along the shore. It was shedding its architectural skin, leaving behind the old and starting anew. A spot of fire flickered behind a rubble pile in this ghost village. Then another, stimulated by need and time of day.

A *pirogue* sailed by, its jib made from used sackcloths sewn together and tied to the mast with baobab rope. The boat's cargo of firewood balanced precariously over its sides.

In the high water of a later season, the River Niger's Lake Débo would be forty kilometres wide. That day, we crossed thirty, boating for hours in its marshes and in a narrow river channel with banks that quietly left the water, moved upward a metre and grew thick with grass, spindly shoots, and white flowers. Two trees appeared, their branches loaded with nests, more than fifty to a tree, and birds darted in and out of the commune.

This seemed to be a prosperous and healthy part of Mali, with villages that seemed, from the river, to be cared for and comfortable. It was the first place we saw fishing boxes, which were like lobster traps. The tributaries of the river flowed into the Niger through tidy mesh screens. Fish were ample, and the fishermen tending the work were young; the elders appeared to be contented overseers. Black ducks, herons with arrow-straight bodies, and kingfishers with much to feast on were everywhere.

The children and grownups teased us for gifts, for welcome, for a chance to chat. I began to see that the more frequently visited a village was, the more aggressive its children. The visitor shifts from guest to prey.

The African woman on our boat sat idle. She was surprised but almost smiled when Ona offered her a handful of peanuts. Our lunch consisted of fish boiled slowly past the quivering stage, and it was provided to those who had paid. It was not given to this woman until Ona indicated that she must be fed. Although sharing was natural among the Malians, it was not presumed to be a trait of paying Europeans and North Americans. Captain Nanaga shared his oranges, and she too received one.

We neared Mopti, the river's major port of call, at dusk. First, a nice village with a tinker-toy mosque appeared on shore. Its prosperity was evident in the mud's colour, rich and dark. The soil was better here than in the other places we had visited.

Soon Mopti came into view. Zak and Nema were delighted with our arrival and bounded onto the shore's boulders in the dark. They shouted commands at one another in rapid Bambara, oblivious to the captain's directives on where to tie up the *pinasse*. Their teamwork pulled the boat around the rocks, and, as I admired their skills, I was thankful that the two of them would be with me throughout the coming ten days. They held the *pinasse* tight and teetering as the six of us prepared to disembark for the last time.

"Packs," Zak ordered, and we passed them from one person to the next along the *pinasse* and eventually over the side of the boat and into his hands. Nema grabbed at them immediately and tossed each into a pile in the mud by the river's edge. The captain steadied the boat, its engine thumping loudly as he kept it edged into the rocks.

"Netherlands," Zak said by way of indicating who should disembark first. He helped each passenger step off the boat onto the jagged boulders and over toward their packs.

"Welcome, Mopti," Nema said as Zak shifted my landing her way. She balanced my arrival with arms much stronger than Zak's and rubbed my back in greeting.

Zak and Nema were staying in a hotel across town but would first walk Anke, Robert, and me to our hotel a kilometre away. Ona and Jose hugged us and went to find a hotel of low repute. They wished me well: "Have a safe hike, *Eric*." Tomorrow, with Zak as my guide and Nema as cook, I would leave for *Le Pays Dogon*. Odd to need three people on a solo trip, but I knew I couldn't do it without them.

Zak and I walked from the Niger on a path that wanted to be a road, a path that ran through a neighbourhood of homes and stores darkened after bedtime. On an even less walkable street was a light and, when we got beneath it, a sign for the Hôtel Le Fleuve. An entrance yard, behind a high wall, had three tables. Two were empty, and, at the third, a boisterous group listened to a domineering Malian who was buying their beer.

"*Allemagne?*" a gruff, friendly voice shouted my way. Why do so many people think I'm German, I wondered.

"No," I replied.

"Ahh, *Anglais?*"

"No sir," I said to the burly man ordering the beer.

"Ahh, *Americaine!*"

"Not!" I said firmly.

He was puzzled, his face blank. I told him.

He boasted, "I am the big chief of the ferry boats on the River Niger."

"Comanav?" I questioned, giving the company name.

He was happy to be recognized. "The *Kankou Moussa*, the *Général Soumare*, and the *Tombouctou*." Sharply he listed the three steamers the company ran, one of which was reliably out of service at any given time, while the other two were known for their unpredictable departure and arrival schedules.

"I've heard good things," I lied. His company, Comanav, is known for its boats, which attract many stories, most concerning their famous lack of both amenities and predictability.

I completed my check-in at the twelve-room hotel and was well up the stairs, across a landing, down a sectioned corridor and three metres from the solitude of my room when I heard my name.

"*Rick*, the captain asked me to get you," Zak announced as he appeared from a stairway.

"Later is fine," I suggested, and kept walking.

"He wants to give you money."

"Now works," I said. And I turned to go with him.

"Is that Dutch women gave him money to go on boat. You paid most. He will give you some," Zak told me as we tramped over to see the *pinasse* captain.

Captain Nanaga was attired in jeans and a fresh T-shirt and he sat with Nema, the hotel's night clerk, and the neighbourhood layabouts. His youth showed in his enthusiasm to share money. I thought, wait till Mohammed hears of this. "Don't tell Mohammed," I said to Zak.

The captain held out a handful of crumpled U. S. dollars, two hundred in all. He was untainted by malice, without any ulterior motive. Before Zak could translate his willingness to share, Nema bolted into the conversation: "You get fifty. He gets the rest."

Zak proposed, "One hundred each is fair."

"Too much," Nema barked. Her prettiness was rapidly fading.

"What does the captain think?" I asked.

"He keeps one hundred and fifty dollars," Nema said, her words a pounce from a sitting position.

"Nema," I said sternly. "Back off. This is not your deal."

I was to blame for what happened next.

Recalling what I thought was a friendship, I smiled and walked to Nema's plastic chair, pulling on the arm to demonstrate her removal. All in whimsy. She only needed a pause button and she'd be welcome to stay. The arm cracked off the chair.

"Ten dollars at market," said the night clerk, dismayed at the split chair.

I wanted a cold beer and patio conversation with the Comanav guy, not this.

"Ten dollars at market," echoed the ever-helpful Nema.

"It'd be nice if you'd shut up," I told her.

"*Rick,*" said Zak anxiously, "the captain. What to do?"

"I'll tell you what, Captain." Zak conveyed my words in Bambara as my eyes silenced Nema. "A hundred each. Found money for both of us." The captain watched as I shuffled the bills in his hand, and smiled with what I left him. We shook hands. It was the first time I felt I'd got the best of a deal in this country. I gave five to the clerk for the broken chair. (I will forfeit money, but not pride.) "Good night," I bid the gathering, and almost tripped over Nema's frown as I left.

The night was now mine, all alone. In the sparse room I repacked my bags for the Dogon trek, trimming my load to the traveller's necessities of health and protection. In the first mirror I'd looked at in two weeks, I noticed my chubby cheeks had disappeared. I made a successful search for the missing toilet seat. Even cracked and broken, it would do — I knew it was the last one I'd see for ten days. I twisted the shower knob and was about to jump under the slow drizzle when there was a knock at the door. I figured it must be Zak. I flung it open, wearing nothing but three-day-old dusty underwear. And there stood the beautiful Anke.

"Come on over, we've got cold beer. Robert ordered chicken."

Following her, I stumbled near-naked down the hallway, trying to pull on my pants. We rounded the veranda. Robert was waiting for food and talking with a slim Australian whose face narrowed from the top of his shoulders toward short brown hair that probably curled when it hadn't been in the desert forever.

"Alistair," he said, his hand extended, his smile conveying a wistful confidence.

Robert's food arrived, and he announced: "Alistair rode a camel to Taoudenni."

Alistair acknowledged the accomplishment. "And back."

That place name stands alone. Taoudenni. If Timbuktu describes out-of-the-way, Taoudenni was beyond such definition.

"How many weeks?" I asked in disbelief.

"Thirty-five days in all."

I parroted to Alistair what I'd heard from two Britons I'd met in Leningrad, decades ago, after they had stepped off a train on the Trans Siberian Railway: "You'd be a fool not to do that once in your life, I guess." Smiling into Alistair's calm disposition, I added their admonition: "And a bloody fool to do it twice."

He nodded, absorbing my unsolicited evaluation. "It was the third time I'd made the trip."

This was travel at its hardest. I had to ask. "What if your guide died?"

"Right," he said, acknowledging that I'd asked a worthy question.

The sailor and slave Robert Adams visited what he called "Taudeny," and his 1814 narrative provided one of the earliest European descriptions of these mines, which were created around 1600. Until then, Westerners were uncertain where the salt that came from North Africa was mined. René Caillié travelled there with the caravan that he'd chased from Timbuktu and then travelled northward as he made his secretive journey's last stretch. Today, the caravans that cover this vastness consist of thirty camels, not the thousands of earlier times, loaded with salt slabs coming south.

There are no trading routes in the desert that compare to travelling from Timbuktu to Taoudenni in the north. It is a dangerous trek, and few attempt it. If there's a "season" to travel, it is from September to April. Each way is a meandering 750 kilometres.

Anke took four beers from the waiter and twisted open the bottle caps as she handed each of us our refreshment. We gulped the welcome brew and settled back with a "tell us" look.

Alistair continued his account. "Taoudenni is set on a plain where a lake that dried out long ago left alternating layers of silt and salt. It's surrounded by volcanic cones and rocky outcrops. There is no town, not even a shop. Taoudenni is not a fixed place;

it creeps across the dry lake bed as the salt is successively exhausted. Ragged shacks, made of mine waste and corrugated iron, move with the mine. The water available near Taoudenni is only suitable for camels. Potable water for the miners is a three-day camel ride away."

It seemed like a place and activity without benefit, even when he added, "Oh, and the miners have first dibs at the camel dung supply, as there is no other fuel available." Fewer than a hundred and fifty people at the mines scrape together an income.

Alistair's experience made his knowledge encyclopedic: each mine is operated by two to four people, is the size of a large room in a house, and ends up being three to four metres deep. Only picks, shovels, baskets, and bare hands are used to remove the rubble and reach the layers of salt, the first of which is about a metre below the surface. A slab of salt is ten to fifteen centimetres thick, one-and-a-half metres long and three quarters of a metre wide. The salt is trimmed of the exterior dry clay and dirt by pick, leaving a four-centimetre thick slab weighing thirty-five kilograms or more. This is now ready for the caravan.

Anke-the-direct asked, "What did you wear?"

"A *bou-bou*, the traditional sky-blue robe, and a *houli*, the length of cloth for a turban. I was assured that the camels preferred me to dress this way."

During the desert story, Anke and Robert left, preoccupied with an early morning departure. We hugged our parting thoughts instead of saying them.

Alistair had had a lot of time to think while travelling in the "vast nothingness" of the Sahara. He continued: there are two grades of salt, one for human consumption, the other animal grade. The blocks are worth about three U. S. dollars, perhaps four, per slab in Taoudenni, but their value increases to about twelve dollars in Timbuktu. The trip takes longer going south because the heavy salt must be reloaded onto the camels each morning.

I became tired as the story went on for two hours. It was clearly also a drain on Alistair, who'd had little conversation for so long.

"On the last night of the journey south we could finally see a blinking red light on the transmission mast in Timbuktu. Ahmed and I rose after the rest of the caravan had departed at the usual 2:30 a.m. We loaded the salt onto his five camels for the last time, and the two of us moved off toward the red light. As we made our way along the sandy tracks, I practised the few words of Arabic I'd learnt and Ahmed practised his English. At dawn we pulled to the edge of town, where the salt was unloaded and the rhythm of caravan life came to an end. As soon as the town's markets and shops opened, the camels were gone. I went to a hotel, had my first shower and shave in five weeks. Then I visited a café and had coffee, baguette, and a cheese omelette. Heaven."

Mopti's morning began early as market sellers and traders clanged their way to work. My waking thoughts focused on those travellers I've seen along the way who had packed carelessly. Maybe a duffel bag or loose packs, as though packing were an afterthought. Some carried tents at their side, boots dangling, sleeping gear flopping.

My own large pack was now restuffed. I jettisoned once-thought-to-be-necessities to lighten my trek in the Dogon. Camera, first aid kit, sleeping bag, sandals, and my last granola bars were stuffed into a pillow bag and empty tent case. It was all I needed, no more. I fixed a thick metal cable around the orange backpack, wrapped the zippers with duct tape, and prepared to leave it behind for ten days. I felt refreshed by the whispering shower, the sense of adventure, and the invigorating start to the day.

Anke had sliced a baguette and was spreading red jelly across it as I walked onto the balcony for breakfast. I was surprised to see her and Robert still there. Robert smiled nervously and raised his milky drink to me, tilting the glass with the angle of his head, and I realized something was amiss. Silence had decended on the veranda. Slowly, Anke voiced her frustration. Mohammed had not arranged the promised ride to Bamako. She fumed: "He promised. And again, he broke his promise."

As if on cue, Mohammed pulled up in a car with a driver. We heard him climb the stairs to the veranda with harder stepping sounds than his light weight would normally have made. He landed with a heavy step onto our deck, overlooking Mopti's low-rising skyline. He ignored Anke's scorn as he leaned against the balcony railing. "This not look good," Robert mumbled so that only I could hear.

As Mohammed stretched a muscle, Robert tried a light opening to conversation. "Bad bed?" he asked.

"I drove all night. Bamako to Ségou to Mopti," Mohammed whined. The villain's overture.

Anke did not offer the sympathy he sought. "Where is our car to Bamako?"

"There is a bus," he replied.

"Our plane leaves today."

"You'll make it by bus," Mohammed stated.

"You screwed us," Anke spit.

"Don't say I screwed you."

"That is true. You screwed us." It's been said that the first person to hurl an insult instead of a spear was the founder of modern civilization. Anke was in their lineage.

Mohammed spurned her. "You changed your plans."

"Bullshit. We bought Bamako to Essakane to Bamako," she said.

Mohammed sulked as he did when proved wrong. He sulked often.

Anke strode across the balcony and down the stairs like a mad butterfly. Robert built a verbal bridge: "That's her mood." I saw in him the peacemaker that was in me. Also a middle child? Over the railing we watched a Peugeot pull up; it was their ride to the bus.

"You paid the airline, not me, for the ride," Mohammed said to the ground below, where Anke walked away.

She shunned him. Nothing could be done. She closed their relationship. "I say no more."

Robert shouldered his pack, and we walked down the stairs. Anke was in the distance. "Now we have also to pay for the hotel," he sighed. Exasperation, Mohammed-style. Robert and I clasped hands and shook. It had been good.

Anke slipped through the door into the car. Last words: "Rick, goodbye. Sorry. We'll e-mail." And then she was gone.

Robert let go of my hand, shifted his backpack to settle it on his shoulders, and walked away.

Mohammed, standing near me, groaned as the Peugeot disappeared. "They changed their plans," he asserted when they were no longer within earshot. He had a tone of voice that could ask you to pass the salt and make you feel like he questioned your parentage.

What to say, if anything? "Mohammed, I can't even sort out my own plans with you. I won't try to fix another's."

He shaped his mouth but not his heart into a smile. "You sent me a note."

He owed me money and he knew it. "Yes," I confirmed. The note recapped our Timbuktu talk. "I have to trust you, Mohammed. Prepare the list of actual costs that you promised. If I did not advance enough money, I'll pay you more." We both knew this was not the case. "If I advanced you too much, you reimburse me."

"I will."

"Don't screw this up, Mohammed."

Anke's anger was still reflected in his eyes. Two wrongs in a morning. It was his style; he lived here and would outlast our comings and goings. It's been noted that every successful company needs three personalities: a visionary, a people person, and an SOB about the money. He lacked the cunning for the first and the disposition for the second; but Mohammed was his company's SOB.

Back on the dirt road, after Anke's dust had settled, we shifted and reshifted packs and people as though in morning prayers. Only four of us were going in the vehicle, so the work seemed without purpose. The garrulous Mamadou would drive; it was good to see him again. His effusive hand-batting renewed our camaraderie. Others laughed their happiness at the Mali rap greeting.

Mohammed, still in need of a friend, unnecessarily asked, "To the Dogon?"

I repeated, knowing his promised recalculations, "For ten days."

He pumped my hand and my hopes dimmed. I said: "See you in Ségou on the twenty-sixth. For an hour."

Mamadou and I drove in the dust to the hovel where Zak and Nema had stayed the night. Looking groggy, they sauntered toward the vehicle, tossed their packs into the trunk, and settled into the backseat. We stopped at a market stall for canned peas and bottled water, and pushed slowly through the busy street traffic, mostly people on errands.

Drive-through banking was invented in Mali. In need of *seffe*, I made arrangements through Zak as we motored across town. The car crept into a shop fronted with sacks of millet, stacked cooking pots, and a long row of spatulas. The low roof gave shade, but the air felt crusty. A hundred U.S. dollars from my money belt rested on the counter as the wizened merchant flipped open several wooden drawers. From each, he removed handfuls of bills. A quick count. He shuffled them my way. A fair exchange, and we drove on through.

Out of town, Mamadou drove along the Bani River until it ended, beside Sahel fields where women sifted grain. Mali is a nation of powerful shoulders, made strong by pounding millet, grinding cereal, hacking baobab trees.

EIGHT

African Lanterns

THE ROAD WE DROVE TO BANDIAGARA WAS PAVED. It wound gently and had only one hill, a 7 percent incline. I felt optimistic about my future. At that stage of the trip, as though it were mid-life, I saw my preparations and quest in context: the river had changed me and my travels. Ahead, without a problem in sight, lay the future. I couldn't wait.

We did not make the hill.

The vehicle's clutch gave, and, nurse it as he might, Mamadou could not crest the hill's summit, which was visible a half kilometre away. It was high noon. We were sixty kilometres from Mopti, still thirty-five from Bandiagara.

I abandoned our vehicle and traipsed alone over the hill as the others debated our dilemma in Bambara. In the next hour, one vehicle passed in each direction. The plateau had extraordinary rock formations, house-sized boulders that were tapered at their base so they appeared to be precariously balanced. One massive stone had been carved out by wind and water, creating a cave that a train could have passed through.

I returned to our vehicle, and as I neared it the traffic increased: a man pushed his bicycle, two grain sacks strapped to its fender, up the hill to its crest, where he could pedal again; five carts, two of which sported the luxury of double donkeys, made the hill laden with sacks of coal, a petrol can, firewood, and pots for sale. Then the traffic jam was over.

As Malians seemed to do in periods of transit uncertainty, they had unloaded the packs from my vehicle on the roadside, perhaps to mark the calamity.

"*Wrick,*" said Mamadou, offering a defeated smile in greeting, and keeping his hands in the trouser pockets.

"*Rick,*" said Zak, laughing despite his concern about my well-being.

"*C'est la vie,*" I replied.

Remarkably, Mamadou's cellphone worked. He had purchased a time card for the two minutes needed, no more. It was another hour before a second car arrived and three men got out, a frustrated Mohammed among them. They had parked on the roadside, not far from where I lay against a rock. Mohammed, who may have thought he'd seen the last of me, looked disturbed at having to acknowledge my presence. "Rick," he smirked.

I tipped what I could of the broad hat brim from where I reposed, the back of my head pinning the hat to the rock. "Afternoon, Mohammed." We were now formally estranged. He walked out of my sight and out of mind.

There were six Malians, enough for a solution. It was in this other vehicle that we left an hour later, eventually arriving in bustling Bandiagara. There, we provisioned more cans of peas, hard-capped water bottles, sleeves of pasta, and soon-to-be-stale bread from the market.

We pressed on through countryside with bush bordering much of the dirt road. This was the preferred route into Dogon, even for travellers from Burkina Faso, from where Dogon trekkers often arrived. We sped past a woman on foot, undoubtedly walking at her regular speed, and I wondered what she made of our progress. She moved slowly; we passed quickly — did she envy us?

A group of boys, a dozen strong and aged perhaps ten to thirteen, waved from the roadside. They chanted to the slapped beat of hand-held *calabash*. The bowls were gouged from dried gourds, used or broken and no longer filled with wooden pieces as noisemakers.

"Why?" I asked.

"They are in second season, you know?" replied Zak.

"School?"

"No, before marriage. Circumcision. They stay out of village one month. Do you want to see circumcision paintings?"

"Why?" I did not see the connection.

"They have a special home for these boys. To learn. For transfer to manhood."

We slowed and Zak gave them money, a poor man helping poorer boys. "They make asking," he said. "All who pass make a gift."

"Marriage?" I was confused.

"They are not ready for marriage," Zak said. "That, for me, may be early twenties; for women, late teens. Men, if in school, often wait. Women are needed at their homes for work." That was the complete explanation.

Then we came to a stop at Djiguibombo, where an intrepid Zak, a reticent Nema, and an eager Rick would begin the long trek on foot. When Mamadou and his car disappeared in swirls of dust, we were on a rocky road that narrowed even more, discouraging use by other vehicles; it wanted to be left alone, as people on foot were more welcome in the Dogon. We hoisted our packs and walked through the village gate into a courtyard. It sprawled wide and was rimmed with stone buildings patched with mud. In the centre was a high structure of dead tree branches, open to the air, braced with twisted metal and loosely covered with thatch.

I found my pipe, tamped in some tobacco and lit it. I smoked in the hot shade, sitting on a chair of slivers smoothed by other bottoms, and spent the afternoon with the village men. A man next to me watched me puff. Then he lit a thin pipe of his own, tamped its small bowl, lit it again, and spoke to me in Bambara. We shook hands often. I nodded in concurrence with whatever he said, as it seemed the thing to do. There was no telling what views we shared or whether I had bought the village tart. He handed me a pinch of his tobacco. In trade, I gave him premium London cuts and got from him a mixture of harsh grinds that, when lit, almost yanked my tongue from my mouth.

The various generations of Malians grow old together, their gatherings synchronized by day and activity. A man of wizened hair and disposition cradled a young girl in a red garment that was laced with blue lines. Smoke curled from his pipe and above her head. His finger rings were silver, hers gold.

Half a dozen men, mostly older, lounged at a game of Wale — "Wally," Zak called it — which was played by two men and directed by the rest. Stones in five divots beside a board were chosen from an initial handful of four gleaned from a wrapped cloth. The game resolved down to empty holes, and the first there was a victor. I could determine no more about the game. When I initially asked Zak in French to name it, he spelled out the village name. I knew then that I must work on my communications.

Nema removed a pouch and a can from Zak's backpack and was gone. She returned with mangos, and demanded my knife, which, when offered, she instructed me to use as a peeler. When she was ready, which had no relationship to anyone's timing but her own, she returned and spooned slippery penne pasta onto three plates. The sauce tasted buttery. She then brought a flat pan of steaming meat accented by a thick sauce made with bouillon cubes. Nema took my knife from my hand with a simple command: "*Reek*, give," then sliced green mango atop the red sauce presentation. Before taking a bite, I mentally thanked Dennis for his recommendation of a cook and, as a backup, said a quick blessing for the health of the meal.

Into the courtyard stumbled a man wearing handcuffs. A metal bracelet shackled his left wrist. The other wrist was clamped, too, but with a slider along a half-metre-long metal rod. He scrounged a cigarette from Zak and talked his way past Nema. "They say he became mad," Nema explained. I wondered whether the manacles were meant to protect him or others. He sat down beside me, and I lit his cigarette. He flicked a finger off his thumb and decapped the flaming match-head, then moved my plate of food and fork away from me and onto his lap. He reached over to scoop more sauce from the pan. Between mouthfuls of dripping pasta, he smoked in long, swallowing drags.

Stretching from an afternoon nap, I saw Zak staring with one eye, asleep with the other, and called his name twice to get his attention.

"I was just between thinks," he said.

"Zak, let's walk in the village." He was more asleep than I had realized and took a while to answer.

Granaries are the most distinctive aspect of Dogon villages along the Bandiagara escarpment and are used to store all manner of things: jewellery, clothing and, of course, millet.

"You'll see many Dogon villages — Kani-Kombolé, Teli, all smaller than this."

I began to walk on my own; Zak relented and caught up.

There were paths, not streets, bordered by stacked rocks or a house wall to give the route definition. Zak and I walked in silence, each still waking to the afternoon, when he pointed to a low-roofed building without walls and called it the *Togu-na.*

"The elders meet there to talk of problems, and about fellow villagers. Gossip." He smiled. "Every village has a *Togu-na*, it is social centre. Only men." He explained the significance of the carved support posts that hold the roof. "In Dogon, we have ancestors, eight main, and that is why eight pillars."

In most every yard, stone-based buildings were set apart, impracticably thin and characterized by peaks of thatch that married the design of European castles and African roofs. "Granaries," Zak replied to my question. "Animals can't get up the rocks to the millet. They are divided inside for different types of storage."

"All grains?"

"Mostly. Each woman has her own and might put there what she wishes not to have in the house. Maybe jewellery."

When I lifted my hat off, the air was cool on my sweaty head. I sat down on some rocks across from a round house. Zak called it by its French name, *Maison des regles*, which is where menstruating women retreat, receive health attention, and stay away from daily village life. "It is respect for their potential as mothers."

"There is always a system to setting a village," Zak said. He chose a thick stick and sketched a diagram in the ground saying, "A picture speaks paintings."

I listened as he outlined in the dirt and then used his body as a village map. "Even when on a hill," he said, touching his stomach, "the layout is like a body. This," he said, pointing to the *Maison des regles*, "is a hand, and if two, they are west and east. The *Togu-na* for elders is here," he tapped his head. "There is where we have an altar, where our forefathers are remembered. It is called *ginna bana*." Zak breathed audibly, saying it reflected the founders, then put his hand to his chest, indicating where in the village this would be found. He called it "start of life."

Time has worn a human path in the Dogon for nearly two millennia. My days there seemed the true goal of my sojourn, the pinnacle. Not the train, not Timbuktu, not the River Niger; for those I had expectations and ambitions. In *Le Pays Dogon*, I had none of those encumbrances.

On the dusty road, half a kilometre from Djiguibombo, a friend of Zak's showed up on a motorbike. They talked; I listened. There was no hurry. Soon, the man left with Nema, whom he'd never met before but who clearly welcomed the longer, but less onerous moped route to that night's camp. On the back of his departing Mobylette, next to Nema, rested the heavy sack of tinned peas and other bulky provisions. Zak and I, left with the hand-helds, strapped them together for our walk, hampered by my earlier decision to bring a large pack for the trip, one that housed all manner of goods but now proved too large for the Dogon trek, and I longed for a smaller, more practical pack.

We made a decision to pack our collective heaviest goods into Zak's proper pack. We'd spell each other off, sharing the load and

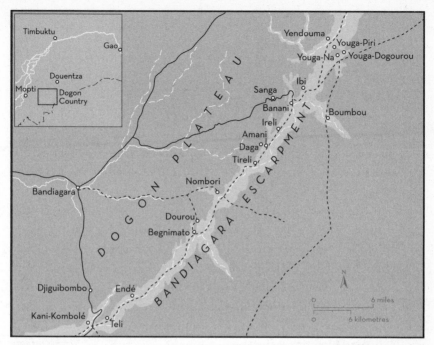

Dogon Country (or more commonly referenced in French as Le Pays Dogon*) includes many villages on the plain or plateau along the two-hundred-kilometre escarpment that abuts the Gondo Plain.*

responsibility. I agreed to carry this large pack for the first few days of our trek in the desert, up and down the rocky terrain.

The Bandiagara escarpment, two hundred kilometres long and three hundred and fifty metres high, is the much-appreciated source of shade, the territory of cliff dwellers, and the base of a sculpted sandstone plateau.

The trail, which was followed by nose rather than decipherable signs, slipped off the road. It was Zak's land, and I followed him into the wilderness.

The plateau is exposed rock on high land and commanding in its seemingly endless expanse. Much of what we used for footholds on the kilometres-long descent into the canyon was large rock, boulder upon boulder, hewn by the elements, and scattered in a disarray that made sure footing a difficult task.

I had a happy sense of being, enjoying the open country, the ensuing days and nights, the strain of muscle and awkwardness of pain. In Dogon, I found much to please me.

Atop large sandstone rocks that had broken loose from the cliffside, I saw for the first time the Gondo Plain, an immense space of great intensity. It was my first long look at the escarpment's expanse. *"Rick,"* Zak said tightly, then poetically, *"le falaise."*

"Zak," I said in a similar tone, *"the what?"*

"Is French word. You say you want learn French. *Falaise.*"

"It means?"

"Escarpment," said Zak. "This Dogon Escarpment. *Falaise.*"

My clicking of film was, I knew, futile. Nothing would capture the grandeur that is that place. I framed one picture to show a rock formed like bread slices, half a loaf in volume, each ten metres tall and a metre thick. They fell open as they would on a serving plate.

I was glad for the pleasant fit of good boots. Their ankle bracing was crucial to a safe descent of the steep hill, and fundamental to my safety and comfort. They were just-right snug, soft in the toe, and I expected them to see me through many a climb and descent over the coming week.

Zak turned sharply on the trail and I followed. My right foot swung wide and stubbed hard against the cliff's stone. It stung and I knew instantly that I'd split a toenail. Blood warmed the sock inside my boot. It took two hours of careful step upon hesitant foothold, handgrips when available — which was seldom — before we descended. The pain in my right foot meant that I tried to use its heel whenever I could, lessening the pressure on the ball of my boot to keep my cut toe from jamming.

The plain began where the canyon emptied out onto the rock-strewn trail. Furrows of thin earth breached the land we walked on. A bicycle bell rang behind me. A lad not more than nine years old was pushing hard on each pedal, grinding sand. His bike carried a heavy sack across a back wheel brace we called a "rat trap" when I was his age. Sand sucked his tires down, but he did not complain.

He passed us with determination, and the bike wavered. Five minutes later, we approached as he propped his fallen bicycle upright and then wrapped his thin arms around the giant sack that had slipped off the bike. It outweighed him, yet there was not a wink of resentment in that boy. It was his task and he would do it. He lifted his quarry and was laying it across the carrier as we neared him. The bike shifted and he stopped its tilting with his leg. The bag slipped but did not fall. I offered my leg as a fulcrum. He mounted the bike, grinned *"Merci,"* and successfully pumped the pedals to force the wheels to churn through the slippery sand.

The chattering of a nearby community greeted us near Kani-Kombolé, where we found a *campement.* Could one feel more welcome? I thought not. It was dark when we arrived and a fire backlit two men who were seated near the entrance of the camp. We were to meet Nema here, delivered from the backseat of the moped.

Flashlights revealed the warmth of lashed-wood chairs and blanket-covered tables. Toehold steps were carved in a log that leaned against the mud home and led to the roof above. There I would sleep in the open, beneath the stars.

Someone brought me a bottle of orange Fanta. It was decently cool, soothing the throbbing pain in my foot. My swollen, bleeding toe had started to outgrow the space available in my boot.

In the shadows, a young couple from France was silhouetted in the corner behind a table and on chairs they surely wished would be comfortable. Quiet, content with being together, they shared a dinner plate.

Suddenly, Nema appeared. She grabbed the collar of my outer shirt and the neck of my T-shirt. She tugged these two layers of clothes off my back. *"Reek.* I wash." I relinquished them as ordered. There was a contented smile on her face; the motorcycle ride had been good for her. She stepped back into the night, black into black. She motioned for more clothes but I declined to strip bare. "Please." She was demanding, "Ruin shorts," she warned of another day's wear. I gave in and handed them over, along with my bloodied sock. Nema was kind and efficient, and irreversibly straightforward. It seemed to me inappropriate to be buck naked before this beautiful woman in the camp's candlelight. She took a swig from my Fanta bottle before she disappeared. I sat in the warm darkness, waiting in my underwear.

The bath was Dogon traditional, a large, mud-walled room without a roof. It was next to, and barely separate from, the toilet hole. The arch was low and the door was constructed of vertical sticks woven with rope. I picked it up, placed it across the doorway for privacy, and parked my boots. I knew this bathing ritual well from my travels in Japan, where you sit on a stool in front of a bucket of water before taking a dip in the hot springs. Here, only the bucket was provided, with a plastic cup floating in it. Bring your own soap, towel, patience, and dexterity, and a refreshing shower-bath resulted. Leaning against the mud, I coated my washed toe with an antibiotic cream and slipped my feet into sandals, strapped them tight and realized that these would be my walking shoes for the next nine days.

When I left the bath, no one was visible. It was so dark, so quiet, you could hear your thoughts. My small flashlight, I now realized, was worth its weight in gold, as I wound back to my chair and rickety table by its amber help. A man who I'd not noticed previously placed an African lantern on my table and lit the wick with a match. Its glow was rich with shadow lines and stories. I listened to the snippets of conversation that began to emerge from the darkness.

It was as though I were listening to a radio program or sitting at the side of a stage, unnoticed. Rapidly, then more slowly, conversations erupted and subsided in Bambara. Here there was more laughter than in Mopti or Bamako or on the road. It was light and touching and genuine. These people liked one another, and my being there was cause for funny asides and politeness — but generally I was irrelevant.

A candle invites sitting. People brought chairs and set them around my lantern. They told stories none of us needed to know. Self-centred Western self-awareness was not even a curiosity to them. Nothing there was indifferent — not the multi-touch greetings, not the high-pulled pouring of tea, not one smile. These villagers meant to be doing what they were doing, and they were content. How often can a Westerner claim that?

I was raised in a family where you ate what was put in front of you. That training had prepared me for Nema. She waited at the end of the table where I was writing, holding a metal bowl covered with a plate. Both steamed. She ladled potatoes that had been lightly fried in lard from God-knows where. Over this she set two pieces of chicken cooked in a sauce of green herbs and tomatoes, which had flavoured, if not softened, the meat. She dribbled the sauce evenly over the chicken and spuds. Grease pooled to the side. She was as pleased as I was cautious. "Eat, *Reek*."

Zak looked on as I finished Nema's meal, pleased at the start of the trip. I belched. "Good groceries," I said.

"Groceries?" Zak asked, the concept a Western conceit.

The tea ritual followed the meal. The tea was green in the lantern's light and was served to me in a glass that had just been sipped from by a Malian nearby. "Tea." I was motioned to accept the offering. It was a prescription, not a question. A man with seasoned hands and a liberal smile held a platter with three cups, into which he poured slowly. He stretched the pot from a low in-the-cup start to reach high — it seemed half a metre away — to release the flavour. It left a foamy head. He did not spill. They *always* got that right.

"Tart," I muttered, finishing. Zak was next. The tea was served in a sequence of three on the spot, as among the Tuareg, each serving with the long curled arch from the spout.

"In Dogon, the meaning is different than in the Sahara. Here, the first is bitter as death," said Zak.

"I just tasted that," I responded.

"The second is soft as life," he said warmheartedly. Nothing is without reason. "The third is sweet as love."

They left the pot after that. The longer it cooled, the sweeter it became. There was no reticence about having a fourth.

In the calm that followed, I opened my pocket knife and sharpened my pencil. The shavings floated to the ground. For nearly an hour I smoked my pipe and relished the soft orange glow of my African lantern. Peace of mind and contentment were my companions, I thought.

My bowels erupted. A gut-loosening sound broke the peace and wind. Was it the mangos? Dishwashing water? Had I been careless? But, in fact, the odds had simply caught up with me: two weeks into the trip — it was my turn to get sick.

In Africa, dehydration is always a risk. But here there was ample water, labelled engagingly as *Tombouctou* and sealed with plastic for reassurance. I downed one bottle, mindful that my evening's sleeping quarters, should nature keep beckoning, meant a repeated acrobatic descent on a nearly invisible post angled in the darkness and notched with tiny footholds. The night resolved itself in my favour.

In Dogon, it is best to sleep on the roof of someone's home. You are not in the way. I climbed the precarious steps. It was too warm to use the sleeping bag for anything other than a ground sheet. On the rooftop across the *campement*, the French couple settled in for their sleep.

Earlier, Zak had looked above us, and seeing no moon, said, "There is no sky tonight." Now, as I settled atop the sleeping bag, a curved sliver showed low on the horizon. There was a sky after all.

The wind was up that night and with it came a cleanness in the air. A prolonged donkey whine, sounding as though it was thrown from behind his temples, woke me. The morning moon was a small crescent. A rooster's cry and the trill of a bird harmonized, and more animals joined in the pocket symphony. It had been this way with the village voices late the night before — a pleasant buzz.

A wristwatch bleated its alarm, and I wondered why one would bring such technology here. There was a brief push of rain. The recorded sound of morning prayers began, scratchily, to play over a loudspeaker. I sat up in my sleeping bag on the roof. On the opposite terrace, a line of rope looped between a treetop and a post to hold the mosquito net that covered the young French couple, curled together in their sleep. Even here, in the land of the exposed breast, a French lace brassiere on the clothesline was a sexy sight.

A donkey's braying was like a tuba clearing the air among the other instruments in the orchestra pit before the real music began. It duelled with a trombone donkey and then fell silent. The village's women lit their home fires, and I rose to the smell of warm bread. Certainly, I was not the first to notice and appreciate it, but I felt as though I was.

Brooms in the skilled hands of women cleared the dirt floors below as I gingerly slipped down the ladder post. They swept the one tidy part of an unkempt country. The streets and public places were cleaner in the Dogon. Less trash, more pride, and a sanitation savvy lacking elsewhere in Mali.

The early morning was enlivened with village mutterings. Nature's statement surged: all was right in this world. I crested toward the village on a teetering mud path that banked on an aging dune. Across the way was a man tending his fire. He was what Zak called "one of the olds." The elder smiled without teeth; it was an invitation. I squatted and warmed my hands around the fire. You travel to see the stories in other people's faces. This man's face told me of hardship, though he grinned; it spoke of wisdom, which I interpreted as patience; it showed knowledge of the past and an acceptance of today as rather special. His smile was the day's punctuation mark.

He picked small twigs from a pile and added them to the fire. His bony fingers tended the kindling to create more heat for me. Mali has a history you cannot quite comprehend, even as you know its facts. Seeing the desert is not understanding it; being in the Dogon explained that waking up with few possessions was not the same as being impoverished. I passed him a few kola nuts — a mild stimulant — from my pocket. His eyes smiled as he accepted them.

Four older women, carrying the morning food, paused to greet me, laugh, and shake my white hand. A man wearing gold-rimmed glasses and with a cloth-covered head walked past me and grinned. Three little boys came and sat with me in silence, whispering to one another and starring at the peculiar man.

Donkey colts played without making a sound, chickens fussed over food, and the goats grazed. Morning had broken; the orchestra was at rest.

We were not far out of Kani-Kombolé, the start of the second day of our trek. I followed Zak on the desert path.

"Zak," I called, and he stopped. I caught up and said, "You're a good guide."

He smiled in his shy way. What I had said was true, and he knew it.

"You can lead from behind," I told him.

"Why?"

Trekking in Dogon Country is often along paths worn wide by donkey carts and by traders making their way to markets, perhaps carrying firewood atop their heads for sale.

"Because I want nothing ahead of me. I need to be alone, Zak. I won't get lost with you behind me." He stood there solemnly as I walked away. In Canada's north, where dogsleds once prevailed and are still used, there is a saying: "If you're not the lead dog, the view never changes." For the rest of the time Zak and I spent together, I enjoyed the advantage.

On the sub-Saharan trail, I bore the heavy pack as we had agreed. I walked with a wide stride as the way was clear and Zak had me in his view. Not unlike my work world, I get to lead so long as others have me in their sight and make sure I don't stray.

I trudged for an hour without looking behind me. When I did, Zak and Nema were quite far back, with two boys sitting on top of a cart hauled behind a donkey, yoked with baobab rope. For once, I wanted them to catch up and pass me. Half an hour later I shifted my heavy pack and looked again. The cart was still with them, and friends of theirs had joined them. When the donkey trotted past me, I realized in a blink what had happened. They had shucked their loads onto the *charette*, and were walking with ease. I ran after it and shed my haversack.

"Once ago," Zak said, "Tellem pygmies settled here." He called these eleventh-century migrants "nomads who found permanent home." They feared the animals that inhabited the plentiful woods that once stabilized the soil and held off the sands. Their defence was to carve caves into crevices high up the cliffs on the escarpment's side. It was heavy work to climb over boulders and pull oneself up the cliff to these dwellings. Because of the shortness of the Tellem people (Zak had earlier asked if I knew the term "pygmies"), they needed ropes, wooden ladders, and each other's help to construct, as well as reach, these homes.

Then, in the fourteenth century the Dogon people arrived, refugees from elsewhere. The first to arrive were farmers, who hunted aggressively to rid the land of predators. The forests, which were once filled with wildlife, were cut for agriculture and firewood by the Dogon and, in time, the Gondo Plain emerged. It now borders the escarpment for its entire length. Villagers no longer feared jackal or hyena attacks, and did not require refuge from predators. They made new homes lower on the land and left the caves, now remote and impractical, except for storage. Most of the Tellem are gone.

Ridding the country of forests, with their ability to store water and sustain an ecosystem, these farmers hastened desertification.

The soil eroded without vegetation or roots to hold it fast. Now, with rearguard thinking, trees are being replanted to drive back the desert. There are tens of thousands of them, a gift to Mali from China.

We walked the difficult *sentier*, Zak's French term for tracks, from the village. Then we climbed over the large rocks to visit Old Teli, well above the present village, and found the hill homes vacant and abandoned. Treasures lay scattered on the ground, not yet scavenged by travellers. A sack rested in a wedge of wood, its tired straps holding a large tin with the faded number "1904" showing through the dust. Upon scrutiny, it was a drum, its leather cracked with age.

I had come to value little things — a firm footing on a sandy walk, washing my mouth with warm water to ease a dry throat, French spoken as a break from Bambara, three branches of shade, even a slight waft of wind, a cool Coca-Cola that I measured in gulp, sip — gulp, sip, sip, sip — and then the last mouthfuls in two glorious swallows.

Tellem villages were built precariously on cliff sides for protection from the wild animals in what were once nearby forests, now disappeared. The deserted remnants of these homes are today accessible with a guide — and exertion.

The joy of the walk with the heavy pack was singular. The path was cushioned by worn grains of sand, too slippery for a foothold, and the steps were difficult. Previous walkers had found this too, and their search for a new path had eroded the berms, packed them down, and left a firmer new trail.

A well and a youngster pulling water came into view. I came near and he smiled. I grabbed the rope between his hands and alternated with his pulls as we drew the heavy rubber sack of water together. I steadied a funnel and the boy filled a plastic container. What water was left in the sack he let me use to wash my face. He laughed at me and I lowered the sack ten metres back down the well, where it sank and filled with water again. Hands over hands, we pulled it up again. I poured some over my head and then handed the sack to him. He filled a trough for the animals, admittedly a more worthy use of the water. I recalled the comment of a friend from Japan, who once told me that in small villages in that country, there is a saying: "When you take a drink of water, stop to thank those who dug the well."

I was far ahead of Zak and knew this not to be particularly good. I trusted that I was on the right path but several options opened before me, each heading in a different direction. No one was in sight. I chose the only tree in view and dropped my pack, eased myself to the ground with it as a prop, and waited patiently for Zak and Nema to catch up.

We never walked at midday. In the early afternoon we found shelter in a small village and dodged the sun. This day we arrived at Endé, with its loose assembly of homes. Immediately a young man brought Nema a live chicken. She held it, scowled by way of negotiating the price, pulled at its wings, and passed it back to the boy. Dejected, he pushed it her way, advancing its qualities in a language I did not know but in a style I recognized. Over to him, back again to her. The chicken squawked its own views in the debate, presumably seeking a reprieve.

We sat down and I asked for a cola. Nema, heading for the cooking area with the chicken she'd purchased, quickly added a *d'jina, jus de pomme.* Thus I learned to run a tab for our threesome whenever we stopped.

During a nap in a shady spot on a cushioned mat in the sand I was awakened by the clatter of plates. The temperature was well over a hundred degrees, a heat that evaporated energy from anyone who moved. Yet a pot, the plates, and a fork were strewn on a nearby table. A listless Nema had transformed a can of vegetables into a feast. It was easier to carry food in your stomach than on your back. Peppers and tomatoes contrasted brightly with the sleepy green of the peas. Nema lifted two pieces of boiled chicken from the pot and laid them on top the bed of off-white rice, flicking her fingers to loosen the food. The peas held suspiciously close together.

Zak, quickly into his, mulled over the first mouthful.

I offered the critique, "This is an old chicken."

Shaking his head, Zak observed, "It's just chicken that had to walk for its food."

Zak was constantly greeting people. Those who walked past me with merely a nod engaged in a detailed exchange with him. It held the lilt of friendship, that I could tell, but the words at first had no meaning to me, almost as though their cadence sent the message, not their literal meaning.

"*Aga po,*" they said to him in greeting.

"*Po,*" Zak replied. This much I could pronounce, and did say, *Po* being fairly easy on my non-linguistic tongue.

Then the banter became warm, never token. I must have heard it a hundred times in those days. It was Dogon, a language like no other. When I was breathless on a mountain path or wanting to be silent while trudging along a market trail, Zak would be involved in this exchange.

"*Aga po.*"

"*Po.*"

"*Seyoma?*" they asked.

"*Séo,*" Zak responded, pronouncing it *seyo.*

"*Gineh Seyom?*"

"*Séo.*"

"*Deh Seyom?*"

"Séo."

"Na Seyom?"

"Séo."

"Ulumo Seyom?"

"Awa, Popo."

And with this final assurance that "Everything's really okay, thank you," the whole exchange was repeated anew, in reverse. Zak, the one who was all answers in the first go, now asked each question in return. There was no short version.

"Hello, how is your work?" Zak asked.

"Fine," was the response.

"How are you?"

"Fine."

"How's the family?"

"Fine."

"How is your father?"

"Fine."

"How is your mother?"

"Fine."

"How are the children?"

"Everything is really okay, thank you."

I relished the *"Séo"* part of this as a gentle exclamation of reassurance. It was never tedious, never abridged. Often this appeared to be the case with strangers, but it was not. Each knew of the other's family, and sometimes the greeting began with a man as we approached his home on the hillside or with a woman toiling in the field. It would finish fifteen metres later, as our trail wound almost out of earshot.

Dusk settled quickly as we made our way up a ravine of steep rocks on a difficult path toward a towering landmark. It was not a trekkers' path; it was the villagers'. They walked here on the way to sell onions or buy coloured cloth, to bring animals for slaughter and tillers to their fields.

A man of Zak's age, his friend, greeted us. Escarpment hospitality dictated that he take my pack and that Zak carry my smaller one. We were in a narrowing box canyon. Two little girls, five years old at most, descended toward us, balancing wide pans of food on their heads. One swivelled to go around me on the tight trail. Her cargo swirled loose and fell over the edge of the container. It all teetered and tumbled to the ground. She did not cry; she bent down and scooped, trying to quickly refill the pan. I shifted to be out of her way and then crouched to help pick the grain from the sand and replenish her load. She did not grouse or seethe. We sifted together and completed the task, and suddenly she and her embarrassment disappeared down the gulch.

The twilight was about to take Zak and Nema from my sight.

The rocky path opened to a long field, well irrigated and green with rice and grass. Zak had stopped to ensure that I was following the thousand rock steps, and then disappeared around a corner once he saw me. All I could see was the fertile field stretched in a bend that entered the rocky hillside, where it stopped and the trail climbed back into the mountain's open rocks, a gorgeous view. The sky darkened, and while my way was easier without a pack, I realized I was separated from both my flashlights.

It was an enjoyable struggle to climb the steepness into the noise I heard above. Zak was there when I pulled myself up by ancient handholds in the rock. Candles greeted me. The village of Begnimato topped the climb, a settlement where we would find food, a rooftop of mud for my bed, and a welcome *douche* of water to wash away the day's sweat, one cup at a time.

We were out of the desert's reach. It was black. After the bucket bath, I scrubbed laundry against a stone to squeeze the dirt out. By the light of an African lantern, I wiped alcohol swabs on my scrapes. Nema moved to a wooden bench to watch. She brought *konjo*, a warm spill of millet beer that was served in a conca shell split in half to the size of a large bowl, passing it across to me after first tilting it to her generous mouth.

Zak returned from another part of the village. "Lamb," he said, shoving poorly wrapped meat across my table to Nema. She left to prepare it, speaking to others as she went by, shaping a dinner of rice, onion, and leaves. Zak found a bottle of cool beer and two dirty cups. The chilling had been done by a refrigerator powered by a solar panel, and I wondered why there were not more of them in

Mali. I poured beer into one of the glasses for Zak and sipped from the bottle. I was learning that travel in the Dogon revolved around food and rest, interspersed with trekking.

There were two travellers talking together nearby. I mistook their speaking Dutch for German, which they corrected upon my asking. Marijke and Renate were on leave from all their usual responsibilities: boyfriends, work, and family. They were in West Africa for seven weeks, and my envy was immediate.

"Burkina Faso was our motivation," said Marijke across her beer at a table for two.

"And we're there in one week," added Renate, talking to Marijke in Dutch and then asking where I'd come from. It was not important to me now to mention Timbuktu, and I mentioned only the River Niger.

"We wished for that, but we have not time," Renate said. "It was to go to Timbuktu, but we had not the extra week." And I wondered what it was that made one destination dear to travellers that other travellers found easy to neglect.

When I headed to bed, I flipped open my wind candle into its protective glass shield. I wanted a light for reading. The village calmed near silence; someone strummed a guitar, not with a twang, but a tremble. Another instrument joined in — a set of jingles, maybe stones in a wooden canister. Then the singing began, and I stood on the rooftop to see where it was coming from. Clustering on the dark hillside where it levelled out above the *campement*, a family was gathered. I watched neighbours walking there and heard a man singing as he climbed down from above, walking a trail I hoped he could see. It was impromptu and I wanted to be a part of it.

I clambered down the post's notches from roof to ground, flashlight in hand. My light caught Marijke and Renate coming from another home, and together we walked up a trail to the music. The villagers found chairs for us, and we were invited to sit beneath the stars, moved from the edge of participation into the circle of singers where we passed an hour surrounded by Dogon innocence.

Later, in the cold of night, we made our way back by flashlight. I'd earlier told them about sleeping on the roof. Before coming to Dogon, they'd been told of the day's heat but not the night's cold and had only slight blankets with which to cover themselves. Having begun by sleeping on their rooftop, the cold forced them indoors, away from the starry canopy.

I woke in the middle of the night, engulfed with new emotions. The sky was both so very far away and clingingly close. A star shot across it; another bolted and disappeared forever. The dark was dry; the wind was lovely. I returned to a comfortable sleep, realizing that you are who you are when you're alone in the dark.

"Nema is sick," Zak said over millet pancakes and powdered coffee, starting our morning on a serious note.

"How sick?" I asked.

"She would like your medicine," he said.

"Only aspirin," I offered, not feeling competent to dispense prescription drugs. We took aspirin to her, and I tilted a bottle against her lips to help her swallow two of the tablets. I pressed the back of my hand to her forehead. Fever. Zak left lemonade, and, as I gave Nema a packet of chicken noodle soup, I saw my hat beside her bed. She'd taken it from me last evening, but this was not the time to retrieve it.

A night's lodging in the Dogon is most likely on the rooftop of a mud home such as this, reached by stepping up notches cut into a narrow pole that leans against the building.

"If she doesn't get better," I asked, "who will be our cook?"

"Don't borrow tomorrow's problem," Zak said matter-of-factly. "She has ride after sleep. Will meet in Dourou for lunch."

I was to learn that Nema never cooked breakfast. Instead, it was nothing to pick three or four *farni* from a pot of bubbling oil where women cooked the dough. A sort of Malian breakfast muffin.

Zak had promised to show me the edge of the escarpment, a short hike from our camp. Now we stood near the brink's two-hundred-metre drop. Zak looked beyond it and said, *"Le neant."*

"I don't know that word, Zak."

"Vast," he explained. "Maybe empty." Then muttered, "The vast empty."

At times the path before me forked, and I needed Zak's decision regarding which way to turn. True to my request that he "lead from behind," Zak often dropped back far. In fact, he often dropped out of sight. On the open plain I often saw him appearing very small in the distance. I waited until he was near enough that I could tell which arm he waved, which fork to take. Then I was off, followed by my leader.

In the hillsides, where Zak's penchant took him and therefore me, I learned to read the trail in the rocks. A series of small boulders at first might seem to block a path, when actually they guided the walker to a lower trail that climbed more suitably. Decades ago, the rocks had been placed to define sections of trail, but rainy-season floods have altered their arrangement and trail repairs were sporadic. This makes them currently of marginal value, and the requirement for an experienced guide more necessary.

I heard Zak's *"Séo,"* as we worked our way up a steep path and heard also the name "Abraham." I listened as the exchange continued for a short while and then stopped.

"*Rick*, you have medicine." The man Zak had greeted put forward a stool for me to sit on and then a pail of water for me to wash with. As he did this, he called to another, who was behind a shack. A wounded farmer limped into view. His leg was badly gashed, apparently by rough metal scything rather than fallen rock. "They ask me your help," Zak said. I had plastic gloves but lacked the inclination to explore the wound. My day pack had proper supplies to ease his pain, if not remedy the gash. Through Zak and sign language I explained the use of anti-bacterial wipes to first clean it, watching as the man began to work on his own leg. It was dirty where he had washed it earlier, before some of the blood had crusted. It would be better to clean and stitch, but that was not a job for today. Once the four-inch cut was semi-clean, I squeezed antibiotic cream onto a small cloth and demonstrated how he should apply it. We did this until the tube was nearly empty, his gash white with medication. I wrapped it with gauze and taped it. Zak translated, "See a doctor," twice — once for the wounded man and once for my own reassurance.

Abraham brought more water for me and I washed my sweating head. When we walked on, he carried our bags to the end of his area, as was the custom.

We met Nema at Dourou. She'd hitched a moped ride there and, while recovering from her illness, seemed to have busied herself with the chore of cooking. She greeted us with lunch.

I hate onions. Nema knew that. The meal was laced with them. With that meal dawned some understanding. What I'd thought were rice fields as we walked were not rice fields at all. We had entered a zone of onions, an odour that would be my companion for days to come. Here, the sprigs and bulbs were pounded into a pulp, and the pulp was formed by hand into lopsided balls that were set to dry. The sun's baking did little to diminish the smell.

"Nema, *sans* onion," I was unsure whether this would establish or settle a rift. It was only one of many attempts. My immediate task became one of weaning Nema from her love of onions in order to accommodate my aversion. This task took the entire trip.

The longest day was that day, with eighteen kilometres of trekking. Nema packed up after lunch and we started across the desert once more, staying close to the escarpment. Zak said to Nema that I was *"quatre quatre"*... "four-by-four," and it was the length of my stride rather than the number of strides that separated us.

We were soon in the hills, and my reading of the trail became uncertain. It was a quick increase in altitude, and Zak picked and pointed our way with assurance. Indiana Jones would be at home here, I thought, among the thick rock roofs and passages. In one narrow place, I pushed my pack ahead of me, eased my body through the pinch of boulders, and took Zak's pack from him, after which he slipped between the wedged rocks. Once we were over the top, there was a brief levelling, and then a steep descent. We plunged down the gully of rocks that took the escarpment's sheer pitch as a path, not unlike the course of a waterfall, which in fact it became in the rainy season.

"Zak, is there another route?" I asked. I wondered about those who traversed these difficult paths regularly.

"Yes," he replied, "but less interest. You'll enough see plain." The sun dried our words, and we stopped talking.

I again pushed the pack through a tight spot, followed it with my body pressed to the rock, my face scraping the headway and avoiding a sharp piece that blocked the passage by ducking under it. The troublesome passage was invigorating; I was loving the challenge. Then two Malian women jaunted up the incline toward us, their pace steady and sure. They each carried cloth-covered baskets atop their heads and were heading home from market, where they'd been since dawn. They negotiated the boulders as smoothly as a square dancer would.

By the time we reached bottom, I was exhausted.

Me: "I'm finished."

Zak: "Yes, spewed."

Me: "Spewed?"

Zak: "Yes. Spewed. By the rocks. Finished."

I looked back up the slope, past Zak's shoulder, to the rock face. "Thanks," I said, meaning for the safety as well as the experience.

"Now, flat but sandy for you," Zak said, and there was something playful in the way he said it. I found the slip of sandals on sand less enjoyable than my graceless scampering on the hillside had been.

Trading and selling and buying happens in Dogon with a system that sees transient markets set for certain days each week. It is so reliable that Zak's uncle can send him a letter from Mopti and, if timed right, can count on it being delivered the considerable distance to his Dogon village within two days on the market circuit.

We came upon that week's market at Nombori. A hundred stalls flashed their wares to five times as many people. There were bright dabs of colour everywhere, not on the market but on every person. The Malians were in gorgeous dress. Each sash tethering cloth to a woman was a different hue. If one sash was yellow with blue clothing, the next ensemble would be a turquoise garment with purple at the bottom. Pinks, reds, and greens knew no bounds. No two outfits seemed related. It was one of the most colourful sights I had ever seen.

We dropped our packs at the trunk of a giant tree, and I folded myself beside them. To me, "shade" is one of the most beautiful words in the English language. I surrendered to it, and began the ritual of picking *krim krim* from my clothes: these tiny bush burrs irritate, their prickle hurts, and any cloth or sock is like a magnet for them.

Zak, who had walked away to greet an older man, returned with half a dozen children in tow and a large wooden jug in his hands. I was given a *calabash* by one of the kids, whose little hands helped me hold the wooden bowl, though it was not heavy. Zak poured millet beer for me. Warm and good, it filled a need not uttered but sensed. I sat beneath the tree, sipped to the gaze of kids and elders, and felt their welcome.

By the time we were ready to leave, Zak and Nema had met two more friends. They carried our packs, and this time I kept my small pack and its flashlight at hand.

Zak and I shared a goat trail. For long stretches of the walk, we were together, and Zak told me what he thought I should know. About the "raisin tree" from which they take oil for their hair and body. He also pointed out the tamarind tree. "Our women pound its new leaves for juice and for millet cream, " he said, pointing to one I'd leaned against earlier. The bush date tree shelters as well as provides food ("Tastes like roasted marshmallow," Zak said, and I wondered at how he would know), and in Dogon is called the Balanzan tree. Above all, there is no more common tree than the baobab. Its bark is used for making rope, its leaves for a soupy food called to, its large branches for fertilizer when its heart is cut for firewood, its

Zak, Dogon guide, teacher, and friend, wears protection against the sun.

fruit burned to make potassium for medicinal remedies, and "the baobab tree's root use for malaria." This reminded me that it was the time of day to take my pills to fend off this illness. When Zak described another children's sickness that it cured, I deduced it to be like chicken pox because he explained that "it makes buttons on the skin."

At camp, we passed a brew between us. "Zak, are you animist?" I had no clue about his religion. There had been no bending for prayer or obvious blessing before a meal.

"My family is. Mostly. And my village."

"You?"

"I'm Christian. Is my choice."

In a country dominated by three religions, one should never be surprised. Every village has at least one distinctive place of worship. Mosques are common, and over 80 percent of Malians practise Islam. But the Dogon people look dimly on external influences, assimilating only what they wish. Animism has been among their beliefs for centuries.

"In my village, does not matter. Every village, is okay what you believe," Zak told me. "Everywhere you find Muslim. Will find Christian. Too, animism. Is all okay what your neighbour believes."

"No one wants get to heaven with no name," Zak told me as though that was what my question was about. Within his family they had all hedged their bets: three were Muslim, some Christian, and some animist. "What if we get heaven and God doesn't recognize one us?"

During the evening's lull, Zak mentioned how different it was in the rainy season, from June to October. "Is lush, if that your word. Very green." I tried to visualize. "And wind strong. Monsoon."

Through the hiss of the *campement* radio came the thump of music.

"National anthem, *Reek*," Nema said, unable to shake her plaintive way of pronouncing my name.

"Our president is going speak," Zak announced, talking above the radio.

And then the two of them began to sing their national anthem, Zak in French and Nema in Bambara. Quiet, not boisterous.

"Mali, it is your pride," Nema said in schoolgirl English, with a hint in her voice that it was a rough translation of one line.

"We will do what is right," Zak sang in English for me.

In 1960, freed from colonial shackles, the historic name "Mali" was selected for the new democracy. Crippled by debt to foreign lenders, with little in the way of export products, slow in developing foreign revenues from tourism and victimized by encroaching sand, it is understandable that Mali is labeled "poor." (Westerners do a lousy job of making nation-to-nation comparisons for hardy spirits, the enterprise of happiness, or indigenous joy, wherein Mali would be labelled rich, even thriving.)

"ATT," said Zak when I asked the leader's name. "We call him that. Real name Amadou Toumani Touré." ATT came to power in a 1991 coup, thrust into the role by public pressure for democratic institutions, a reflection on neighbouring countries' miscues in Africa. He is among the few leaders of a coup who have won not only their country's ballot, but also international respect. Too much of African diplomacy rests on the patronage of former colonial powers, and Mali accepts help without bowing. It is one of Africa's fifty-three nation-states and among the few that make sense as a sovereign nation on the world stage. Mali does not attract cynicism. It does not have problems that are beyond the reach of Western help. In a continent of 670 million people and among its fellow members in the African Union, Mali is one of those countries worth the world's patience.

And now, on the radio, ATT's voice began a speech, not preachy, yet with an air of precision and pace that betrayed his military background.

"What is he saying?"

"It's Bambara. Talking about Army Day. Is anniversary. This it. A holiday."

Initially ATT did not seek to rule, preferring to leave that to political parties. But they sought to bring ATT back into leadership as president in the 2002 election. In the view of my hosts, the expectations of this non-politician, non-partisan leader's ability for stewardship had largely been met. "Our country gets better," said Zak. And that was the most politics we talked.

There is peace now. The Tuareg, once lords of the Sahara, no longer fight for autonomy, a struggle that caused bouts of unrest and civil strife for decades. Mali would benefit from a mentor nation, a first-world big sister who would help nourish its potential with dedication rather than sporadic aid. The country shoulders a foreign debt of $900 million U.S., provided by the African Development Bank, the International Monetary Fund, donor nations, and the World Bank. As with most of Africa, Mali survives through what Shakespeare would call "the courtesy of nations" and walks more slowly under the weight of this help.

Tourism may be part of the solution, as a source of both foreign revenue and foreign understanding. It need not be "pro-poor tourism" other than that the benefits of visitor spending need to stay local, and traditionally little of what visitors spend trickles through to residents of a developing host country. Perhaps here tourism can contribute to the alleviation of the nation's poverty, a reduction of crime, a rising literacy rate, and enhanced rights for women. It might reduce global inequities through education (of both traveller and host) and exchanges of more than currency.

The world tries to make Africa right — children helping the mother continent. Africa sits in the world's margins; noted, commented upon, and somewhat unwillingly included in the family of meaningful land masses. Most North Americans and Europeans never get remotely close to it. Those who do, report to the rest of us and help us think differently, reaffirming that travellers are the world's synapses. Africa is not yet what it will be at its brightest, but the wait will be long.

Mali's survival, like travel, is about adapting to the inevitable.

The broadcast ended brusquely, and the radio blared anew, partway through a Pink Floyd song. The incongruity of the moment struck me, but it also distracted Nema. I snatched back my favourite hat, determined it would go home with me.

The next day, we stopped in a village to rest and came upon three men building a house. A newly dried mud wall came to a framed corner where its wooden braces meshed laterally and vertically in a latticework. The wall was being filled to make it stronger.

I offered to help.

The men smiled — in the international way of saying "whatever" — and showed me to the mud-making area. I was given a trowel to move back and forth in order to mix the guck. I swirled and scraped with it. The mud was pliable, yet firmed nicely in the heat.

There were straw-and-mud bricks that had been made days earlier by the water hole, where the floods had moulded a washed-out workstation. They'd been blocked and dried and cut into moveable pieces that stacked easily. When my muddy mortar was ready to secure them in place, I was shown how to position these large bricks. Lending my back to a building process that was hundreds of years old, I placed half a dozen bricks on the wall and troweled mud into the gaps.

An older man walked over, pushed a long sleeve up his arm and away from the dirt, and tested the newly laid bricks. Finding them suitably set and firm, he smiled. He laughed. He shook my muddy hand. It was all a ploy to keep me building this Dogon home. One day I'd like to sleep on its roof.

It had been an unusually regular week: darkness came at six-thirty, dinner at eight, and bed at nine-thirty. Another night. Zak and I smoked and picked our teeth. He explained his demons.

"We are often afraid, and stay close to the village at dark."

"Afraid of animals?" I asked, feeling that reasonable.

"No. Of people with black magic."

I was intrigued. "What people?"

"Powerful people who use things we don't understand."

"Like?"

"Black magic."

"And ...?" I wanted to hear all about this.

"If on the road now, bad black magic powers could kill. If left my pack in last village, I not go get. Not now. For fear."

"Only at night?"

"Sometime — once when celebration, bad people put danger in food. To check, we feed to sacred tortoises. If don't eat, is poisonous. Make your skin sick."

"But here, we are safe tonight?"

"Very safe in Dogon." And I looked into the eyes of the man who said this, seeing their truth and serenity. About us, people walked who could not be seen, only heard. There was no moon.

"Do you have a fire?" Zak asked, holding out his cigarette.

The closest I came to personally "connecting" with Mali had occurred when I held the centuries-old manuscripts in Timbuktu. Somewhat similar had been my sensation on a dark night on the dry mud bank of the River Niger under more sky than I knew existed. But Mali had not yet riveted itself to me, not made an indelible impression. Then, it came to me one morning. Not in the sands, as I'd thought it would, but through shy, undemanding children. Not in the sun's gaze, as I'd expected, but in the easy darkness of Zak's grandparents' home.

We trekked past Tireli's vegetable plots and climbed straight up over two hundred metres of rock to the ridge of the escarpment, clinging to rock holds and pulling ourselves up over the outcroppings. Sweat beaded my brow and stained my hat's brim as we took on the elevation. I raised my hat a few centimetres to

234 TO TIMBUKTU FOR A HAIRCUT

funnel cool air over my forehead. I hiked as though I were moving on scaffolding, nervous of the fissured trail. My stride was tentative, even more so near the chasms.

Then a young woman waltzed around a large rock, on her way down to the village with a pot on her head, its contents covered by the lid. On feet bare and sure, she swayed by me without concern, generations of confidence and balance in her genes.

On top of the cliff was a *campement*, owned by Zak's uncle. In the middle of this sun-baked, desolate nowhere was a two-room shack. Zak's grandparents were in the next village. His little brother, Étienne, arrived as we rested under his uncle's wooden lean-to.

With Étienne in the lead, we walked over the hot escarpment, dipping periodically into paths formed by centuries of water flow. We stepped across wide fissures that dropped thirty metres into an abyss and were bridged with a single large stone, precariously wedged. Earlier bridges were clearly visible below, where they'd tumbled.

One eroded path led to the hollow of a valley and stepped down and along for half a kilometre of rock pathway. A village was at the end of the path, where it climbed back up the sandstone shore of a gully. Children gawked at me and did not laugh. They let me pass, their eyes fixed on each stride I made, each footprint I left. They were fearful of the unknown; they did not often greet trekkers. None reached out to me until I stopped and opened the palm of my hand to them.

"It's okay," I said, hoping my soft tone conveyed my meaning, since my English words surely would not. A toddler ran up and touched my hand with a finger that I gently cupped. We smiled at one another. My right hand was tugged by another child, and these two children led me into the village. Zak and Étienne were nowhere to be seen.

Entering the ageless village required the children and me to climb over large rocks. Their tiny feet often gave me the right of way, as though they were unsure of my ability to cope with something they accomplished daily. I looked at some older kids, and they looked away. Eventually we made eye contact, which I took as a mark of acceptance.

Zak reappeared from a doorway. Ten kids and I reached the threshold of this wood stave house, and I entered it to be greeted by an old man's hand and a Dogon phrase I did not understand, except for its ending in a smile that bade me enter farther. The man made as if to rise from his chair, but clearly had no intention of doing so. His hair was metal-grey and his goatee hung in strands, a growth of many years on his weathered face. His wife stood at the height of my chest and held my arms, one in each of her strong hands, pressing them to my side and speaking into my eyes. She clutched each arm, back and forth, in grasps that meant acceptance. I was Zak's friend.

She sat.

"This the grandfather," said Zak. "This the grandmother." He smiled as a grandson would.

I sat next to his grandfather, one whom the French would call *pampaloom* — the "sweet grandpa." He smiled, spoke of something in a different Dogon dialect than did Zak, who smirked with all his teeth. It was about me, and I was not supposed to know.

Zak's grandmother twisted a stick of raw cotton, pulling it into useable thread around a wood holder; this activity predates the cotton gin by centuries. She tugged it tight to make it true, and her lips all the while curved in a grin. She stared.

Zak said, as though he needed to be sure I realized this: "We live not only this century, *Rick*, like you. We live last. Even one before. All at once."

Ten children had come into the house and stayed on the grandmother's side of the room. The girls sat on a bed next to her, and the boys leaned on posts. The expectation was that I'd sit, be observed and talked about. Nothing else need be done. The child who had first taken my hand looked timidly at me. I opened my hand his way again. He moved closer and I gently lifted him to my knee. His head slipped against my chest. He rested, eyes open, in confidence that this was safe. I just sat there, feeling pleased.

When we took our leave, I held Zak's grandfather's hands and caught the flickering of his eyes. We both knew we'd meet only this once, never again. Grandma stretched from where she sat, clasping my forearms, and when my hug did not embrace her enough, she rose to hold me, smiled, and held me more.

Out of Africa has come the theory that your heart is the size of the village you were born in, and I left Zak's village knowing it was the largest.

Zak had become as much my sidekick as my guide. We returned to Tireli for lunch, from where we'd later depart for a long afternoon walk. Nearing our *campement*, I spotted a village sign that said *poubelles*. Later, we arrived at a stone box with the same word on it.

"What is a *poubelle*?" I asked Zak in French.

"A dustbin," he replied in English.

"Zak, the whole country is a dustbin."

He was right, though. It was a garbage receptacle, the first I'd seen in nearly a month. It seemed redundant.

It was Zak's day to carry the heavy pack.

"I think we should get a porter," he announced.

"A porter?"

"Yes. The way is rough tomorrow."

I said, "This is today."

"A porter will be good. I arrange here."

"How much?" I asked.

"Is my solution," Zak said. "I take care of it."

Fifteen minutes later I looked over my shoulder to see Oumar on the road, coming from the village, with the tightly tied pack balanced on his head. The pack's bulk was not at all out of proportion to his gratitude for the job.

I walked all afternoon through a landscape I had only imagined while reading books about this continent: tall grasses, sand dunes, and stony paths with occasional trees and random people. This part of Africa has little wildlife to fear, and that knowledge made my hiking alone, nearly a kilometre ahead of my guide, feel comfortable and safe.

So the crocodile was a surprise.

It waited on the shore of a large pond, beside the trail, a little too close for comfort. There, too, were its crocodile friends, fellow caimans — small crocodiles, about two metres in length. Nearby, two men sat behind a souvenir table offering: "Observation 500, Photographs 1,000."

I continued my walk and waved to them as they moved to recapture the escapee. An hour later, when we were back together, Zak explained that there are hundreds of caimans in the pond, revered by the locals and hedged behind a stake fence on the perimeter. Once a week a trekker actually paid to take a picture, so it was worth the men's patient wait. The caiman that had surprised me was a rogue; it would be taken care of. Not to worry.

"Well fed?" I asked, having seen valuable goats within range.

"Yes. Food in the water. Sometimes they eat their young."

"It caught me unprepared," I said. "I should have known better."

Then came another of Zak's eternal truths. He said, "Only travellers in danger those who think they experienced."

Feeling nauseous at the end of the day's walk, I shivered in the cool evening. I'd worn no protection against the sun that afternoon, so it was likely my carelessness that was at fault. But many children's hands had held mine — where had those little hands been before? This was not the flu, but it felt like it. I swallowed a muscle relaxant, as my day pack had been tight and tingly on my hands for the last six kilometres. Maybe using a plastic coffee mug washed in local water had been the cause? I considered the Gravol in my pack, but the label warned users to avoid alcohol, and I craved one of their cool beers if I could find one. I showered, washed my scraped feet, and put antibiotic salve on them, especially on my right centre toe, which was still blood-encrusted with sand. My throat was a bit sore. I set aside a packet of Neo-Citran and an eight-hour Tylenol to put me to sleep.

Nema strode toward me and said, "*Reek*, couscous. Chicken." This was a relief; I'd been expecting caiman stew. I'd come to realize that if you wished to have chicken, it was killed for you to ensure freshness (if not tenderness). If you wanted beef or other meat from a large animal, you would get it only if your timing matched the needs of the village. Often I missed variety by a day or two. Now that I knew what was being prepared for dinner, I asked that the chicken be cooked over an open fire. "Barbecue," I said as a stupid Westerner.

"Onion?" Nema retorted.

We were among chickens, tiny and noisy. A larger one squawked and was taken to serve Nema's latest epicurean twist. Plucked and washed, it was set in a pot to boil. Salad leaves arrived in a sack and were soaked in water, plucked in their own fashion and readied for consumption.

Nema cooked over the wood fire and, following my request, removed the chicken from the pot and placed it on the grill. She tossed in a bit too much *piment*, reddening the water. Into this she put potatoes. She'd arranged to receive fresh bread from the *campement*'s brick stove. She boiled a green pepper whole, then tossed it in a pan to sauté. The concoction was enriched with ash. Nema defined close-to-the-earth cooking. She'd also found something called *l'aid* (a term I'd never heard and have not heard since), which Zak said was like onion but wasn't. The brat.

I found a not-too-warm Flag beer offered by a helping African hand. With it, the young man brought an African lantern, unsolicited, as he had noticed my note-taking. The lamp's chimney was grey-brown with use, the mantle hesitated. Then wind got beneath the air vent and the flame glowed, but never brightly.

A youngster watched my scribbling. He peered close to the smoke from my pipe and pinched his nose and spoke. Zak, nearby, guffawed. "Smelly stick," he translated.

Orona is what the family called their home, my *campement* for this night. It was owned by the local doctor. Dusk descended on the open courtyard in its nightly ritual. Tamarind wood fed our fire; this was not always so, as some in Dogon view it as a sacred wood. Its smell drew me and I stood nearby and watched Nema at work, flashlight clenched in her lips, bent over to tend both fire and food. She was young, sensuous, and talented, and her life would only get harder.

The wind was up, sending dust flying. The lanterns and the cooking fire gave a soft glow to the *campement*. I couldn't shake the thought that Mexican-American cowboy towns were more like this than like the Disneyfied versions portrayed in the movies. Two green-leafed trees separated the bare courtyard into thirds. Fields surrounded the walls with crops and animals. A farm cart wheeled by, and I could hear the donkey's wheeze. A mother and child came and sat close to me, readying their dinner in an aluminum pot. The woman joined a group of other women, who prepared dinner while I made light talk with their men. My lantern flickered. Tea was served in long draws.

I was the lone traveller in the village of Ireli, where Orona was located, and I liked the feeling.

Zak asked if my trip was what I had wanted. I was trying to find a way to say yes when he said: "You ask life, it give."

The wind bristled the air and began to howl. It was a wilder wind than I'd known in the Dogon. Zak was cold and suggested that I sleep inside the house. He and Nema would bunk down on the earthen floor, sheltered by walls and a door. The roof above them was where I'd earlier laid out my sleeping bag, which now ruffled in the wind. There was a slight buffer in their house design that left a low rim half a foot above the roof's surface. It furled rather than deflected the wind. I did not give in to the temptation to sleep indoors.

Zak corrected my mistakes several times on the next morning's trail, shouting when he saw me meander down the wrong fork. He might yell from far behind; or, if it suited his pace, he'd wait and when I turned to look at him he pointed wildly, trusting that I saw him, and indicating that I must trudge across the plain to regain the proper trail. Extra paces in the hot sun. Then he'd shout to suggest a rest that he felt I needed. He knew that travellers need to pause most when they know it least.

Travel in Dogon was, for me, often about detours. I was singing to myself, happy with my pace for over an hour, when a small boy ran up shouting, "Sir, sir, *la geed. La geed.*" (That is how I heard it.) It was a new phrase to me, and I struggled to interpret its meaning. He motioned back along the path I'd come from and repeated the term *"Geed."* That would be "the guide," Zak by most definitions, but there was no one to be seen. The lad tugged at my T-shirt, and I had enough sense to follow. Thirty minutes later, he'd retraced my walk to where Zak rested and offered trenchant advice: "*Rick*, time. Stop. You too far." That's all there was to know.

It was later explained to me that in remote parts of Africa they have a perspective about travel based on reliance upon one another and safety. When you leave a village on a journey, you have a choice. If you wish to go fast, then go alone; if you wish to go far, then go together.

A trekker from Germany walked by in a Dogon hat, a bonnet of sorts that drooped on either side, tassels hanging. It was incongruous. Few things reminded me more of our shrinking and distorted world than a Malian in a Chicago Bulls T-shirt or a waif drawing well water while wearing a Manchester United jersey as a smock. I had brought with me a handful of ballpoint pens from a stash at home, their designations Ritz, Fairmont, Four Seasons, and, as I handed them out on this trip, their names had become as insignificant here as the third-hand branded clothes the Malian

A woman pounding millet, or goats grazing, are ubiquitous scenes in the farming economy of Dogon Country.

shepherds wore in the desert: Nike, New York Yankees, Marlboro. At first those reminders of home seemed like an intrusion, until I learned that such attire made its way there through American and European donations, from when we clean out our closets of no longer wanted clothing.

You do not drink in Dogon just because you are thirsty. Water must last the journey. You do not whistle, do not make idle chatter, because it dries the throat — a discovery I would take home with me. From the water bottle, you at best get a wilting quench. I learned the difference between warm water and *warm* water — my standards shifted like the sands. Water was always a serious issue in Dogon; little of it fell to the ground without further use. Where I encountered people at wells, I passed my hat to them as they pumped and cupped it back over my head in a spill they approved of, but only once. More was too much.

And the breeze was never benign. As it cooled the walker, it blew sand against the gardener. Although people built slatted fences to thwart this, the fences functioned more to sift the sand. They were only ramparts, a temporary, permeable barrier to the ever-patient sand battalions. Agriculture is at the heart of Dogon's subsistence economy — those who can grow, do so and put their products into the cycle of trading food for rope, car parts, utensils, or labour. What cannot be sold for cash is bartered.

That day at noon we passed at least three hours in the shade, sleeping or sitting silently — the need for midday conversation evaporated. Zak called this *nitege*, which might be Dogon for *siesta*. The temperature was thirty-five degrees, ten more than it was comfortable to move in, however, Nema made a fire, cooked spaghetti, and served it with a thin gravy. She prepared a leafy salad, high on the warning list for travellers to avoid: breeding ground for bacteria, washed in local water. The dressing was onion juice with herbs.

Zak showed his proficiency in languages when we stopped among his kinfolk or other travellers, transferring from one language or dialect to another with the turn of his head. He had been true to his word that we'd talk in French while in Dogon, though my linguistic laziness in the heat made me less diligent than I'd intended. Our food talk and planning for the afternoon had been in French for the past half hour, and I was the oft-corrected student. We did not misunderstand each other because our respective home countries' French accents were different. Rather, I misused words, made up words, and bracketed French terms with English explanations.

Zak was a patient man; only when he tired of my predatory approach to language did he interrupt as I attempted to speak in French. Zak sighed at my fractured phrases. "*Rick*, I have broken English," he said. "You have unfixable French."

As we left the outskirts of a village we saw four low buildings, each with two rooms. "*Rick*, is the school," Zak announced. One structure had a third room attached; as we walked toward it Zak said, "You must meet my teacher." And so it was that I met the teacher of my teacher.

A strapping, handsome man, perhaps thirty-five years old, smiled at Zak. His hand reached far into the space between them. The man's look of inquiry was no doubt related to the question of whether I was visiting out of genuine interest or happenstance.

"The headmaster wants show you students," Zak said as we crossed the schoolyard to one of the classrooms.

I ducked into the dim room, its windows open to the air. Facing the blackboard at the front, sixty-nine students suddenly went quiet (I counted them before I left). Their teacher was pleased to see me, a welcome diversion that sparked attention. I was welcomed in French and replied in kind. It was clear that he wished me to speak to the class.

"I am from Canada," I said in French, and there were nods. "Canada is a very fine country. Mali is a very fine country." They smiled as a class often does, together. "Mali and Canada are friends." The students liked that.

"Let me take you to the English class," the headmaster said. He led me past another classroom window, into which I peeked as we walked by, causing laughter. Many of the students rose from their desks to see me better. The gentle reprimand of their teacher drifted out the window, and they sat back down. There was a wall and another window, so again I poked my white face in, just because I could, and again a disruption resulted and the teacher quelled the disturbance I had caused.

There was no recess here. The children were not at play; it was serious study. "Many of them walk nine kilometres every school day," said the headmaster. "Difficult."

"I understand, given how difficult the sand is," I observed, citing my own weakness (and not understanding at all).

"It is not that. It is that most have no lunch to bring. No food," he said. "That is difficult. No one learns when their stomach is noisy."

Zak elaborated on what I had not grasped: "Nine kilometres walk home again, before they eat."

In the English class there was more for me to say, as they were eager to hear a native speaker of that tongue. Rummaging through my pack, I found maple leaf stickers and a few iron-on flags, which I gave to the teacher. Spoiling all sense of propriety, I gave one each to three girls in the front row and walked down an aisle to share stickers at random.

In this classroom dozens of wooden desks were blocked together, with narrow aisles between them. Each desk had at least one student — two, where there was room for their slim bums to share a seat. Against the walls lounged students who wanted to learn but for whom there were no seats. I counted: one hundred and twelve students in the room. One teacher. I felt a Westerner's shame, while at the same time feeling a great admiration for the teacher.

The students let me look over their shoulders and into the texts they were studying. They were not ten years old, and the books they studied from were heavy on the pictorial. There were two pages on AIDS. It was clear in the visuals how AIDS is contracted and how it is spread and why the students must practise safe sex, when and if. I looked at Zak, then at the teacher and was told: "It is important that we protect our young people."

A little girl smiled at me and I stopped to pay closer attention. To demonstrate my interest in her work, I flipped the pages of her textbook. It opened at a section on female circumcision. The message there was a clear statement that it was not a tradition the government or doctors wished to see continue. It was not her responsibility, was not an obligation; it need not happen to her. There was an added sticker on her page, the internationally recognized NO symbol: a red circle with a diagonal line applied to everything from NO smoking to NO car parking, and here it encircled the French words for "Female Circumcision."

And, I was forced to ask myself, what of the vulnerable children who don't get this education, of the nations that knowingly perpetuate the ignorance and humiliation? They need never learn the term clitoridectomy, but they do need to learn the concept, "my body, myself."

"*Au revoir*. Goodbye," they said as I stepped outside.

Zak, the English teacher, myself, and the headmaster stood outside in the daylight, beneath the lone tree. Nema had caught up to us on the walk, and stood next to me, her hip cocked in a slouch. They moved so that I got the shade; they were more used to squinting. To Zak I said, "I will send money from home if you think that would help with the food."

"Is my school," he replied. "Headmaster my biology teacher. Now he boss. If you can, *Rick*, that be good."

Getting home with such intentions and actually sending money a month hence was going to be complicated. I knew the gesture might fade in importance. If a traveller is to help, most often one must do so immediately. I slipped off my money belt; there was U.S. currency in the hidden sleeve. The first folded batch came loose as I unzipped the sleeve. They saw the entire roll, and I could not peel away only a portion. I felt some embarrassment for actually having hid it. Or perhaps guilty that I had a Western well of money from which to replenish my stash. I began to straighten the wrinkles in the bills, and quickly realized how much money was there. I flashed a calculation, estimating what amount I'd need to keep for the remainder of my expenses before I left some of it with them.

Nema, ever helpful, took the first layer of bills from my hand and began flattening them, lifting back the curled edges and making them tidy. Then, she handed over the entire pile. To the headmaster.

He, Zak, and the English teacher smiled a broad grin of "Thank you." Nema, at whom I stared, smirked in her role as Mali's answer to Robin Hood.

"You will feed many students," said the headmaster as he pocketed the cash. "They will learn better."

That night we were in a charmed *campement* near the village of Ibi. There was a large family to greet our arrival, and they quickly set us up in comfort. A man, who appeared to be the father, shook my hand.

Nema prepared a spaghetti stew unlike anything I'd had before. (Who else but Nema could concoct it?). There were mixed meats (some leftover, some fresh), *piment* crushed into a sauce with the milk boiled loose from its rice and cooled to jell before being warmed again for serving. It tasted sugary, and while that surprised me, Nema was good at surprising me. I might have written this as Chicken Supreme if there had been a menu to write that on, but Mali is not a menu country. You ate what was there, and it might not be available the next day.

Dinner over, this evening was mine for relaxation, without obligations. It was now quite dark but I had my wind candle out to read. My glasses, now bent from too often shoving them into my pack, must have curled in an odd angle over my nose. I took them off to clean them on my shirt, and they were dirtier to see through when I put them back on. The plastic nose bridge fell off in my hand and the metal poked my skin.

"*Rick*, they offer you their dance," said Zak, carrying an African lantern that brightened the spot where I sat.

"They? Dance?"

"Yes."

It was not enough of an answer, and I prodded for more.

"The family. They have song. The man written them. They tell what you should know."

"He's a musician?" I asked.

"Sort of."

I sensed there was more to this, and Zak confirmed: "Is ten thousand *seffe* for performance. You pay. Is help with education. For the children. For village."

"And how long is this show?" I asked, feeling silly in my desire to read when Africa was about to unfold in front of me.

Nema defines close-to-the-earth cooking.

"*Rick*, is good, you should do. Don't worry about time. Is dark now." The family started to appear, never a doubt in their minds about the evening. The father — who had earlier welcomed us to his home, had shown me about the large yard, and had passed my bag up to the rooftop that was my night's sleeping quarters — came into the open area about five metres from where Zak sat beside me. Zak blew out my candle, trimmed the lantern and handed it to the man. I fell into the night as Zak continued to show me his Africa.

Two long-skirted children came to their father and an older daughter in a halter top and western shorts walked out from the other side of the yard. The man played a three-string guitar that a traveller had left behind. His chords were a cue: four male teenagers entered the courtyard, jostling one another. They appeared from behind an outer wall as though waiting there for my decision, or Zak's, that we'd watch their performance.

Ten children arched around him, joined by a boy, who held a two-sided drum between his legs. The mother, who had helped Nema cook and wash the dishes, came closer but Nema stayed away. There was no clapping to start the performance, nor any obvious direction. Immediately they were joined in song. Strident. It was a kind of spontaneous combustion.

"Is about first aid," said Zak.

"Happy topic for a song," I observed.

"No, not that. If a person has hurt, they can fix. Is important because gives new life."

It was lesson time for me. The second song flowed with little break from the first, except that two toddlers shook their *calabash*, the beads inside the gourd rattle setting a rhythm that the man picked up. Then the movement had words and became a chorus. "This about medicine," Zak instructed, and I thought how unlikely these songs were to hit local folk-music charts. "Is that there is no medicine, so make precautions." It was for the children he wrote the songs, and it was through these that they would learn.

In the bustle of the dark, using only their low-lit lantern, I could see fifteen performers. Zak leaned toward me, "They will do song on family planning. Is about birth control. You understand birth control?"

"I know the term."

Their way of adding instruments to the song one at a time was moving, with all of them working together with voices that appeared to relax while also demanding attention.

Zak explained that the fourth song would tell of a feared illness. "If child has headache, maybe is malaria. Is not big. It passes. But medicine and treatment needed. Or won't pass. They don't have medicine. So is dangerous sickness."

When it was over, no one moved for a full minute. I did not look at Zak. No one breathed. Then there was a rattle. Then another. And a third. The song, for the first time, began with the drum's insistent beat. It lured before it entertained. But this was not about entertaining. The song was about female circumcision. Three young girls walked closer to me, each holding one of the introductory rattles. They waltzed only to keep the beat of their rattles and the drum in sync with their words. The story-song was not from the father this time, but from them, for them. I thought back to my earlier visit to the school. Clearly this was considered an important issue in Mali as well as in the outside world.

Zak spoke only when the instruments played without vocal accompaniment, between the sung lyrics of the three smallest girls. Then there was an interlude set for the listener's contemplation of the song's impact. "The girls know their circumcision not need be. Before, felt they must. Was tradition. No more."

"No more?"

"Yes, often. But not need be," he repeated. "Is important to no longer be important."

Female circumcision, deemed unnecessary by today's government, frowned upon by medical authorities, shunned by Western women's groups who sponsor highway billboards to communicate this, is nevertheless widely practised in Mali. The genital mutilation disfigures the girls, and the frequent use of a blunt instrument for the procedure is both painful and a disease spreader. While socially and sexually the circumcised women become more acceptable to many African men, the trimming is fraught with individual trauma. Although it is campaigned against, and sung against, it will not abate easily.

What we may say is mythology, the Dogon hold dear. When the God, *Ama*, finished making the universe, Earth was to be his female mate. Their sexual intercourse — which would complete the world — was symbolic of fertility and *Ama*'s manhood. This copulation was prevented by an earthly termite hill. The clitoris is seen as the impediment, cast as the termite mound in Dogon history, their myth. The termite hill-clitoris was in the way and must therefore be removed. Female circumcision became the symbol of man's dominance. It became mandatory to remove the clitoris of young women, both to ensure unimpeded consummation and to further the myth's perception of truth.

I wondered what world these little girls were dancing into. To end the song, the littlest girl sang, and I asked Zak what the words meant. "She teaching, this is wrong."

"Isn't she young to teach?" I said.

"Teach what you want to learn," he said.

Then the man sang alone, as if directly to me. "They wish health for their family. Welcome you. Wish your family good health," Zak interpreted the concert's closing. It moved to a louder, happier tune, as though to end.

The mother and three teenage girls, wrapped in shawls, sprang up and held hands. They swirled as the happy music pumped through the courtyard. Everyone began clapping. The women twirled close to where I sat on the ground with Zak, and their circle broke. Hands reached down and pulled me to my feet and into the dance.

It was not raucous, not fancy, just our moving with the music. I leaned my head back, balanced and held secure by their hands, looked up to the million stars above and watched their faces smile. I felt the sand between my toes, let my body sway in the least self-conscious dance possible, moving only to the beat of the drum, the rhythm of Africa.

When I sat down, sweating, Zak said one must celebrate life, and the best way to do it was to do what I just did. "When dead, you can't dance."

A young cock crowed me awake. I was unexpectedly curious about this day. There was a sharp pink flower in sight, a twig reaching from a tree branch at the rooftop, all the more enchanting for the contrast to brown mud. This was another special day. The Dogon is a land of masks, and nowhere more so than where we were to travel.

"Let's away," said Zak, handing me a water bottle. Zak and I were to hike alone for a morning to Youga-Dogourou, not far away. Youga-Dogourou was one of three name-related villages in close proximity, the other two being Youga-Piri and Youga-Na. It was already hot when we left. "Ready, *Rick*?" I was eager for the open fields, so I bolted, leading. After a kilometre, the trail meandered into the rocks, and I picked the path out for half of the escarpment's heart-beating rise. Our way became unclear. "All yours, Zak." I bowed, and he flowed through boulders and around giant rocks, up, always up. Steps were in place everywhere; the route had been used forever and always. My knees bent, my calves cursed, my thighs pushed. Up. Up.

Masks dominate the Dogon's spiritual landscape. They are not ornamental, but spiritual necessities. Each village has an altar around which services and ceremonies are held, performed by males, preferably those directly descended from (often deceased) religious leaders. The face covers are hand-held and represent animals, people of either sex, and various ages and assorted village craftsmen, such as the blacksmith.

"*Sigui,*" Zak said, as though I should know.

"*Sigui,* what?"

"*Sigui* is most important ritual," he said. "In Dogon, all else will stop for this ceremony."

"Will I see it?

"You must come back. Next time 2027."

"Next!" I said, surprised. "And the last was ...?"

"Many years ago." It was in Youga-Dogourou, where we walked. "Only every sixty years."

Zak explained that the festival requires the carving of a Great Serpent Mask. "Six times your height, *Rick.*"

Zak's explanation of the sixty-year cycle for this ritual oddly fits with science. Sirius is well known to Westerners as the sky's brightest star, often cited by amateur astronomers and professionals alike, and common in literature. In fact, it is Sirius A that we see. There is a speck of a star, Sirius B, about which the Dogon people have known for centuries and which Westerners "discovered" in 1970. That much is fact. And what is the source of the Dogon's irrefutable knowledge of this second star, which Europeans and North Americans did not believe existed? Information was provided to them hundreds of years ago by the *Nommo*, twin masters in the creation myth of the Dogon. The *Nommo* told them of the star's existence, citing its periodic (you guessed it: sixty-year) cycling on the horizon — a tiny light, often initially red. This triggered the start of the *Sigui* ceremony in Dogon. And for those who enjoy intrigue, note that the *Nommo* come from the system of stars we call Sirius. Their telling of, and the Dogon belief in, a Sirius C star has yet to be corroborated by Western astronomers.

Zak was brushing his teeth with a stick when I found him at our campement the next morning. I was ready for another discovery, perhaps another revelation. We were soon joined by Nema and Oumar.

We left the village of Youga-Na and were almost immediately climbing through narrow passages, scrambling over crevices and slipping between fissures, all done with an exhilarating sense of risk. Far above the plain and onto the flatness of the Dogon plateau, we faced a long day's heat, trekking to Sanga across seventeen kilometres of barren but beautiful isolation.

Zak looked at the long stretch of hike and time before us, and said: "Tomorrow comes this way."

There was little to confuse us on the trail, hard stones all the way and as hot as the surface of an oven. Undisturbed rocks marked the path, as no one wished to perish on this plateau. This walk, the longest uninterrupted stretch we'd made in the entire month, reinforced my conviction that the purest form of travel is on foot.

Oumar, Zak, and Nema caught up with me in the last kilometre. I had relished walking alone but was happy for us to share a meal. We shucked our packs and dusted off when we came to a village on the outskirts of Sanga. The four of us took lunch at the Katsor Restaurant. The proprietor brought three servings of beef cuts, three bowls of au jus, and three servings of rice coloured by the water used first to cook the green beans that sided our plates. Oumar followed the custom; his eyes looked at the roof. I asked for the missing fourth plate and was told by the server that Oumar would get whatever Zak didn't want from his plate. I looked to Zak, as this was not to be. Zak understood immediately and before I could do anything with the food on my plate, Zak took his best pieces of beef and placed them with a cut of fresh bread on a napkin and passed it to Oumar, whose eyes blinked an appreciation that would not have been more clear in Dogon, Bambara, French, or English.

Sanga was not far along after lunch. The mission, one of several villages that form Sanga, is specific-built: a compound. Everyone knew the game here. Guides gather to hunt clients, travellers come here to be found. It no longer felt right.

A Dogon man walked over to where I sat, sulky at trek's end, and said, in English: "Masks?" Then, indicating with a flung arm where they were, he said in French, "My place." Curious, I walked with him around the village hill and over a field to his home, where another man sat in a chair made of woven plastic slats. Unlocking the door of a small shed, the second man said to me in English, "Many old things."

Fresh wood shavings covered the floor, among freshly carved masks that had not yet been made to look old. Off the wall I chose a mask with a bulbous nose, long cheeks, and scattered baobab bark, which hung from it as hair. Chunks of dirt fell off in my hands.

In a corner, behind more masks and partially hidden by newly carved wooden doors, peeked spearheads. I moved two elaborately designed window shutters to get a closer look and saw more clearly. There lay a quiver of arrows as long as my arm.

"Were for hunting," said the man who had been waiting when we arrived. "And war. From his family fighting years ago." Striking metal tips with ridges had torn through the quiver's pouch, which was hardened by time and dry air. Bundled and sharp, the spears poked out the opening they'd made. The leather was cracked and in danger of falling apart; ripped portions were curled and hard. Unlike the doll-sized carvings rubbed with dirt or stained with roots to fake age, this felt honestly old. Age is a relative concept in an ancient land. My guideline for "old" — forty years — had been suggested by a Malian website, an age after which an object belongs in a local museum.

I asked how old the weapons were.

"Forty years," replied the man who walked me here, with great reluctance. His eyes shifted to the other man as if to say, "It is not so."

I accepted his answer too willingly. It couldn't be true, but I wanted these things. I was no better than those I chastised.

The other man moved to close the sale (it was not his heirloom). "His family has agreed to sell this from their ancestors." This tinged the arbitrary date more than I liked, but I bought. Locals always know the travellers better than the travellers know the locals.

From the mission came beautiful songs. It was Sunday. Oumar saw my inquisitiveness as we walked away from the place where I'd purchased the weapons. In Bambara he said what I understood in English: that it was okay, even good, for me to enter the Christian church. I sat down on the first bench by the door, where I figured it would be easiest to leave when the music stopped and the preaching began. Oumar leaned over a woman and tapped my shoulder, winked at me, and we moved across to the right side of the church, where all the men sat. During the following hymns, the worshippers kept arriving one by one until the initial two dozen had increased to more than a hundred. Song after song began with a child tapping on drums at the front of the church and an elder shaking a baobab tree rattle. The preacher sang confidently, his baritone persuasive. The women clapped, their voices joyous. Little children came through the door, all clad in the brightest cloth. Men and boys entered and sat silently, feigning the odd clap in the thunder of women singing. But each time a song ended I feared a lengthy sermon would start. I wished to avoid being either trapped or rude.

When I finally bolted, seven songs after my arrival, the drums were hit and another song began. More people arrived as I exited. It was now half an hour since I had first sat down. If there is a Second Coming, Christ might want to allow a little extra time for the Malians to show up.

Already I missed sleeping on rooftops. I missed the openness of the night sky in all its inexplicability. Missed being humbled by the insignificance of my preoccupations. Missed, too, lying awake at midnight in Africa, jogging away my childhood images of being there.

I left *Le Pays Dogon*, as they call it, not Dogon Country as we would, wanting more. That was not how I felt about the train journey, about Timbuktu, about the River Niger. What could be better than travels that leave one wanting more?

NINE

A Good Night for West Africa

FROGS DARTED ACROSS THE DARK ROAD, THE meagre light of our car giving little warning to them or us. The crunch count was high. This reminded me to resolve financial matters with Mohammed. No one I'd met had yet come out on top of a deal with him. In Mopti we'd set the date to meet in Ségou, and that was now a day away. It skewed my travels, but Mohammed had promised to be there when I arrived and to make amends for my complaint. First, though, Nema, Mamadou, Zak, and I prayed to our respective gods that the car would make the night crossing and deliver us to Djenné.

The tires squealed suddenly and the brakes hissed. They did not grab securely or uniformly. Donkey-driven carts appeared only when we were almost on top of them, so deep was the darkness and so poor were our headlights. Honking did as little to warn them as it did to help the frogs, so we veered often.

The narrow road became even tighter for one-lane bridges. A stop sign popped out from nowhere; we lurched through it and over an embankment, where a lantern shone. The Bani River ferry crossing. We slid to a halt beside a lorry, got out and joined other Malians waiting beside their truck on the barely discernible shore, one we could have easily driven over and into the river.

Two men used *pirogue* poles to force the small ferry to the embankment, using flashlights to guide them. Bats flew among us, and one dove at me. The lorry was called for. Its lights flickered on as it rambled forward with big baskets dangling two metres over its backside. A dozen people clung to the wooden posts on the piled flatbed. The truck lumbered over metal guides to mount the small ferry. Once it had boarded the ferry, a throng of people jumped from the lorry to the deck to stand as passengers for the half-hour crossing. A Dutch voice came from the only other waiting vehicle and spoke into the dark: "Lonely Planet says this ferry should already have sunk."

"Stay out of vehicle," Zak suggested, unwilling to board while we were in ours. "Walk on." The truck's lights were all we had to discern water from land and determine direction. Once we were on the river, they were turned off. What little light we had came from the tiny flashlights held in the mouths of the pole men.

Darkness returned to the launch site as we heaved away. We crossed the water powered only by the pole men. The farther shore appeared when we were only metres away from it. I was leaning on the Land Cruiser when the ferry's metal prongs speared shore and jolted the boat and all those on board. The land lit up when the truck's ignition sparked. Exhaust pummeled the air and the vehicle's passengers scrambled back on top, clinging to it for their lives as it bounced off the ferry and swerved in the slippery ground.

Our landing was less choreographed. We climbed in. A waiting motorcyclist was told to park on shore and to aim his light at the place where the crew fastened a rope. Mamadou gunned the engine, and we pumped forward into the mud. Our wheels spun, the treads grabbed, and we catapulted up to the harder surface. Then we were in the dark, all alone.

Mali's most photographed image lies in the heart of the Niger inland delta. The Djenné Mosque symbolizes history, architecture, religion, and discovery, as the world's largest building of clay-mud construction. Since 1280 it has been repeatedly repaired. Having lasted this long, patched and smoothed by masons over the centuries, it has earned a place on the United Nation's list of World Heritage Sites.

Djenné has been Timbuktu's sister city, albeit a sibling rival, for centuries because of each city's reliance on trade. Each is as much a living archeological site as a community of traders and residents. It was to Djenné that the salt of Timbuktu and other trade goods moved for broader distribution centuries ago. Djenné both preceded Timbuktu and endured economically after Timbuktu's decline. Today, it has ceded primacy to Mopti, where the River Niger now has a thriving transport economy, away from the Djenné marshes.

My stay was contrasted not by a disappointing return to sheltered accommodation, but by a return to eating fish, a taste I'd nearly forgotten in Dogon. The morning market enthralled as much for its array of products and personalities as for its humble presence beneath the imposing mosque. That morning at the market I saw Mamadou open the car's trunk, where my bags were stashed. He pushed two live chickens into the small hollow between the canvas and the metal siding. The birds squawked until he closed the lid and darkened their lives, whereupon they shat all over my backpack.

The day's drive from Djenné to Ségou was marked by car breakdowns, all mysterious. At the first, I hung around the little village where our vehicle gasped and shuddered and stopped. After thirty minutes it was coaxed to resume its journey. An hour later it spluttered again, as engines do, and halted, in the middle of West Africa, with nothing to be seen in any direction except desert, stunted trees, and more desert. I walked away, knowing the others would catch up to me on the only road, assuming it started again. An hour later, while I was strolling down the lonely byway and loving my walk, Mamadou slowed the car — afraid to actually stop — and flung the passenger door open to me. I had to run alongside and hop in.

Eventually, hours later, we came upon a town with shops that would be of interest to a mechanically challenged vehicle. As was Mamadou's way, the car was brought to a rest where it suited him — this time, in the middle of the road. He got out, we all got out, and repairs began with seriousness. Parts were offered, parts were rejected. It was not just any road that Mamadou chose to park on, this was a main thoroughfare within Mali, and the cars, trucks, and tractors that wished to pass our vehicle veered around it while Mamadou shouted beneath our raised hood. I found a chair, sat by the roadside, and breathed dust, to the amusement of the children. I would not give up the thoughts and sights that came — certainly not for efficient travel.

When we pulled in front of the office-cum-bedroom-at-hotel-cost back in Ségou, Mohammed was not there. "Mohammed is coming," was the mantra spoken upon my arrival — and the last thing I heard that night.

Upon rising early the next morning, I heard that "Mohammed is coming," as though he were the messiah. However, no one knew when he was actually coming. The office lady told me she should come to Canada with me each time I used her phone to leave Mohammed a voice message or used her computer to e-mail him.

He was unresponsive.

When I returned from my morning walk and a successful search for a breakfast of hot bread and cold Coca-Cola, the office lady said Mohammed would be there. "Today, at four." Hours away.

"Does he know I want to see him?" I asked, to reinforce what she already knew.

"You want to see him?" she asked.

This was my fourth Tuesday in Mali. Why in the world would I have expected Monday's plan to still exist?

While waiting for Mohammed, I found myself walking along a dry road in a silent setting. A wounded building sat at the dead-end of the road. Its stairs led to a verandah reminiscent of distant days, of times when students gathered here, when the colony had wealth and the decisions were made in Paris. The colonnade posts begged for paint that perhaps would never come.

I walked over fields and roads strewn with litter. In Ségou, garbage ruled, shards of bright-coloured plastic poked through everywhere. But even my few weeks in this country forced me to accept the shabbiness, the torn living-room furniture the homeowner overlooks but guests notice. It was as though Mali had become the world's rubbish bin. Malians were as likely to talk about the never-changing weather as about the never-changing mess. I should be no more appalled at the litter there than they would be at the plentiful table scraps we Westerners put in our garburators.

I returned to the office and was told by the woman who wanted to come with me that Mohammed would not be there that evening. He had phoned her, she recounted, about "car problems." He had promised to meet me the next evening in Bamako, at the Hotel Wawa. "Maybe you'll have dinner together," she proposed.

Zak, who was standing nearby, saw my frustration. *"Rick,"* he said, "we should walk." So we returned to the garden where I'd first smelled the mighty River Niger weeks ago and thought of Mungo Park's sighting of his nemesis. This was also where I had forgotten about Mohammed and had started trusting Zak.

A timed shutter might have captured that day's close, such was the momentary composition of sun, cloud, sky, and refraction. Everything, then nothing. An orange wick trimmed out. There was the cinder smell of an old fire. Zak said, "Sunrise, promise; sunset, memory."

We left the gardens, left the river, and knew that we would not have much more time together. Still, our emotions remained unspoken as we walked side by side in the dark until the trail narrowed. Then Zak stepped aside to let me pass, to let me take the lead as had become our pattern. It was dark and the route was uncertain, and I deferred to my teacher. "You lead," I said.

At our partings, I was feeling misty about both Nema and Zak. She was practical and appreciated the utensils and food I left with her; she even thanked me for the used clothes I would no longer need. Mostly, she liked the money. She kissed my cheek with quivering lips and walked away, looking over her shoulder only once. Then she was quickly in front of me again and hugged me with her strong brown arms. In the momentary calm, Nema reached over me like a poem, took my hat, and that was when I last saw her.

I hugged Zak as a son, wanting to give him what was of value to me — my compass, the flashlight, a medical kit, and safety supplies, which we went through piece by piece. He accepted money but did not fuss; it was the knife that he held longest. I have not often had a more memorable handshake — not for business or friendship or family. Maybe that's how one says goodbye to one's teacher.

"*Amadgugou,*" Zak said, using my Dogon name, which I'd taken to mean "dearly good to know."

"*Gana,*" I replied, in Zak's dialect — "Exceptional thank-you."

The road rumbled beneath me all the next day. I was returning to Bamako, roller-coastering on the heat-heaved pavement. The desert routes, once charted by stars but now paved, still suffer the vagaries of sand dunes and shifting landmarks. Into this comes a plan for the Trans-Saharan Highway.

Mali is again at the heart of an African dream. It is here that the Sahara must be crossed if the route from Lagos, Nigeria, on the Atlantic Ocean, is to run north to Morocco. René Caillié would be astounded. Asphalt. Four Wheel Drive. "Just follow the signs, René."

There will always be more desert than road, fortunately. The proposed highway is mapped, and much of it has been surveyed. From Nigeria to Benin, through Burkina Faso. Mali, of central importance, connects the south of Africa with the west and from there, the north. Mali's linking of these regions is being done in tandem with its neighbour, Mauritania, where the real work is already underway.

An *International Herald Tribune* article quoted Mauritanian official Sid'Ahmed, calling the nameless highway "The Road of Challenge." In a land of prophets, this man prophesied, "When it is realized, the whole world will be connected."

Indeed, we would be. All that is good and bad about the convenient flow of peoples north, south, east, and west would become increasingly apparent. But only if the crushed-stone base topped with asphalt can withstand the desert's will. Only if the sand-defending trees lining the highway survive and the protective nylon tarps defy the drifting grains. Only if the desert wishes it to be so.

I took dinner alone in Bamako at a restaurant that had earlier proven to be a prize. Brazier chicken, french fries, vinegar, salt, sliced tomato, cold Coke with lime, and no onions. Burkina Faso and Mali were playing in the Africa Cup of Nations game, and I caught portions of the match as it was the thing to do: a black-and-white television set was brought to me, the restaurant's only patron.

The restaurant was family-run, a young woman and an old woman doing the cooking and serving. When a gruff man entered, their chatter went silent. He looked about the counter and rummaged below it. I heard the spilling of roasted beans onto metal. His right shoulder arched, and his arm drove a hand grinder. Immediately the room smelled of coffee. I sniffed loudly at the aroma to get his attention. His eyebrows tweaked together. I tilted my head in request and his lips pushed a smirk toward his nose. Minutes later my first cup of authentic Malian coffee steamed before me. Rich, thick, and dark.

The sun outside my window was gone in a sip.

A coffee brand had once sported the name *Klekolo*, in tribute to a Bambara word for "rules to live in peace and harmony." With that recollection, I left for my rumoured meeting with Mohammed. As I neared the Wawa Hotel, I was happy to see a vehicle parked in front. Finally, justice would be done.

"Mohammed is in Ségou," the desk clerk informed me. "I just talked on phone." I mulled over this predicament while watching CNN break news that was no longer news. Earlier in the day I had e-mailed Mohammed and left a phone message. Both communications emphasized my trust that he'd do right by me, meaning cash back. I decided to call him one last time, as he was obviously in an accessible district if he'd just spoken with the adamant clerk. Taking the hotel's cellphone, I walked into the dark, star-covered courtyard. And I called Mohammed who, against the odds, answered.

"Rick, did you get my e-mail today?"

"No, when?"

"I replied to you. We'll send you the money. I'm working out the costs right now."

"I'm pleased to hear that, Mohammed."

"It is not a problem, Rick. You've had a good trip to Mali, and nothing should spoil it."

"Mohammed, the best advice I got was to take ten days in the Dogon." (I was sucking up to close the deal, giving credit where it wasn't due.) "When I come back, I'll spend two weeks there."

"That is good. And good that you'll come back."

I inadvertently shrugged. There was no quarrel in me, nothing I wanted to prove. We agreed to meet in Berlin two months later as we both planned to be at ITB, the mother of all travel trade shows.

"Rick, e-mail me the details for where you want the money, and I will send to you."

"Thank you, Mohammed. We both know roughly what it'll be, so please send five hundred Euros to start and we'll come to a final agreement soon."

"Good."

"Good," I replied.

"Bye, Rick."

"Bye, Mohammed," and I turned from the darkened compound to the low lights of the two-storey hotel and passed the cellphone back across the desk.

Then I took my last walk under a Malian night sky. All the dirt roads near the hotel were couched in dark except where a lone cooking fire burned, a bent-over woman scrubbed dishes, and a TV glowed. Clusters of people sat by the side of the road, most without speaking, others laughing quietly.

A grey-walled store made of recycled wood rested under a tin roof that reflected a warming fire. A refrigerator stood in the store's doorway. I bought a Fanta and sat outside with the children. A mother strapped her baby to her back and the men watched a fuzzy image of the football game on the store's TV set. Giggles, many a "*bonsoir*" and stares. When I finished the soda, I left. Then, a few metres away, I paused to treasure the sight of these people so enjoying each other's company.

In all my travels in Mali, I never found despair. Hardship, disappointment, poverty, indifference, and resignation were always evident, more so than hope. But never despair. The people have one another. "Westerners don't understand Africa," I was told. "They say everyone's poor. That is not it. Africans are very happy in the good countries. Poor, yes, but what is that? They are happy." The visitor's reward is to witness the resilience, the wealth, of the human spirit.

Fumbling in my pack, I stuffed the remaining tobacco into my pipe and lit it. This produced an unfamiliar dusty smoke that burned dry and went out quickly. I repacked the pipe and lit it again, only then realizing that my last stash had come from the tobacco exchange with the elderly *peep* smoker in Djiguibombo the day I entered *Le Pays Dogon*.

Cheers broke into the darkness. A man squatted in the shadow near a mud wall, the volume low on his radio as I walked by. I asked the game's final score, and he announced happily that it was Mali 3, Burkina Faso 1. A good night for West Africa.

A Gentle Harshness

I LEFT AFRICA PERSONALLY CHANGED BY THE gentle harshness I found and a disquieting splendour that found me. Mali was the journey I needed, if not the one I envisioned. And I learned that there's a little of Timbuktu in every traveller: the over-anticipated experience, the clash of dreams with reality.

For some, the greatest gift of travel is anticipation. For others, its benefit is the journey, personal or physical. Many travellers relish the occasions bound in, not for, a destination. There are those who comprehend travel best in the aftermath, in the memories of difficulties met, and in reflection over photographs and home food. There is no recipe. Not all travels are a quest, not every student learns.

True travellers (that's an unfair term, but hear me out) find any landscape of interest, passingly so, perhaps, but still of interest. One may develop preferences and value some spaces more than others, yet every place, journey, and view holds potential. And there is never a more real landscape than the one where you stand. All else is memory, imagination, or a cobbled-together expectation of what might be.

Travel reflects the care one takes in building oneself, in identifying the spirit of living as one sees it. A journey is not complete unto itself; the physical start and end are only arbitrary statements of time, useful for spatial definition. As a traveller, one passes through and around stationary places; the traveller is the stream, not the rock. Travel is about caring for those who welcome you, who grant you passage, who take care of you, who share their work and play, their homes and meals. It is not about waving painted fingernails at the locals as you drive by.

At its core, travel holds immense hope for a better world. It has been said that "Tourism is the right hand of peace." I hold that to be true. Two hundred and eighteen countries call this tiny planet home. Each of us is but a step or two away from a person in every one of those nations; they may be family, perhaps a friend, or a fellow traveller. Tourism, more than any other industry, can break down barriers to understanding, can bring people together to celebrate differences.

In my journey, I was fortunate enough to avoid the misfortunes of Adams. I did not find in myself even a modest measure of Park's persistence, not an iota of Caillié's preparation, the conceits of Laing, or the rigours of Barth. It was good that I explored Mali at the dawn of the twenty-first century; I did not have to compete with those paragons of travel. Their impression of Timbuktu, however, echoed across the canyon of the two hundred years between us: "Is that all there is?" Timbuktu was not what any of us thought it would be. Few destinations are as fascinating as the journeys they inspire.

Now is the Needed Time

IT HAS BEEN NEARLY A DECADE SINCE I SLEPT on the rooftops of mud homes in the Dogon villages, got lost in the streets of Timbuktu, and wiled away time with Zak. I will always remember that when I was antsy about a delay or other issues arising from foreign travel and sought a solution or his advice, he'd simply say, *Inshallah* ("If God is willing").

My travels to Timbuktu would be forbidden today if the jihadists had their say. A traveler would find him or herself in harm's way for all manner of reasons, constantly deterred by both the military as well as their own common sense. As I was leaving Mali in 2004, the Islamic extremist groups were already convening in the north, the Tuareg were restless, and the Arab Spring was in gestation. Events then unfolded as they always seemed to unfold in Africa, as portrayed by the Western media — at their own peculiar pace of unrest, brutality, and disappointment.

Traditionally, Africa annually garners immense hope from observers in the Western world. The Band Aid theme song, "Do They Know it's Christmas?" is a perennial reminder of hardship and conveys the power of Western guilt ("we have more") with thumping sympathy masked as empathy. Yet we can't escape the song's sentiment: "Thank God it's them instead of you …" It's often hard for me to reconcile the Timbuktu I visited to the atrocities that have occurred since I left, especially when current events have had such a significant impact on the people I met on my trip.

Beginning the month after my journey, Zak and I remained in touch via e-mail infrequently, whenever he could make it into Mopti. As time went on and with the expansion of Internet access, e-mail became more convenient for him, and now we can even speak on the phone.

When I first returned from my travels in West Africa, Mohammed e-mailed me regularly, offering meaningful promises: "I will get back to you very soon with further details and reimbursement." Then, "I am having my people check our records for your refund." Eventually, "I am very sorry it has taken me so long. I will be in Europe in one week and from there I will send you money." One day the messages stopped. No reply came to the e-mails I continued to send. Eventually I heard from Zak in response to my asking about Mohammed: "Nothing. No one says. Gone." It seems Mohammed's business went bad and out.

Nema e-mailed me once to say that she was taking a computer course and would I please send sixty dollars.

Zak was never paid by Mohammed for his work as my guide. I covered the amount because it was my shout, as they say, and asked him to share it with Nema.

Alistair and I traded notes after returning home. He kindly sent along some of his writings, a version of which appeared in a later edition of the valuable book *Sahara Overland*, edited by Chris Scott. His sharing of this draft ensured that I did right by him when reviewing my own sketchy notes of that evening's conversation on the hotel balcony in Mopti.

And a few months after this book was first published I arrived home one evening to find a large bouquet of flowers on the front porch and a card that said, "Thank you. Love, Anke." I've been unable to make contact with my three Malian and two French train companions, though I hope this story finds its way into their hands so they know how they furthered the awareness and understanding of a fellow traveler.

Ali Farka Touré died in March 2006, after a long battle with cancer.

In late 2007, I received an e-mail from Zak: "*Rick*, I am married. Name is Marie." I was thrilled for him and Marie, and asked about his plans. "Will live in village. Dogon." When I asked about his guiding business, he responded, "Is difficult. Is slow."

And when I asked about Mamadou, Zak replied, "No work. Now not."

Around the same time, I asked Zak for his comfort with my writing about him and our travels together. He replied, "Good you write. Make more people for guide." And after the book was out and I'd sent him gift books as a thank you, he wrote: "Six Timbuktu books. Arrive Mopti. Will share." And so it went. Of the copies I'd sent him, he gave one to Nema, he said; and because her English was limited, "I told story. She laugh." And that made me happy.

In the spring of 2009, Zak sent me a smiling e-mail, one of those messages you glean great happiness from because of how the words jump: "Son Kaleb. New. Born to Maria. And me. Am happy."

His family was now rooted in the Dogon village he'd called home forever. But all the while, events outside his world were curtailing his work as a guide as well as the increasingly essential income for his growing family.

Occasionally I put readers of the first edition of this book in touch with Zak, but none of them actually ventured to Mali: difficulties started to arise, hesitations set in, trips were postponed and finally cancelled. Kidnappings occurred in nearby countries, and Mali was rumoured to be a place for hiding those captives, a country from where lucrative ransoms were negotiated. Tension escalated in June of 2009 when Malian armed force's Colonel Lamana Ould Dou was assassinated at his Timbuktu home, in uniform, his purported AQIM assailants fleeing into the desert in 4 X 4s.

In November of 2011, two Frenchmen were kidnapped not far from Timbuktu, nearer Mopti. Two days later, four tourists — one each from The Netherlands, Germany, Sweden, and South Africa, were having lunch in a café on the Timbuktu square, a place I'd walked by casually and confidently feeling safe. They were approached by gun-toting men who forced them into waiting vehicles. When the German baulked and refused to go with his captors, a gunman turned, aimed, and shot him dead.

When his work as a guide for trekkers dried up, it became Zak's ambition to create a garden business for his village and to provide a job for himself and for fellow villagers.

Timbuktu's tourism numbers hit a sharp decline — to near zero — in an industry that once accounted for fifty percent of the local economy. Zak's guiding business, even in the Dogon, dried up.

Occasionally I sent him money. Not a lot, and I never tied this to Christmas or to an anniversary of our travels, or to anything that indicated it would be annual or even repeated; it was just a little bit to help a friend.

When the Harmattan winds died down one year, an e-mail from Zak sprouted with an idea: "I build business. Village. Garden to sell." I wondered if I could help somehow. "What do you need for your new business?" I asked. His garden was growing, he replied, and he had the land to expand, but he needed a larger cistern to hold water for irrigation. The well needed to be deeper, too. Both projects would mean he could give jobs to people in his village.

Months later he sent two photographs. They showed his large garden, and Zak's message: "*Rick*, one day you visit. We sit in garden. You. Me. We eat garden. Is onion."

"Onion?!" I wrote back. "Zak, I hate onions."
"Is onion garden *Rick*. You like."
I vow to one day sit in Zak's garden and eat onions with him.

In 2011, as Libya fell from dictatorship into disarray, many soldiers who had fought alongside Colonel Moammar Gadhafi's troops — armed, well-trained, and eager for action — fled south and west through

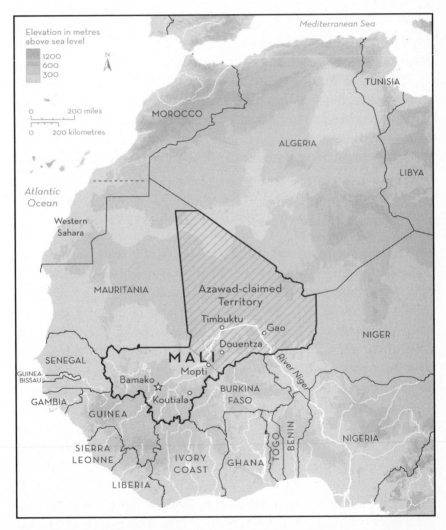

The Tuareg have long wanted a country of their own. Today that would require separating Mali in two, with the new nation becoming Azawad.

Niger and Algeria. They found a refuge in Mali and changed that country, perhaps forever.

The Tuaregs — nomadic desert dwellers who form about a tenth of Mali's population — have long called this part of the Sahara their home. As recently as two decades ago, they took up the battle for an autonomous territory, one they envisioned as a self-governed homeland. Azawad, they call their proposed new country. Since Mali gained independence from France in 1960, the Tuareg had mounted four armed and aggressive calls for autonomy. Mali, a democratic country, stayed firm that it should remain whole. Each Tuareg attempt at separation ended with a ceasefire, resulting in peaceful, if disgruntled, coexistence. Until the next time.

Tuaregs know death. Before teaching me how to ride a camel at an oasis near Timbuktu, my Tuareg companion wrapped a blue turban, a *cheche*, around my head and neck. It was to keep out the wind-whipped sand, he said: "Is necessary. Or you will die."

When the Tuareg survivors of the Libyan rebellion returned to Mali, their National Movement for the Liberation of Azawad (MNLA) aligned with AQIM, the opportunistic front of a jihadist movement targeting occupation and control of the huge sub-Saharan region known as the Sahal. The Salafi militants were bent on destroying the status quo in Mali, a country known for its tradition of religious tolerance. Their aim was the establishment of a theocratic state and "terrorist sanctuary." The consortia moved southward with the common purpose of pushing away the ill-prepared Malian army, taking control first of the desert and then of the Sahel's trading city of Gao, in the eastern part of the country. And their incursion soon made parts of Mali — certainly Timbuktu — "one of the most dangerous places in the world."

To bring that about, several strands of history played out in sequence — all were separate, yet related. The Malian army felt that the government, led by former general Amadou Toumani Touré (affectionately known as "ATT"), provided them with poor equipment and inadequate resources to fight this civil war. That discontent led to a military coup on February 6, 2012, which deposed ATT and replaced him with a mid-level captain, Amadou Sanogo (a graduate of U.S. military training programs for Mali), who was then declared president. (Later, this junta would itself be forced to relinquish power in another transition.) While the cabal fought their own government, the distraction provided the alliance of Tuareg and Taliban-like militants with open ground.

The Tuareg–AQIM partnership methodically seized control of three of Mali's regions — Gao, Tombouctou, and Kidal — and surrounded Tombouctou's capital city, Timbuktu. The old town's shrines and mosques came under threat, as did its 700,000 manuscripts from the 14th and 15th centuries. The rediscovery of these Arabic and Hebrew language documents has been called "the most important archeological discovery since the Dead Sea Scrolls." Most of the manuscripts are brittle and curled by humidity and time, many of their bindings weakened by bugs. I had cradled some of these ancient books in my hands while visiting Timbuktu.

One day the insurgents entered and took control of Douentza, the town where I'd played soccer with the free-spirited village children on a patch of dirt road, and I was struck by their immediate loss of innocence. Wherever they went, the AQIM imposed what the *New York Times* called "hard-edged Islamic rule." Women were to clothe themselves from head to ankle and to cover their faces with veils. Non-compliance was punished with flogging. Public amputations for minor misdemeanors were but one demonstration of the militants' fanaticism. They would carve off an accused person's hand, at the wrist, in public.

Timbuktu was for many centuries a centre of Islamic teaching and learning, a place where curiosity led to the study and acknowledgement of differing world views and cultures.

Irony steps in at the oddest times: it was here that the insurgents' alliance split as the Islamic militants turned on the ethnic Tuaregs, forcing them to flee or be killed, and making Timbuktu a flashpoint during what *The Economist* magazine termed "bloody repercussions." The Ansar Dine's black flag now hung unchallenged in Timbuktu.

The first amateur photographs coming out of the invaded Timbuktu in 2012 showed spades held high and pickaxes being swung against the mud walls of shrines and mausoleums constructed hundreds of years ago. It was not enough that these monuments had been built and maintained by devout Muslims, or that they had survived the ravages of many centuries. As chunks of earthen plaster fell away and littered the ground, frenzied hands pulled at exposed structural frames. The frames crumbled.

Timbuktu was once called The Town of 333 Saints, and there are dozens of shrines and mausoleums and mosques, all of them targeted for destruction by the jihadists after they took control of the remote and famous city. (STR/AFP/Getty Images)

Of the shrines, considered idolatrous by the jihadist vandals, Ansar Dine spokesman Sanda Quid Boumama told *Agence France-Presse* that they would be destroyed: "All of them, without exception." The International Criminal Court barked in reply, "This is a war crime."

The world responded with words. The United Nations Educational, Scientific and Cultural Organization (UNESCO) expressed concern about "the looting and smuggling of artifacts," to which Boumama replied, with a terrorist's shrug, "All of this is *haraam* [sinful]. We are all Muslims. UNESCO is what?"

In the spring of 2012, Zak's e-mails took an ominous turn. For the first time, he asked for assistance: "Can help village? No food. No work. No garden."

Then, weeks later, another message: "Am to Burkino. Look for work. Maybe flee."

When he returned from Burkino Faso, the country just south of where he and I had trekked in the Dogon area of Mali, he wrote that there were already too many people there looking for work. He and Marie might instead go to Mopti.

Within days I read on a BBC website that Mopti was where the rebels were heading next in their surge westward in Mali. And it was then that I asked Zak what I wrote in this book's preface: "Are you safe?" He replied, "Am safe. Village has fear." It occurred to me that another fear held by Zak's fellow villagers would be that someone as strong and diligent as Zak might leave them. And that's what he did.

Zak and his family fled their Dogon village and headed west and south to the town of Koutiala, somewhat north of Mali's border with Burkino Faso. His next email read: "In Koutiala, time is little quiet, I think that is better to stay here because all west Africa is in danger so going in new adventure inner Burkina or Côte-D'Ivoire will not change about the security."

Then: "The village is 05 km from the town but every morning I go there to look for job! My family and myself are OK today." As they adjusted, Zak wrote: "Now we have the habit of life from here! At the beginning (02 months) ago it was hard with the mosquito and the wedder." (Here I have to repeat one of his misspellings, revenge perhaps for the times we spent together in the Dogon when he announced: "*Rick*, you have *unfixable* French!")

I do not wish to trade on his colloquialisms, charming as they are, nor on his candour — but always he is pure, lovable Zak, the fellow who was my teacher, and always patiently so. It brings a wry and sad smile to my face when he writes, "Please my friend if you can help me; I need to buy cereals for eating food and build a toilette. Because the toilette we are using is in somebody house and they getting boring with us now."

And, when he's been assisted, "Thank you very much for the help; this will arrange my situation." In the midst of war, amid uncertainty, living in trying times and danger, Zak's life with Marie and Kalib moved along.

Not once has an e-mail from Zak ended without his best wishes in some version of "I hope you are good with your family!" And recently Zak wrote of his prayer "for liberty of survive..."

I told Zak I was preparing an update of the text for this book's "second edition." It was important for me to ask about his comfort with, and his permission for, my writing about his life in these difficult times.

He replied, "That I survive or no from this war, that book will be a very good memorial thing for all around the world but more for the future generation from my country!" What he wrote next tore at my heart: "It's a work you are doing for my people for the world know us and do not forget us!"

The great fear among both the region's residents and outside observers is that all of the Sahel will become unstable. Robert Fowler, the UN special envoy to Niger in 2008, was kidnapped by the AQIM in the Sahel in that year. Now freed, he says the AQIM's ambition is to make the vast swath of territory from Mauritania to Somalia "one great, chaotic, anarchic mess in which they believe their jihad will thrive."

Everything I'd enjoyed in Timbuktu has been curtailed or condemned. The Djinguereber Mosque I'd been allowed to visit, the Festival au Desert, the freedom and confidence to trek in the Dogon, the smiles on the faces of children saying "*un cadeau, un cadeau*" — all were gone for the time being. Nothing strikes me as much, though, as the loss of Zak's carefree "will fix" attitude concerning any difficulty. Instead, his wish became "that we cross this difficult and terrible time..."

After my trip I became more attentive to the efforts aimed at easing the plight of Timbuktu's endangered manuscripts. Those efforts garnered the attention they deserved, notably in a front-page article in *The New York Times* and a page in *National Geographic*. Coverage was well intentioned but only sporadic. The current difficulties have brought these artifacts to the forefront of international media attention. The known collections of manuscripts are spread among sixty family and private libraries; even these locations are thought to account for only a portion of the manuscripts. At the height of the AQIM control of Timbuktu, the survival of every single ancient manuscript was under threat.

There are many private libraries in Timbuktu, most in the Old Town part of the city, as shown by the location tags on this aerial photograph (which compares to the drawn map on page 157). Some of their collections are not well known, yet each is important and in need of financial assistance and trained workers to help preserve the ancient manuscripts. Location assistance and French names provided by Ali ould Sidi, Chef de la Mission Culturelle de Tombouctou. (Map c. 2013 Google; Imagery c. 2013 Aerodata International Survey, Digital Globe, GeoEye)

At that time, I came across the story of Mohamed Diagayete, a refugee from Mali, a peripatetic scholar, a covert conniver, and bibliophile with spy-caliber nerves. The computer that Diagayete had left behind in Timbuktu housed digital images of thousands of the manuscripts. As tombs in Timbuktu were being defaced and people were being subjected to the lash for minor infractions, he returned to Timbuktu, "snuck in," retrieved his hard drive, and escaped once again. But he has reproductions of only a small portion of the estimated 700,000 manuscripts at risk in Timbuktu. Of the rest, he said: "When we lose them, we have no other copy. It's forever."

A few years ago, I was in California and met with Professor Musa Balde, of the Timbuktu Educational Foundation. He took me to his neighborhood African restaurant for a meal of the most delicious chicken and couscous. The professor had just returned from a trip to Timbuktu and when I asked if he possessed any manuscripts, he said, "Yes, in my family." When I pressed, he replied, "I have some myself." I did not ask about either the quantities or the locations of the manuscripts. Over a lunch enlivened by much talk and many handshakes, Professor Balde spoke of how my arrival was the wish of the heavens and that there was a role for me to play in helping the Timbuktu foundation move forward. I did not have the same sense of heaven's hand, nor did I feel a nudge, and we left one another without any implied obligation on my part, though I'd made the foundation my first choice for the promised donation of funds resulting from my book royalties and had provided them to him. The TEF had once operated a "preserve a manuscript" program that was admirable and easy for one to support. Lately I've tried to connect again with it, but I've had no luck making contact or receiving a reply. I suspect the foundation is not operating any longer, and its once handsome website is now down.

In 2008, a beautiful book of photographs and text was published as *The Hidden Treasures of Timbuktu*. Written by John O. Hunwick and Alida Jay Boye, it included lavish photography by Joseph Hunwick. I'd met Alida Jay Boye over the Internet when I came across the work she was doing through the University of Oslo and its program to preserve Timbuktu's manuscripts. She generously provided two photographs for my book, and then her own book came out, leapfrogging to the top of the list of Timbuktu books as the most descriptive, most important way for all of us to understand the wonders and importance of these artifacts. In 2010 Alida facilitated my modest donation to La Bibliothèque Mohamed Tahar, a library in Timbuktu under the careful custodianship of Abdoul Wahid Haidara, advising that $600 would complete the library's roof, providing a necessary shelter for the library's work and helping to house more books in a stable environment.

All of that changed, and then changed back.

Irreplaceable treasures in peril, even when added to the horrors of forced prostitution and punishments that include amputation, drew the world's outrage but not its intervention. As Mopti came under the plotting gaze of the insurgents, France's president, François Hollande, responded: "It is in leaving AQIM ... free to flourish in the Sahel that I would be taking risks with my country." An international military response began with the arrival of French Mirage and Rafale fighter jets in Malian airspace in early 2013.

These workers are employees of the Ahmed Baba Institute, and when the time of day is appropriate for their prayers, they conduct them within the library's collection which holds rare and unique books and pamphlets, including ancient Arabic and Hebrew manuscripts. (Alexandra Huddleston)

African soldiers welcome working with French forces in northern Mali as they begin maneuvers in mid February, 2013 to oust the insurgent extremists from not only Timbuktu and Gao, but from all of Mali. (AP Photo/Pascal Guyot, Pool)

And it was swift, the way the French went about taking control of each city first by securing its airport and then surrounding or arcing through the town. Most insurgents were reported to have retreated to the desert, to hide away in its mountains and rely on intimidation from a distance.

Amid all this came an email from Zak: "Hello my friend, we are so happy now that FRANCE is taking out those peouple [sic] from of MALI!!! We hope to be abble [sic] to go back home very soon."

And then the rumours started. "Rebels torch Timbuktu manuscript library." The Reuters news service quoted the town's mayor: "Islamist fighters fleeing Mali's ancient Saharan city of Timbuktu as French and Malian troops closed in set fire to a South African-funded library there containing thousands of priceless manuscripts." These were the treasures in the Ahmed Baba collection. Inside I cried. These writings by Muslims, cared for over centuries by Muslims, watched over and interpreted and revered by Muslims — were destroyed by other Muslims for the simple reason that they passed along history and told of science and conveyed knowledge.

Yet as quickly as that news came in, it was immediately followed by conflicting reports: the extremists were unsuccessful in their efforts to destroy the ancient manuscripts of Timbuktu. The attempted arson had failed, the flames unable to take hold. Instead, the sturdy stacks of pages proved too bulky for the fire to burn effectively and engulf the books and wooden shelves. Rather, the fires smoldered long enough for residents to extinguish the threat. The library was scarred and many writings were lost, but there was reason to look at the lessened damage optimistically.

In this time of heightened awareness and renewed interest, individuals and foundations and Malian scholars will embark anew to protect the ancient manuscripts, and they will build on much good work that exists already. Among the most important is the University of Oslo's Timbuktu Manuscript Project managed by Alida Jay Boye, which successfully completed its scope of work in 2009 including a preliminary inventory of collections, and

First reports out of Timbuktu in late January 2013 warned of the fires set by the fleeing Islamists in an attempt to destroy Timbuktu's trove of priceless and irreplaceable manuscripts. Such reports fueled fears that libraries were ablaze and that the damage would be overwhelming. Though many manuscripts were partially burnt or others turned to ashes, these at the Ahmed Baba Centre were being recovered and the resulting damage was limited. (Eric Feferberg/AFP/Getty Images)

the creation of an electronic database for ongoing cataloguing, as well as training for workers in the delicate task of handling these historically unique pieces. Also among those active is the Tombouctou Manuscript Project through the University of Cape Town, supported by the government of South Africa and the Ford Foundation. Just as UNESCO has announced that it will find ways to rebuild the destroyed shrines, so too will there be fresh and meaningful endeavours to preserve, translate, and understand these treasured manuscripts.

Soon the French announced plans to leave Mali, their surge of 4,000 troops no longer committed, though they stated the intention to leave 1,000 military personnel in the country until year's end. Their role on the ground was supplanted by troops from nearby African nations, notably Niger and Chad. New forces claimed their own early successes as they pursued the jihadists into their desert hideaways. The Malian army, with a history of accusations of human rights abuses, began new training in hopes it will properly protect those they are tasked to help. Into the mix of well-intentioned efforts would come 12,000 UN peacekeepers, arriving during the summer of 2013, and deployed with the unanimous endorsement of the UN's Security Council.

And in the north of Mali, the Tuareg realigned their transitory loyalties to assist African troops in driving away the now unwelcome insurgents.

But did they all retreat into the desert as was claimed? *The Economist* asked: "Where have the jihadists gone?" Some were said to have shed the markers by which they could be identified and to have melded in with the locals. It is here they have a reprise, for the moment. One may surmise that a re-tailored extremist may be leaning against the broken wood door jam of a mudded home watching a Gao carver make furniture, or standing in line to buy fresh baked bread from a street-oven vendor in Douentza, or might even be bended in prayer next to a fellow Muslim whose lifestyle they despise.

When I first returned from Timbuktu, it seemed to me that few people, private citizens and government officials alike, were paying

Before they left for a safer place, Marie, Kaleb, and Zak Kouriba are at their home in a small village in Le Pays Dogon, with a television set in the corner under protective cover from the swirls of sand and wind.

any attention to Mali. The nation wasn't much more than a point-to reference as a functioning democracy on a dysfunctional continent. The Western world has an unfortunate tendency to ignore Africa and its ongoing struggles under all but the most tragic circumstances.

While writing this afterword, I received another email from Zak: "I am very happy to know that new pages of writing will appear soon about my country, and all things happening in Timbuktu and all around Mali." And yet later, "We are happy to inform you that we are back to Mopti. We are healthy and in security!" He could not know that Mali and Timbuktu were regularly leading the commentary in the West's major daily newspapers and on evening television news broadcast around the world. He could not know that right now we are a world wrestling to find a way to care for, and to contribute something useful to, the wellbeing of people like Zak, his family, and his country in their time of desperate need.

On the phone just before this book went to press, Zak told me that he, Marie and Kaleb will stay in Mopti. He is starting a new business there. He has five female chickens and one male, and is building a chicken house and will get more chicks to add with his current dozen. He plans for 100 females and 15 males in order to be a sustainable size. Then his brothers and sisters can join with him. This will be his new work – and theirs, though he will keep the onion garden in his remote Dogon village. I asked after Nema and he had seen her "just one day before." She has a good job with an African bank in Bamako, and what is more – she and her husband have two healthy young sons. This bright news was balanced with talk of Zak's father passing away recently, as had his grandfather a year ago, leaving Zak, 33, as the family's patriarch. "We do not live long lives in Africa," he said.

And talk of Nema reminded me how often readers of this book have assumed that she kept my hat when she last grabbed it from me. I agree I left that impression. While I never saw Nema again once we parted, the truth is that a little later I noticed the hat leaning against the wooden elbow of an arm chair. I took it. I love that hat, and have it still. It makes me smile.

The suicide bombings began as soon as France announced the scattering of jihadists. Five suicide bombers attacked Malian troops near Gao, wounding several and killing themselves. Next, a loner on a scooter targeted soldiers, leaving five dead when he exploded. Within the same time period came news of two bombings in Timbuktu and two in Kidal. All this of course channels memories of other conflicts when the war was won and the peace was lost. Tolstoy wrote that "All victories are temporary."

With Africa on my mind, lately I've been tuning into a radio station which frequently plays West African music late at night. And it brought to my attention striking songs of soft words and haunting truths that I'd never heard before. *Brothers in Bamako*, a selection of songs played and sung by guitarists Habib Koité and Eric Bibb, are songs "shared by an African and an African-American that no wind can separate." In one song, *Send us Brighter*

Days, they share words that must resonate in Mali today: "Send us healing ways..."

That sentiment is echoed in the oddly upbeat song, "Needed Time":

> *Now is the needed time*
> *We're livin in the needed time*

Timbuktu as it appears today, looking north along the Route de Kabara. In the nineteenth century, the French explorer René Caillié wrote: "Still, though I cannot account for the impressions, there was something imposing in the aspect of a great city raised in the midst of sands."

Chronology

circa 1000	–Nomadic Tuaregs use Timbuktu as a seasonal camp.
circa 1100	–Timbuktu is a permanent marketplace intersecting River Niger and Sahara Desert trade routes.
1324	–Mansa Kankan Moussa, emperor of Mali (since 1312), visits Timbuktu with a caravan of tremendous wealth; builds mosque in Timbuktu, and twelve years later makes this territory part of the Mali Empire.
1353	–Ibn Battutah, the great Moroccan traveller, visits Timbuktu.
1373	–First European reference to Timbuktu occurs in an atlas.
circa 1400	–Mali Empire loses control of Timbuktu to Tuaregs.
circa 1470–95	–Nadir of Timbuktu as a centre for trade, religious learning, scholarship, and wealth.
1496	–Pilgrimage of Askia the Great (Songhai Empire) from Timbuktu to Mecca; destabilizes Egypt's currency by giving away hundreds of thousands of gold pieces.
1526	–Visit of Leo Africanus to Timbuktu.
circa 1600	–Decline of Timbuktu's wealth begins.
1788	–Founding of the Association for Promoting the Discovery of Inland Parts of the Continent of Africa (Britain), known as the African Association.

1795–96	–Mungo Park's first expedition to Timbuktu fails.
1805	–Mungo Park's second expedition travels near, but not to, Timbuktu.
1811	–American Benjamin Rose (Robert Adams) is held as a captured slave in Timbuktu, the first non-African/non-Arab to see Timbuktu, a claim that is disputed.
1814	–The Committee of the Company of Merchants Trading to Africa, known as the African Committee, publishes Robert Adams's book.
1826	–10,000 franc prize is offered by Société de Géographie de France (Paris) for a "first person" account of visiting Timbuktu and returning.
1826	–British Major Alexander Gordon Laing visits Timbuktu and is murdered.
1828	–French explorer René-August Caillié reaches Timbuktu and returns safely to Europe.
1853	–German Heinrich Barth reaches Timbuktu and returns safely home.
1880	–French military expedition to determine Trans-Saharan Railway route ends in disaster.
1890	–French declare Soudan as their colony; Timbuktu falls to the French in 1893–1894.
1960	–Independence from France for Republic of Mali; Bamako capital; Timbuktu under Mali rule for the first time since the early fifteenth century.
1988	–UNESCO declares Timbuktu a World Heritage Site.
1990	–Timbuktu is placed on the list of World Heritage Sites in Danger.
	–Tuareg rebellion against the Malian government.
1992	–National Pact.
1996	–On March 27, a formal truce declared following the civil war with Tuaregs who sought an independent homeland, Azawad (Azaouad).
2010	–Beginnings of Arab Spring in North Africa.
2011	–Rebellion erupts in Libya.
	–October 20, Libyan leader Colonel Muammar Gadhafi killed.

-Tuareg's National Movement for the Liberation of Azawad (MNLA) aligned with Ansar Dine (Defenders of Faith), align with Al-Qaeda in the Islamic Maghreb (AQIM).

2012   -March 20, coup d'état in Mali, President Amadou Toumani Touré deposed; Captain Amadou Sanogo seizes power.

-Post coup, the Economic Community of West African States (ECOWAS) works to negotiate a return to democracy, and in November authorizes possible military intervention.

-May, Tuareg declaration of independent nation of Azawad, an Islamic state.

-May, AQIM/Alliance captures Goa and Timbuktu.

2013   -January, February, French air bombardment in Mali, French troops arrive retake Goa, Timbuktu and Duentza.

-February, March, ECOWAS deploys troops in support of French troops.

-April, French begin withdrawal from Mali.

-April 25, United Nations Security Council passes resolution creating peacekeeping force for Mali

-France's President Hollande calls for country wide election in Mali for July

-May, five suicide bombers die in attack on Malian troops near Gao

Acknowledgements

AS MY TIMBUKTU JOURNEY ENDED, MY BOOK'S journey into your hands began. It exists because many people helped me along the way, though I ask those not mentioned to please know that I also deeply value their roles. Stephen Darling and John Korenic were among the first to encourage my travels; Paul Grescoe, Rob Sanders, Scott Wayne, Margo Pfieff, Allan MacDougall, Jim Douglas, and Jim Hutchison prodded my writing; and Steve Henrichsen, Professor Musa Balde, and Brian Antonson spent time reviewing materials and nudging the author to improve. My narrative was informed through swapped travel stories, and several tellers, though not all, will become known to the reader — they enabled a better book. The author takes responsibility for any flaws or errors in the text, including those in paraphrasing and interpretation.

All photographs are identified and credited at the book's end, yet I wish here to thank their creators: Dennis Shigematsu, Catherine Devrye, Jose Mandigers, Anke Biermans, Don Cayo, Alida Jay Boye, and Christine Elliott — seasoned travellers all, and good with the click of a shutter! They kindly lent their images for this book with the understanding that a donation has been made in their name to "help preserve a manuscript" through the Timbuktu Educational Foundation's program and, separately, to further the important work of The Timbuktu Manuscripts Project, financed by Norway with the goal of preserving and promoting Africa's literary heritage. And also Don Waite, who gave a friendship full of guidance on photographic quality and consistency.

The book is enhanced by cartographer Eric Leinberger, whose maps will assist future travellers as well as readers. Also, portraits were commissioned for several figures related to the history of West Africa to further the reader's understanding of their individual character. Illustrator Simon Anderson-Carr's ink drawings provide the first fresh perspectives in nearly two centuries. He worked from known visuals for each, except Adams, for whom only written descriptives exist, resulting in a speculative portrait.

Geoffrey Lipman's willingness to write the book's foreword provided the author with a warmly welcomed vote of confidence.

Certain partners stand out when it comes to assisting and motivating the author. John Eerkes-Medrano is a sage and candid editor who believes that he has equal responsibilities on behalf of the writer, and on behalf of the reader — and he befriended my book's journey. Robert Mackwood of Seventh Avenue Literary Agency read the manuscript over a weekend and committed to represent it on the Monday morning, finding the best publishers for this work.

The decision to publish rested with Michael Carroll, and ultimately, Kirk Howard, respectively editorial director and owner of The Dundurn Group in Toronto. The care of Shannon Whibbs as the book's copy-editor proved to be one of professionalism, patience, and wisdom. The striking cover design by Jennifer Scott furthered the book's stature, as did the thoughtful book layout by designer Erin Mallory. My respect and appreciation to all three.

New York's Skyhorse Publishing's Tony Lyons and Cory Allyn took the decision to publish this Second Edition and encouraged the new Afterword. In doing so, Liz Driesbach created a new cover design and Oleg Lyubner oversaw the book's introduction and promotion. Also, I very much appreciate Dania Sheldon's work to secure access and permission for the new photographs within the Afterword. My thanks to them all for helping convey the importance of Mali's difficulties and the need to help protect the ancient manuscripts.

I extend my gratitude to the people of West Africa, those written about and those inferred between the lines of my story; they are remarkable.

Advice from my sons, Brent and Sean, was fundamental to both my trip plans and writing ambitions. Foremost, as will have become apparent to the reader — and something for which I will be eternally thankful — this book would not exist without a certain question from Janice, my wife, when she asked, "Why don't you just go to Timbuktu ...?"

About the Author

RICK ANTONSON, THE AUTHOR OF *ROUTE 66 STILL Kicks: Driving America's Main Street* and co-author of *Slumach's Gold: In Search of a Legend* and *The Fraser Valley*, is president and CEO of Tourism Vancouver, has served as deputy chair of the Pacific Asia Travel Association based in Bangkok, Thailand and is a former chair of the board for the Destination Marketing Association International based in Washington, DC. He serves as president of the Pacific Coast Public Television. He has traveled widely with his wife, Janice, including a trek with a guide-driver by four-wheel-drive from Lhasa, Tibet, through the Himalayas to Katmandu, Nepal. In five trips over the past dozen years, Rick and his sons, Brent (author of *Of Russia: A Year Inside*) and Sean, have circumnavigated the northern hemisphere by train, beginning and ending in London, England—including travelling by rail from Beijing, China, to Pyongyang, North Korea (a country today visited by few Westerners). Recently, Rick joined an expedition team to the 16,854-foot summit of Mount Ararat in eastern Turkey, followed by travels in Iraq and Iran, the subject of his forthcoming book. Rick and Janice make their homes in Vancouver, Canada, and in Cairns, Australia.

Sources and Recommended Reading

Adams, Charles Hansford, ed. *The Narrative of Robert Adams, a Barbary Captive: A Critical Edition.* New York: Cambridge University Press, 2005.

Africanus, Leo. *The History and Description of Africa.* London: Hakluyt Society, 1896.

Allen, Benedict, ed. *The Faber Book of Exploration.* London: Faber and Faber, 2002.

Asher, Michael and Dean King. *Death in the Sahara: The Lords of the Desert and the Timbuktu Railway Expedition Massacre.* New York: Skyhorse Publishing, 2008.

Barth, Heinrich. *Travels and Discoveries in North and Central Africa.* Edited by G.T. Bettany. London: Ward, Lock, 1890.

Battutah, Ibn. *The Travels of Ibn Battutah.* Edited by Tim Mackintosh-Smith. London: Picador, 2002.

Benanav, Michael. *Men of Salt: Crossing the Sahara on the Caravan of White Gold.* Guilford, Ct: Lyons Press, 2006.

Bennett, Nicholas. *Zigzag to Timbuktu.* London: John Murray, 1963.

Brook, Larry. *Daily Life in Ancient and Modern Timbuktu.* Minneapolis: Runestone Press, 1999.

Caillié, René. *Travels Through Central Africa to Timbuctoo.* 1830. Reprint, London: Darf, 1992.

Christopher, Robert, and Erik James Martin. *Ocean of Fire: Through the Garden of Allah to Timbuktu*. London: George G. Harrap, 1957.

Davidson, Basil. *Africa: History of a Continent*. New York: Macmillan, 1966.

De Gramont, Sanche. *The Strong Brown God: The Story of the Niger River*. London: Hart-Davis, McGibbon, 1975.

De Villiers, Marq, and Sheila Hirtle. *Sahara: A Natural History*. Toronto: McClelland & Stewart, 2002.

De Villiers, Marq, and Sheila Hirtle. *Timbuktu: The Sahara's Fabled City of Gold*. Toronto: McClelland & Stewart, 2007.

Di Cintio, Marcello. *Harmattan: Wind Across West Africa*. Toronto: Insomniac Press, 2002.

Fitzpatrick, Mary, et al. *Lonely Planet: West Africa*. 6th ed. Footscray, AUS: Lonely Planet Publications, 2006.

Fleming, Fergus. *The Sword and the Cross*. London: Granta Books, 2003.

Fremantle, Tom. *The Road to Timbuktu: Down the Niger on the Trail of Mungo Park*. London: Constable & Robinson, 2005.

Gardner, Brian. *The Quest for Timbuctoo*. London: Readers Union/ Cassel, 1969.

Gwyn, Stephen. *Mungo Park and the Quest of the Niger*. London: John Lane and Bodley Head, 1934.

Hemingway, Ernest. *Green Hills of Africa*. New York: Scribner, 1935.

Hudgens, Jim, and Richard Trillo. *The Rough Guide to West Africa*. 6th ed. London: Rough Guides, 2006.

Hunwick, John O. and Alida Jay Boye, with photographs by Joseph Hunwick. *The Hidden Treasures of Timbuktu*. London: Thames and Hudson, 2008.

Jacobs, Michael. *In the Glow of the Phantom Palace: Travels from Granada to Timbuktu*. London: Pallas Athene, 2000.

Jeppie, Shamil and Souleymane Bachir Diagne, eds. *The Meanings of Timbuktu.* Cape Town, South Africa: Human Sciences Research, 2008.

Keenan, Jeremy. *The Tuareg: People of Ahaggar.* London: Sickle Moon Books, 2002.

Kryza, Frank. *Race for Timbuktu: In Search of Africa's City of Gold.* New York: HarperCollins, 2006.

Kurlansky, Mark. *Salt: A World History.* New York: Alfred A. Knopf, 2002.

Mackintosh-Smith, Tim. *Travels with a Tangerine: A Journey in the Footnotes of Ibn Battutah.* London: John Murray, 2001.

Mills, Lady Dorothy. *The Road to Timbuktu.* London: Duckworth, 1924.

Novaresio, Paolo. *The Explorers.* London: White Star, 2002.

Ondaatje, Christopher. *Hemingway in Africa.* Toronto: HarperCollins, 2003.

Palin, Michael. *Sahara.* London: Weidenfeld & Nicolson, 2002.

Park, Mungo. *Travels into the Interior of Africa.* 1799, 1815. Reprint, London: Eland, 1983.

Pitt-Kethley, Fiona. Introduction to *Classic Travel Stories.* London: Bracken Books, 1994.

Ross, Michael. *Cross the Great Desert.* London: Gordon & Cremonesi, 1977.

Salentiny, Fernand. *Encyclopedia of World Explorers.* London: DuMont Monte, 2002.

Sattin, Anthony. *The Gates of Africa: Death, Discovery and the Search for Timbuktu.* New York: HarperCollins, 2003.

Seabrook, William B. *Air Adventure: Paris — Sahara — Timbuktu.* London: George G. Harrap, 1933.

Scott, Chris. *Sahara Overland: A Route and Planning Guide.* 2nd ed. Hindhead, UK: Trailblazer Publications, 2004.

Seddon, Sue. *Travel.* London: Alan Sutton and Thomas Cook, 1991.

Selby, Bettina. *Frail Dream of Timbuktu.* London: John Murray, 1991.

Schwartz, Brian M. *A World of Villages.* New York: Crown, 1986.

Shakespeare, Nicholas. *Bruce Chatwin.* London: Harvill Press, 1999.

Shapiro, Michael. *A Sense of Place.* Palo Alto, Ca: Travelers' Tales, 2004.

Velton, Ross. *Mali: The Bradt Travel Guide.* Bucks, UK: Bradt, 2000.

Welch, Galbraith. *The Unveiling of Timbuktu: The Astounding Adventures of Caillié.* 1939. Reprint, New York: Carroll & Graf, 1991.

Zinsser, William. "Visiting Timbuktu." In *On Writing Well.* New York: Harper Perennial, 1976.

Illustration and Photography Credits

A Plea to Preserve
the Past

Photograph © 2008 by Alida Jay Boye, coordinator of the Timbuktu Manuscripts Project, University of Oslo.

OVER THE CENTURIES, IGNORANCE HAS IMPEDED the preservation of the 700,000 Timbuktu manuscripts. A continued lack of awareness facilitates their slow disappearance — the loss of history's book, one page at a time. Without these paper treasures, we will know immeasurably less about a glorious time in sub-Saharan Africa some six hundred years ago.

It is a race against time to save these irreplaceable riches, which in this book are described as "Islamic pamphlets covered with sand ... scholarly pages a phase away from dust." A portion of the author's royalties from *To Timbuktu for a Haircut* will be donated to preserving the Timbuktu manuscripts. Some of the most notable preparatory work has been done through The Timbuktu Manuscript Project undertaken by the University of Oslo which completed its important work in 2009, coordinated by Alida Jay Boye. Other impressive progress is being undertaken by the Tombouctou Manuscript Project by the University of Cape Town in South Africa and the Ford Foundation, www.tombouctoumanuscripts.org

Of personal importance to me is the work of Abdoul Wahid Haidara who oversees bibliothèque Mohamed Tahar, and I thank Alida Jay Boye for the introduction.

Index

Praise for Rick Antonson's *Route 66 Still Kicks*

"One of the best books of the bunch..."
—2012 round up of holiday travel books by the *New York Times*

"A must for Route 66 aficionados."
—*Chicago Tribune*

"The most impressive account of a road trip I have ever read."
—Paul Taylor, publisher of *Route 66 Magazine*

"A middle-age Woodstock in motion, an encounter with an America that isn't as lost as we think. And in the end, Antonson proves that Route 66 indeed still kicks - as does America."
—Keith Bellows, editor in chief, *National Geographic Traveler*

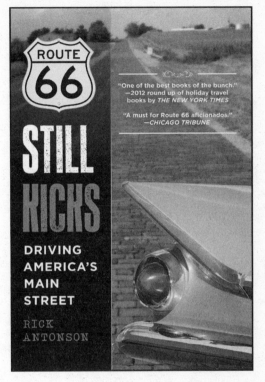

"This is America's favorite highway talking, and Antonson is a superb enabler, so sit back and relax as Route 66 gives up its legendary stories."
—Peter Greenberg, Travel Editor, CBS News

"*Route 66 Still Kicks* was by far the best book I have read about the Road in many, many years. Highly recommended."
—Bob Moore, co-author, *The Complete Guidebook to Route 66*

A bricklayer's nightmare or a roadmaker's dream? Route 66's early surface varied from dirt to pavement, from loose-set gravel to craftsmanship like this still-maintained stretch of brickwork. Today, the once-upon-a-time Road of Dreams wanders warily through the heart of T America.

Introduction

The Most Famous Highway in the World

"Actually, all I know about it is that song . . . "
                                        —World traveler

Years ago, I was sitting in a California tavern. One of the men I was chatting with, a truck driver—bald, squat, and a bit sassy—told me, "You'll never understand America until you've driven Route 66—that's *old* Route 66—all the way. It's the most famous highway in the world." He lifted his eyes over his Samuel Adams beer before revealing: "It runs through six states."

"Eight," said the lady he was with, as she sifted peanuts from shells.

"Seven," he countered, as though it were negotiable.

She began to hum, "Get your kicks on Route 66 . . . "

The truck driver mouthed the song's words as the fingers of his left hand tracked place names, while those of his right hand kept count of how many states were implied. His friend dropped the peanut shells on the tiled floor, freeing her own fingers in order to compete, first wiping them on her checkered slacks.

"Chicago," he said.

"Not a state," I offered.

"Illinois. Missouri, Kansas," he rattled.

"Texas," she said, pointing a finger to the wooden ceiling for some unknown reason.

"Missed Oklahoma," he said.

"New Mexico. Arizona," she added.

"California," they said in unison.

"Eight." She nodded to herself.

Their game over, the truck driver observed, "It's America's Main Street."

I didn't ask why Route 66 was important; being a teenager in the 1960s, I recalled the song made famous by Nat King Cole and remembered the television series named after the road. I knew little else, and what stuck in my mind was a question: Why did he think it was "the most famous highway in the world"?

The years passed. An excess of nostalgia for Americana ensured that Route 66 became known, if not understood, in the ensuing decades. Freeways had circumvented many small towns on the route during half a century of "progress," leaving a hodgepodge of memories where a roadway of hope had once run diagonally across the United States of America. Route 66 retreated to the back of my mind.

But not long ago, just months before what was intended to be a joint journey to Asia, my buddy Peter and I admitted that trip was hobbled by time constraints. We decided to abort it. Dispirited, we retreated to a bar, where we watched the waiter approach with a succession of pale ales.

Suddenly Peter brightened. "Maybe we do something closer to home. Shorter. Within the U.S. Maybe Canada. Mexico?" A long pause. "Maybe a cruise?"

I choked. "That'd be like spending seven days at a wedding reception." I was beginning to wonder about the wisdom of traveling with someone who'd even propose this.

But Peter was not so easily stopped. "What about Route 66?" He considered it a bit, having surprised himself, and then tried again, to make sure I got it. "Let's drive Route 66!" he said. "It goes through six or seven states."

"Eight," I said.

And drive it we did: on a crisp October day, five months after Peter and I made our ale-inspired decision to seek out the rough and lonely spots that remained of what was once a hectic Route 66, I was at the wheel of a top-down convertible, rumbling across a back road of gravel and cracked earth, out of sight of any other people or vehicles. The sun was bright and the wind was fast. I pressed the gas pedal for more speed. A bullet-riddled marker on a fence post confirmed that this remote and bumpy stretch of hidden history was old Route 66. I looked over as Peter scratched his unshaven chin and adjusted his sunglasses against the glare. He removed his baseball cap, held it out over the side of the car, and let it flap in the onrushing air as a little kid would on a family vacation.

We were halfway through our twelve-day road trip, commonly noted as 2,400 miles, although claims range from 2,200 to 2,448 miles—which tells us a lot about the variation of alignments over the years. By that time, I'd already shed enough misconceptions about the United States to fill our car's trunk, but I'd also confirmed that the myth is as important to America's self-esteem as is fact.

That nuance had been captured for me in a conversation the night before with a middle-aged waitress in a roadside diner. When I told her that Peter and I were intent on seeing "every part of the old road," she said, "I hope you're driving a Corvette convertible!"

"We're driving a Mustang. But it's a convertible."

"Ah. At least it's red, right?

"Why red?"

"Because red was the color of the Corvette those two guys drove in the TV show!"

I didn't have the heart to remind her that the program had been broadcast in black and white.

My equation of a nation is straightforward, I think: land + people + climate + commerce = country. America, the world's superpower, has a more elaborate formula, complicated by its distorted sense of importance. Many foreigners suspect that the United States rewrites its history away from facts—recasting them in a favorable light, and revising them to suit its sense of greatness. As a result, America is often accused of celebrating make-believe legends instead of the duller truths. But whatever the reputation of Americans in foreign lands, this national "species" is best viewed close up, in its indigenous setting, if one wishes to take its measure.

Many travelers begin their journeys, whether in their own country or another, with biases based on hearsay. Many of these people, both outsiders and residents, see America as arrogant, and getting away with it, in a world that often respects America's commercial thunder and little else. But if there is a place to see America at its truest, it is Route 66—the road first renowned for its attractions, then for its deterioration, and now for its attempts to reassert itself in the eyes of those who seek an authentic America. Americans love an underdog. Even more, they love stories about people who rolled high, lost it all, and fought to regain respect. In that way, Route 66 *is* America.

The road has an uncommon presence on the world stage. Route 66 is not a runner-up to any contender; it is *the* highway of highways. North America's Alaska Highway, Baja Highway, and Trans-Canada Highway are icon-lite by comparison. Route 66's peers are on other continents: perhaps the Asian Highway from Singapore to Bangkok, the Road of the Emperors from Prague to Budapest, or the Golden Road from Baghdad to Samarkand.

Many tourists today want an instant "experience." Route 66 does not grant that. Tourism frequently offers up over-managed travel; Route 66 eschews that. It is possible to drive from Chicago to Los Angeles in three days on the interstate: you just need to get up each morning and chase the pavement. However, as a fellow traveler told me, "Seeing Route 66 in three days would be like having a smorgasbord on a coffee break."

Peter can be a stickler for daily minutiae (which drives me nuts). He set the tone of our drive by announcing, "If we're going on old Route 66, let's take the time and do it right. That means finding where it's ignored and abandoned, unpaved and unhappy—not just the smooth parts." That gave him a motive for the trip, a mini-quest that satisfied his need for a rationale that took him away from more reasonable obligations.

Our ambition became to search for the left-behind and forgotten pieces of Route 66, not merely to "touch it" between speeding along samples of cared-for sections. We aimed for the remnants and dead ends of 66 for no reason other than that they are dead ends—and were once of magical importance. Although today these fragments are often overgrown by weeds, they are compass points to the past. They remind us of pioneers and provenance.

While speaking to others—even world travelers—about our plans, I would hear, "I'd love to do that! I've always dreamed of driving Route 66." Then there'd be a hesitation, followed by: "Actually, all I know about it is that song . . . " Driving Route 66 was not infrequently a romantic notion accompanied by amnesia.

This cannot avoid being a tale of two boomers at the wheel—one with a love for America in all its exaggerations, the other with a sense that America had become the sum of its flaws. This is us: two friends, simple as that. We are chalk and cheese, Peter and I; he veers right politically, and I lean to the political port. A friend, hearing of our Route 66 adventure, sized the two of us up as "road scholars, not Rhodes scholars."

Peter stretches taller than most men, weighs more than most men, and has a head described by his mother as "large and capable," which his body grew to match. He feigns pride, when in fact he is modest. He casts a long shadow on family and colleagues. He bought a grungy shirt and ill-fitting jeans specifically for this trip, but only brought them out when all his collared shirts and pressed pants had had their day. His hairstyle is unchanging—coiffed for years by the same barber, although his gray is becoming grayer (something he will not bother to hide). His lifestyle is overengaged, overcommitted— he'll be everywhere he's expected to be; he'd go to the opening of an envelope. He's generous to a fault, and gregarious—he could have a conversation with a stop sign. He believes that "the good things in life are easy not to do." And he is loud, and laughs vigorously—often in the face of potential danger, like a freight train whistles before a vehicle crossing.

And I should say that he's done a poor job in life of making time for himself a priority; he's more bound to an office than to the wilderness, more tied to a Daytimer than to the open road. This would be among his few attempts ever to spend a couple of weeks untethered.

Me? I didn't need to go far to find a grungy shirt or ill-fitting jeans; my closet is full of them. I bracket Peter's age by five years—five more in chronology, five less in emotional reliability. I dream of a life without restrictions or obligations. A man of many enthusiasms, I'm not always focused. I've hopscotched U.S. state lines throughout my life, visiting family, friends, and back roads, but seldom with a plan. I travel to reconcile my dreams.

I was witnessing workmates and friends afflicted with suffi- cient money and not enough life. That startled me. "You should save money; you're getting old," Peter said one day while we were driving on Route 66.

"I'm getting old, but I'm not old yet," I replied only a little defensively.

"Seriously, money can be important."

"I've never wanted to be the richest guy in the cemetery," I said.

Woody Guthrie wrote of the man who "lives for work's sake and works to dig up more work." I'd been guilty of that, and I wanted to change it.

Travel is my mistress. I sleep in forty or fifty different beds a year, pull up that many strange blankets, turn out that many bedside lamps, and wake up to that many different curtains, some torn.

Peter and I are in the autumn of our lives. I am still this side of curmudgeonly and, as Peter would say (and has said) of me, "You really can be a bit of an ass." That makes us each a little set in our ways.

Road trips, like marriages, are about compromises. We went in search of America without being sure exactly what that would mean. Might it mean seeing the country in pockets often overlooked? Perhaps hearing truths spoken by people who don't often get listened to? Maybe opening our closed minds to the wisdom of the open road? Freedom was our byword, and the extent of our planning was agreeing on our completion date. But we swore we'd avoid prepackaged foods, prearranged experiences, and predictable America.

En route, a conversation with an old-timer captured the openness of the road and of our plans. In a remote Oklahoma town on Route 66, a tall woman with weathered skin looked at our parked car with its top down and asked, "Where're you going?"

Peter replied, "Wherever the wind takes us."

The lady leaned forward, laughed with a hint of cunning and said, "Travelers *are* the wind."